TREASURES

FOR THE

Heart

TREASURES
FOR THE
Heart

A 365 DAY DEVOTIONAL

ROXANNE EILERS

JANUARY 1

"Arise, shine, for your light has come, and the glory of the LORD rises upon you. See, darkness covers the earth and thick darkness is over the peoples, but the LORD rises upon you and His glory appears over you. Nations will come to your light, and kings to the brightness of your dawn" (Isaiah 60:1-3).

THE DROUGHT IS OVER

I CAN HEAR THE Lord speaking to us saying, the drought is over. The drought is over, and that He will restore all those years the locust have eaten away in our lives. He says, *"Arise, shine for the Light has come! And the glory of the Lord is risen upon you!"* He is leading many into uncharted waters, but He will be our Compass. He is leading us—all those who say, *"Yes,"* to Him, *"I'll go with You."* They will experience phenomenal answers to prayers, and experience the realm of His Glory where things happen that cannot be explained. Don't settle for less. *"Go deeper,"* He says, *"Go deeper."* You will be dropping your jaw in awe at what He is about to do now, and in your future. Just say yes to Him. Lay all your "stuff" on the altar and follow where He leads even if you feel uncomfortable mentally or physically—it is temporary discomfort.

What more can I say—tears are running down my face as I write this because God is here, and His Glory compels me to share His heart with you. Will you say yes? Then do it.

January 2

"You crown the year with Your bounty, and Your carts
overflow with abundance" (Psalm 65:11).

For the New Year

In this New Year the Lord desires to lead and guide your steps. He has ordered them and has prepared you for this next year. Isaiah 48:17 says that He is the Lord your God and He will teach you to profit. That word "profit" in the Hebrew is *yaal* which means "to gain profit, to benefit you, to confer or discuss with the Lord" something that is important so that a decision can be made.

Not only will the Lord show you how to profit in business matters and work, but also in everyday affairs and relationships. He will bring all your suffering and trials around full circle where you are benefitted by them. What was meant for evil, God will work for the good of you. And on top of this, the Lord, Himself, will always be available to discuss over your matters with you and He will guide your decision making. He will lead you as a Shepherd His sheep, in the way you are to go—He already has prepared the way and will take you there step by step.

January 3

"Oh how I love Your law! It is my meditation all the day"(Psalm 119:97).

Love God's Word

*G*OD DESIRES US to fall in love with His Word. The psalmist loves the law of the Lord. The "law" in this case is referring to the Word of God which is our rule and standard for living. One way we can learn to fall in love with the Word of God is to hide it, to treasure it up in our hearts through committing it to memory. Those Israelites, in days of old, who loved God, were adamant about keeping God's words before them throughout the house. They would post the Word of God around inside the house to keep reminding themselves of what He had said. Their hearts and thoughts turned often to the law of the Lord.

If the Lord's words are in our hearts and minds we will have a storehouse to draw upon when we need to be encouraged, directed, cleansed, strengthened and restored. I encourage you this day to fall in love with the very words of God which are sweeter than honey.

JANUARY 4

"This is what the LORD says to His anointed, to Cyrus, whose right hand I take hold of to subdue nations before him and to strip kings of their armor, to open doors before him so that gates will not be shut: I will go before you and will level the mountains; I will break down gates of bronze and cut through bars of iron" (Isaiah 45:1-2).

WALK THROUGH THOSE OPEN DOORS

FOR SOME OF you this year is the year that God is going to open doors that have been closed for a long time. Isaiah 45:1-2 says that God will open doors and the gates will not be shut; He will go before you and will level the mountains; He will break down gates of bronze and cut through bars of iron so that you can enter into your new phase of life and spiritual growth. He will provide people for you, and give you faith to remove mountains that have stood in your way. You will break down the gates and cut through bars of iron through praise and thanksgiving.

The Greatest test of faith is when you don't get what you want, but still you are able to say, Thank You, LORD.

JANUARY 5

"See, I am doing a new thing! Now it springs up; do you not perceive it? I am making a way in the wilderness and streams in the wasteland" (Isaiah 43:19).

A NEW THING

DON'T KEEP DWELLING upon things in your past. Keep your mind free from images of the negative experiences that you had years ago. Even the positive things are past and over. Look up and anticipate! I am about to do a new thing right before you! It will happen quickly, for you have waited upon Me. You will know and recognize that it is of Me. It is My hand performing this. Where there has been days of dry wilderness experiences and wandering and wondering, I will make a plain path that you can walk on. I will give you an anointing of My Spirit that will carry you through the desert places you will encounter. All things will work together for your good and for My glory. You will grow spiritually as you walk with Me, and you will bring renewal and revival to My people, and they will drink deeply from My well of living water—the people I have chosen to declare My praises.

January 6

"...and He said to me, 'My grace is sufficient for you, for My strength is made perfect in weakness'" (2 Corinthians 12:9-10).

Grace Sufficient

*A*ND JESUS SAID to me, *"I am always leaning towards you, not away from you. My arms are extended to you saying, I am here to assist you in your need. When things appear to be greater than what you can handle, My favor and gift of strength is always available for you to draw upon in order to carry you through and sustain you. As you choose to come to Me and depend on My strength, you will be able to do those things you thought you could not do before. When you are feeling your weakest, in need of power and energy to go on, I will be there holding you up and gifting you with My strength and ability to handle your circumstance and situation."*

"So, dear child, have a full and happy heart today and lean on Me and My sufficiency. Whether you are physically or emotionally in pain, I will help you through. I will lift you up on healing wings. And if you are lacking in anything, ask of Me and I will provide for you out of My abundance, but remember even if the answer doesn't appear to be coming—keep believing because the answer is surely on its way to you. If you are being reproached or persecuted for My name's sake, dance for joy because My joy is your strength! And don't forget, whatever your distress is, I have overcome and I will teach you to also. So walk in confidence and lean on My sufficiency."

JANUARY 7

"Do not get drunk on wine, which leads to debauchery. Instead, be filled with the Spirit, speaking to one another with psalms, hymns, and songs from the Spirit. Sing and make music from your heart to the Lord, always giving thanks to God the Father for everything, in the name of our Lord Jesus Christ" (Ephesians 5:18-20). (Colossians 3:15-17)

HOW TO LIVE THE EXTRAORDINARY LIFE IN CHRIST

*Y*OU HAVE HEARD the saying "God uses *ordinary* people to do *extraordinary* things." I like to say, "God calls *ordinary* people to live *extraordinary* lives in Christ." What is this extraordinary life?

It is living in the spiritual realm with Christ and being sensitive to the voice of the Holy Spirit, living in the anointing of God, moving, living and walking in the Spirit, allowing God to do mighty feats through your life. The Apostle Paul tells us to *"be filled with the Spirit."* This means that it is a daily filling that God wants us to live in. How are we filled up with the Spirit of God so that we can live extraordinary lives as Jesus did? The Word of God gives us the answer in Ephesians 5:18-21 and Colossians 3:15-17.

First of all, we need to know that it is God's will that we be filled with the Spirit. We are to speak about the Lord and His magnificent works among other believers; we are to sing to the Lord and worship Him, giving Him thanks for all things and being careful to cultivate a humble heart. This is how we are renewed by the Holy Spirit and filled up—Hallelujah! Glory to God! And as we let God's peace rule in our hearts, allowing His Word to dwell richly in us, we are filled. So then, edifying fellowship, worship, reading, studying and meditating on the Scriptures are the ingredients to being full of God. It is all spiritual food that fuels us to live an extraordinary life in Christ—the life of faith and love.

JANUARY 8

"The LORD will surely comfort Zion and will look with compassion on all her ruins; He will make her deserts like Eden, her wastelands like the garden of the LORD. Joy and gladness will be found in her, thanksgiving and the sound of singing" (Isaiah 51:3).

GOD SPEAKS COMFORT TO THE BROKEN IN HEART

I WILL COMFORT YOU My Son, My Daughter, in all your brokenness and places of emptiness and endless grief, all the deep sorrow you keep hidden away in your heart, all the days of carrying the heavy burden of a broken heart, a shattered soul. I will create life and newness out of your deserted wilderness. I will blow My Spirit of life and healing into your heart and you will begin to bloom again in your garden. Where the flowers and vines have died, I will create new living buds that will burst into being. Where there has just been dry parched land, I will open up a river. You will have joy and gladness when you meet with Me in your garden. Thanksgiving will flow from your heart. Allow Me to come into the deep recesses of your soul and bring this profound comfort. Take the bars off the doors and the locks. Open to Me and I will go in and fellowship with you in a new fresh manner. It is in your desert place that you will find a garden.

January 9

"Have I not commanded you? Be strong and courageous. Do not be afraid; do not be discouraged, for the LORD your God will be with you wherever you go" (Joshua 1:9).

Be Strong and Very Courageous in Your Faith

*A*RE YOU EXPERIENCING difficulties that appear hopeless? You must not keep your eyes focused on what is going on around you or you will be discouraged. God tells us to encourage ourselves in the Lord. Now what has God promised you concerning your situation? If you don't have a promise, get one in His Word. Then cling to that promise and the other promises that God has given to you like, *"all things work together for good"* and *"now unto Him who is able to do exceedingly abundantly above all that we ask or think."*

Don't become weak in your faith. Don't allow your faith to waver through unbelief and doubt. God is keeping watch over your faith and He will honor it. Grow strong in your faith and give glory to God. Worship Him, for He is faithful who has given us His promises. Be persuaded that He is able to perfect that which concerns you. We walk by faith, not by sight. Quit trying to figure it all out and become overwhelmed at what you see with your earthly eyes. Call those things that are not, as though they were. Look and act and speak in faith, for faith always pleases God.

"The LORD is my shepherd, I lack nothing.
He makes me lie down in green pastures, He leads me beside quiet waters, He
refreshes my soul. He guides me along the right paths for His name's sake.
Even though I walk through the darkest valley, I will fear no evil, for You are
with me; Your rod and Your staff, they comfort me. You prepare a table before me
in the presence of my enemies. You anoint my head with oil; my cup overflows.
Surely Your goodness and love will follow me all the days of my life,
and I will dwell in the house of the LORD forever" (Psalm 23).

Psalm 23 Revisited

THE LORD IS my Shepherd. He is the One who takes care of me. He knows what I need every moment of every day. I know His hand will provide for me abundantly, so I don't have to worry. Sometimes He has to move me to places where I can flourish and grow—it is there He promises peace and provision. He gently leads me to the places where I am spiritually refreshed and renewed. He continually fills me with His Holy Spirit. He brings soundness and healing to my weary heart and mind, and faithfully keeps me walking on the paths that lead to life, health, peace and joy. He does this so that His name will be glorified.

Whenever I pass through a dark and overwhelming valley, where shadows of doubt and fear lurk, I can hold up my head and pass on with fearless confidence because my Shepherd's presence is with me. He comforts me, corrects me, and protects me. He deals with me as His own child.

When I am experiencing trials of many kinds, and the enemies of my soul are set around me, I can enjoy a spiritual feast in the presence of my God—His Word feeds me and my eyes are set on Him.

I can feel His sweet anointing being poured out all over me! I am so full of joy and thanksgiving! I know for a fact that good things and blessings, God's merciful compassions, will always be there for me to receive. And then finally, at the end of my earthly life, I will see the face of my Shepherd and live with Him, whom I've walked with by faith, forever, and ever and ever.

JANUARY 11

"You will restore my life again from the depths of the earth. You
will increase my honor and comfort me once again" (Ps. 71).

RISE UP FROM THE PIT

HERE IS A scripture for those who feel like they will never rise up from the dark pit they have been in.

What does this scripture mean? It means that God is keeping track of all you have been going through, and He knows what He is going to do about it. He will lift you up and set your feet on solid ground. He will take away your shame, disappointment and weariness, and will bring you to a point where you are thriving in His Spirit and in your home. He will comfort your troubled heart. So take these words and write them where you will remember His promises. Thank Him now that it will be so.

January 12

"Therefore, since we are surrounded by such a great cloud of witnesses, let us throw off everything that hinders and the sin that so easily entangles. And let us run with perseverance the race marked out for us, fixing our eyes on Jesus, the Pioneer and Perfecter of faith. For the joy set before Him He endured the cross, scorning its shame, and sat down at the right hand of the throne of God" (Hebrews 12:1-2).

In Serving Him

WILL YOU GO all the way with Jesus, never turning back? If you have put your hand to the plow you must go forward and stop continually looking back. God is doing a new thing on the earth these days and He has called you to be part of it.

Will you pay whatever cost it will take to have more of God in your life? Will you faithfully love, trust and serve Him, even if terrible calamity bombards your life? Will you lay down all that you have on the altar of His love?

Will you let Him burn out of your heart all that is contrary to His holiness? He will fill you back up with the fire and passion of His love.

Never lose sight of why you are here—Press on with all of your might, towards the goal of your high calling to serve Christ. Lay hold of eternal life and don't get so caught up and entangled, entrapped with this life's hassles and problems. Keep a God perspective.

JANUARY 13

"And when you pray, do not keep on babbling like pagans, for they think they will be heard because of their many words. Do not be like them, for your Father knows what you need before you ask Him" (Matthew 6:7-8).

THOUGHTS ABOUT MY HEAVENLY FATHER

HOW TENDER THE Father is towards His children. How secure we are in His arms. How undying is His devotion to us—we are His delight and song, and He fusses over us as if each of us were His only child.

I looked into His eyes last night and saw a Father that truly understood my struggles and humanity—a Father who reached for me when I fell and went astray. I believe now, that I really have come to know Him a little more intimately. I first believed in Him by faith alone, but now I have come to really grasp a glimpse of His heart for me. I can feel comforted and content that He will take good care of me, do what is best for me, direct my wobbly feet in the right direction, and keep my thoughts from being self-destructive. He will draw my heart back to Himself when I am deceived and have found myself in a stronghold and snare of the enemy. My Father takes His holy rod of reproof and scoops me away from the evil. He delivers me from evil. I love You, Oh Lord, my strength and my Rock.

January 14

"Cast all your anxiety on Him because He cares for you"(1 Peter 5:7).

Give Him All Your Worries

*G*OD IS ASKING us to let go of what weighs us down and causes us to fret. No matter what it is, no matter how terrible and urgent it seems, God is not in a panic, and He always knows what He is going to do about each of our deep concerns.

I choose to throw all my concerns, worries and fears upon the Lord. He is great and He will handle them. And so I rest in His promise that He will sustain me each step of the way. Surely I am convinced that He will never let me fall.

*"For the LORD taketh pleasure in His people: He will
beautify the meek with salvation" (Psalms 149:4).*

HOW DOES GOD BEAUTIFY OUR HEARTS?

*T*HERE ARE TWO main ways that God beautifies our hearts for
His glory. They are: by His Salvation and through Suffering.

Psalms 149:4 tells us that the Lord will beautify the meek
with salvation. This word *"salvation"* in the Hebrew means "to rescue, save
and deliver." This means that because Christ took our place on the cross for
our sins that we are rescued from the clutches of sin, and our sins are forgiven. We are saved and beautifully reborn spiritually. Plus we are delivered
out of the kingdom of darkness and placed in God's Kingdom of light.

The word *Yeshuah* is also closely linked to the word "salvation." *Yeshuah*
means "God is Salvation." So God Himself is our salvation. Therefore He
beautifies us with Himself, His presence, His person, His anointing, His
Holy Spirit. He beautifies us with JESUS!

In the Greek *"save"* means "to save, deliver and to make whole." This is
so wonderful to me! God not only forgives our sins, delivers us out of the
kingdom of darkness, but He also begins to make us whole in our person.
He begins to heal the fragmentations in our lives—the broken areas. This,
my friends, beautifies our spirits to the glory of God. God wants us to be
whole and healed people!

Tomorrow we will look at the second way Jesus beautifies us—that is
through suffering.

JANUARY 16

*"...to appoint unto them that mourn in Zion, to give
unto them beauty for ashes, the oil of joy for mourning,
the garment of praise for the spirit of heaviness; that they
might be called trees of righteousness, the planting of the
Lord, that He might be glorified" (Isaiah 61:3).*

GOD BEAUTIFIES OUR HEARTS THROUGH SUFFERING

*A*RE YOU MOURNING over someone or something today—loss of a loved one, friend, relationship, job, finances, health? Has your trial been so grievous that you feel overwhelmed with sorrow in your suffering? God tells us that there will come a time when He says, *"Enough!"* He will draw you up out of the many waters and place your feet on ground that is stable. He will take the ashes from the things burned up in your life—burned and refined through the fires of trial, and He will trade them for spiritual beauty and great joy! Praise will be on your lips to the Lord for His kindness and graciousness to you. Why does God give good things in place of things that have been working against us? It is for His glory, that all may see that it was His hand that comforted and delivered you.

There is something in the process of a trying situation that strips us of our pride, self-efforts and self-dependence. As the fire begins to burn, the Great Refiner sits and keeps careful watch over your circumstance and your heart. As you draw near to His heart and actually look into the fire of suffering, you will see the image of Jesus looking back at you with eyes of compassion and love. As you continue to mirror what you see, you become spiritually beautiful in His time.

Beauty for ashes—beauty, for the things you have lost in your life. The Oil of Joy for mourning—I don't know how it happens. Just that one morning you will find life is good again and all is well with your soul. Praise, instead of the spirit of heaviness—that oppressive, depressive spirit that has been weighing you down will be lifted, and praise will come from a heart that is thankful and delivered.

January 17

"Be exalted, O God, above the heavens; let Your glory be over all the earth" (Psalm 57:11).

O God Be Exalted!

O GOD, MY HEART is unshakable! My faith in You is unmovable! I will celebrate Your love for me. I will sing and praise You, Lord. People will see me and be drawn to Your great love. It is so great it stretches out to the highest of heavens, and Your faithful loyalty to me reaches to the skies. O God, be exalted in Your heavenly abode, and let Your glory cover and be seen throughout the entire earth! Amen.

JANUARY 18

"He [Abraham] did not waver at the promise of God through unbelief, but was strengthened in faith, giving glory to God, and being fully convinced that what He had promised He was also able to perform"(Romans 4: 20-21).

FAITH THAT DOESN'T WAVER

MY FRIEND, DO not waver at the promises God has birthed in your heart—those precious promises that He has highlighted in His Word to you personally. Do not fluctuate with any kind of doubt. Do not step into unbelief because of your unchanged situation. Rather grow exceedingly stronger and stronger in your faith. Keep your focus right on, and be fully convinced, completely persuaded, that God will, in fact, *do* what He has told you. He is more than able, so surrender the matter to Him, trust Him to the uttermost and watch for the answer!

"On another day the angels came to present themselves before the LORD, and Satan also came with them to present himself before Him. And the LORD said to Satan, 'Where have you come from?' Satan answered the LORD, 'From roaming throughout the earth, going back and forth on it.' Then the LORD said to Satan, 'Have you considered My servant Job? There is no one on earth like him; he is blameless and upright, a man who fears God and shuns evil. And he still maintains his integrity, though you incited Me against him to ruin him without any reason.' 'Skin for skin!' Satan replied. 'A man will give all he has for his own life. But now stretch out Your hand and strike his flesh and bones, and he will surely curse You to Your face.' The LORD said to Satan, 'Very well, then, he is in your hands; but you must spare his life.' So Satan went out from the presence of the LORD and afflicted Job with painful sores from the soles of his feet to the crown of his head" (Job 2:1-7).

WHY?

SOMETIMES WE DON'T understand why God has allowed certain trying situations to touch our lives and try us to the very end of our rope. There are so many unanswered questions—we ask why? Why? The Bible gives us some reasons why our lives may feel upside down and turned around at times. Among these are: to prove our faith, strengthen our faith, build and refine our character, so we can be a witness to others, to draw closer to God, to teach us a spiritual lesson, to cause us to get into God's Word, to spiritually grow. However, there are some cases where nothing seems to make sense as in the story of Job in the Bible. He was a righteous man and strove to do what was right. He stayed true to God even though he experienced severe calamity in his life. Job did not understand or know why he was put in the boiling pot of hard troubles. His friends tried to tell him the reasons they had for why he was being so utterly tried. God said they didn't speak what was correct concerning Job—they didn't have the answers. As we get to look into the life of Job we are shown that there was something going on in the spiritual realm between God and Satan. Satan wanted and asked to cause

havoc in Job's life. He told God that Job would forsake his faith if he was put into the fires of trial. But we can clearly see in the Scriptures that God, through Job's suffering, was proving Job's allegiance to Himself. Job could not see this insight. All he saw was the terrible tragedies that struck him when he lost all he had, including children and health. He didn't know why this had come upon him, and God did not choose to reveal this to him. However, to us He did, so we might learn that there is always a God-purpose for whatever we go through, and that all God asks of us is to trust Him completely and obey Him no matter what is going on or how things appear.

I know there are things I will ask Him when I get to heaven, because I will never really understand them here on earth in this mortal body and finite mind. So in seasons of continued agitation, grief, suffering, pain and frustration we must trust God that He knows what He is making out of our lives. We can ask Him to show us what He wants to teach us and how to handle our situation, but overall we are to trust Him when nothing seems to make sense.

JANUARY 20

"(For the weapons of our warfare are not carnal, but mighty through God to the pulling down of strong holds;) Casting down imaginations, and every high thing that exalteth itself against the knowledge of God, and bringing into captivity every thought to the obedience of Christ" (2 Corinthians 10:4-5).

RENEWED THINKING

WHAT WE ARE thinking about is so important for victory living in Christ. The Bible says to be transformed in our thinking by renewing our mind. We are to pull down strongholds in our mind and cast down imaginations that are contrary to the Word of God. A stronghold is that area in our thinking where we find ourselves stuck, oppressed, depressed and controlled. It always brings the message of some kind of negativity, sin, fear, or anxiety.

With our imagination we can conjure up all kinds of scenarios that bring doubt and fear into our heart. *What if this happens? What if that happens?* God says to be single minded and focused on Him, and to think on what is good, pure, lovely and positive—things that will make for victorious living.

In the name of Jesus, we can break the stronghold of these negative thoughts and imaginations and train our brain to develop thinking that will bring good fruit unto the Lord and not work against ourselves. If we find it difficult to rid ourselves of stronghold thinking, it is wise to have someone pray for us.

Watch therefore, what you are thinking about and choose to talk to yourself in your mind with words and images that will bring victorious living in Christ.

JANUARY 21

"Do not fret because of those who are evil
or be envious of those who do wrong;
for like the grass they will soon wither,
like green plants they will soon die away.
Trust in the LORD and do good;
dwell in the land and enjoy safe pasture.
Take delight in the LORD,
and He will give you the desires of your heart.
Commit your way to the LORD;
trust in Him and He will do this:
He will make your righteous reward shine like the dawn,
your vindication like the noonday sun.
Be still before the LORD
and wait patiently for Him;
do not fret when people succeed in their ways,
when they carry out their wicked schemes" (Psalm 37:1-7).

A PSALM FOR DAILY LIVING

DO NOT WORRY about those who are dishonest, unloving, selfish, and that have evil motives. God is their judge. Just keep your focus on the Lord and keep doing what is right and good. Make wise choices that will lead to life and peace. Live your life and depend on God's faithful provision for you. Make Him your number one priority. Spend time with Him, telling Him you love Him because He loves you so much. He will answer every cry of your heart and fulfill your desires. Whatever is weighing on your heart, commit it to God's hand, and rely on Him to take care of it. He will always do the right thing for you. Now be at peace inside your heart and quit striving—just keep waiting expectantly for God to move on your behalf.

JANUARY 22

"Believe on the Lord Jesus and you will
be saved, you and your household"(Acts 16:31).

SALVATION FOR YOUR FAMILY

I BELIEVE THIS VERSE in the Bible was written as a lesson for all believers. *"All Scripture is profitable for doctrine and instruction."* What does this verse mean to us today? I believe it means that when we come to faith in Christ, and accept Him as our Lord and Savior, that we have a right and obligation to pray for the salvation of those in our household. I also hold to the belief that God will answer and honor those prayers. We are to stand in faith claiming this scripture as our own promise for us and for our loved ones.

I have believed and stood on this scripture and others for my own family, and out of nine brothers and sisters, seven have come to know Jesus as their Savior, my father and mother also. Two more to bring into the Kingdom! God is faithful and will have all come to repentance and to the knowledge of Him.

JANUARY 23

"God is our refuge and strength, an ever-present help in trouble.
Therefore we will not fear, though the earth give way
and the mountains fall into the heart of the sea,
though its waters roar and foam and the mountains quake with
their surging. There is a river whose streams make glad the
city of God, the holy place where the Most High dwells.
God is within her, she will not fall;
God will help her at break of day" (Psalm 46:1-5).

GOD IS OUR HELP

GOD IS OUR place of absolute safety and incredible strength. He is ever present with us always alerted to our moments of feeling overwhelmed by trouble. He is near to assist us with whatever we need at that time. Whenever we encounter difficult mountains of trial, and our situation seems to be more than we can handle, God asks us to be still and rest in Him. Even if our world has become extremely challenging with financial struggles, stressed relationships, loneliness, fear, the continuous strain of waiting, lingering illness, and broken dreams, God says we can still have a place of peace in His arms. And even though the great waters of sorrow and loss threaten to take us under, and there is a shaking of our inward and outward stability, we need not be afraid, because God says that in Him we can find refuge from the storm and cool streams in the heat. In Him we can draw upon true joy and dance in the midst of it all, because the joy of the Lord is our inexhaustible strength! We are to draw near to the heart of God with pure confidence and find emotional stability and spiritual security, for God is our present help in times of trouble.

"See, God has come to save me. I will trust in Him and not be afraid.
The LORD God is my strength and my song; He has given me victory.
With joy you will drink deeply from the fountain of salvation!
In that wonderful day you will sing: 'Thank the LORD! Praise His name!
Tell the nations what He has done. Let them know how mighty He is!
Sing to the LORD, for He has done wonderful things. Make
known His praise around the world'"(Isaiah 12:2-5).

JOY

CAN YOU THANK and praise God in the difficult days as well as the cheery days? Oh, but the pain and discomfort of the difficult days, at times, seem unbearable—we don't like it at all. It is very hard to have joy when you are hurting. However, the Lord tells us in Nehemiah 8:10 that the joy of the Lord is our strength. It is not our joy that brings us victory, but God's joy. As we spend time in His presence, for He also says that in His presence there is fullness of joy, we can experience His joy which overflows into our hearts. It is the joy of the Lord that gives us the ability to praise Him in the tempest. Again, how do we get His joy? By spending time alone with Him, receiving His love and joy by faith—being grateful, thankful and worshipful before Him. Joy is contagious! Remember that the Kingdom of God is righteousness, peace and joy in the Holy Spirit (Romans 14:17)! Choose His joy today!

JANUARY 25

"God will instruct me and teach me in the way I should go.
He will guide me with His eye" (Psalm 32:8 NASB95).
"My steps are ordered by the Lord" (Psalm 37:23 NASB95).

LEAD ME, JESUS

*I*N TIMES WHEN we need direction and guidance, the Bible tells us over and over that God will be our guide, and He will direct our steps. Isaiah 28:29 says that the Lord is *"wonderful in counsel"* and He is an excellent guide. He knows just how to show you where to go, what to do, and when to do it. He also knows how to get your attention. Sometimes the Lord will bring an idea or thought to your mind over and over again until you step aside and think about it. We have to be quiet enough at times so we can hear God speaking and directing us in our matter. In Psalm 32:8 we are told that God guides us with His eye upon us—He watches us to see if we are indeed going in the direction He wants us to, and if we are not, He will put us back on the right track.

God's Word is a *"light unto our path"* and as we spend time in His Word He will speak to us intimately through the Scriptures. A verse will jump out at us and grab at our heart. God is at this time illuminating our way. He is either, giving us instruction, direction, confirming what He has already told us, or encouraging us to keep steady no matter how things look. The sweet Holy Spirit is our Guide who prompts us inside our spirit. He uses our intuition, and our perception. He gives us supernatural peace at times—or joy.

I am about to make a very important move in my own life, and my ears and eyes are open to hear and see what God is doing. As I venture out and test the waters, and as I wrestle with my thoughts and feelings, He will direct me in the way I should go. When God moves—we need to move also. When God stands still and tells us to wait—we need not be in a hurry. Remember God talks to us:

1. *Through His Word*
2. *By the Holy Spirit*
3. *By circumstances*
4. *Through our own thoughts*
5. *Through an inward peace*
6. *Through our brothers and sisters in Christ*
7. *Sometimes He uses supernatural means*

Lord, help me to hear You, and lean on Your Word and the Holy Spirit, to lead me to the place You would have me to go. Lead me to where the end result will be peace. Lead me with Your goodness to the place I will thrive and flourish like a green tree. Work out the circumstances and confirm my steps. Speak to me in the night watches when it is quiet. Lord, reach me the way You know how. I ask this in Your Name, Amen.

JANUARY 26

"One thing have I desired of the LORD, that will I seek after; that I may dwell in the house of the LORD all the days of my life, to behold the beauty of the LORD, and to inquire in His temple" (Psalm 27:4).

GOD'S BEAUTY

THE BEAUTY OF God can be seen in the stars shining with all of their might,

And it can be seen in the moon glowing in the sky at night.

The beauty of God can be seen in a flower, brilliant in color and hue,

So exquisitely formed and painted by God—something only He can do.

The beauty of God can be seen in a bug as it parades along on the ground,

And in the weightless butterfly that skips and dances around.

The beauty of God can be seen in the waves, unafraid and pounding on shore,

And in the great sun that rises and sets, and oh, it's in so much more.

The beauty of God can be seen in His face, the face of His one only Son,

And as we behold His presence each day, we are transformed by this beautiful One.

January 27

"Cast your cares on the LORD and He will sustain you; He will never let the righteous be shaken"(Psalm 55:22).

GIVE IT TO GOD

DO YOU HAVE cares that are weighing you down? A load of worries and problems that seem unsolvable? The Lord instructs us to cast all our cares on Him, and He will sustain us. It takes practice passing the ball into His hands and out of ours—this must be done moment by moment. Whenever you grab it out of His hands give it back—throw it back to Him, away from you. Let Him bear and carry you and your burdens. He is able to do exceedingly abundantly above all that we ask or think. Don't just sit or walk around worrying—pray about your situation, then cast your cares on Him because He cares for you (1 Peter 5:7).

The Bible doesn't tell us to do something for its own sake. It is for our sake and we are always told to do something that we *can* do. All things are possible with God. Exercise those faith muscles and give your load over to the hands of God. Now leave it there. Keep doing this until you are experiencing peace and relief. You can do this. Cast your cares on the Lord, and He will carry you, sustain, strengthen, refresh, and infuse you with His power. He will keep you afloat in the raging waters and safe in the storms, and give you just what is required for you to continue on in your daily journey.

JANUARY 28

"May the God of hope fill you with all joy and peace as you trust in Him, so that you may overflow with hope by the power of the Holy Spirit" (Romans 15:13).

THAT GLIMMER OF HOPE

*B*E AWARE OF the hope thoughts that God brings into your mind. These are meant to inject hope into your spirit, and with hope, comes the strength to go on. It may be a small little voice inside your heart, or it can be a person encouraging you. It also can be through God's creation, through pets and loved ones, and of course, through a powerful comforting scripture. It is the silver lining in the dark clouds, the rainbow after a stormy rain fall. All I know is that the message is always the same, *"You will make it through this; there are good things in store. God really does care about you and your needs. Don't lose heart!"* Look for those snapshots of hope. They seem to appear right in the middle of a difficult, impossible situation where you feel you are on your last leg. Filling our minds with positive uplifting thinking pleases God, but that doesn't mean we have to pretend all is well, and we are feeling just wonderful. However, as our faith embraces hope, in whatever form or way it is given to us, we become more confident in what God is doing around and in us. This does raise our spirits and brings joy to our hearts.

"Hope doesn't mean the absence of grief, sorrow, fear or worry. Hope is knowing you are not alone and that you will make it through. You can have grief, sorrow and worry and still have hope." (Taken from Hope in a Season of Suffering, R. Eilers)

"Through these He has given us His very great and precious promises, so that through them you may participate in the divine nature, having escaped the corruption in the world caused by evil desires" (2 Peter 1:4).

THE PROMISES/THE DIVINE NATURE

*a*S WE PARTAKE of God's exceedingly great and precious promises, simultaneously, we become partakers of the divine nature. How does this work? I believe, as we allow the Word of God to become part of our very nature and being, Christ's image increases in our lives. The sweet fragrance of Him flows out of our manner of life, our thoughts, words and actions. How do I partake of the promises of God? By taking them as my own, embracing and believing them, then acting upon them. Faith mixed with the promises of God is like dynamite and when accompanied by action ignites into an explosion in the spiritual realm, bursting out into the physical realm—and the impossible is accomplished.

My circumstance may or may not change, but I know I am definitely changed in my spirit and nature. If I take God's promise that He will supply all my needs according to His riches in glory by Christ Jesus, and I meditate upon it, repeating it to myself until it becomes alive and powerful within me, my faith is released. I then find I am trusting God in that particular area. I am at rest. Peace and trust are part of God's nature. His nature of trust and confidence is being worked in my spirit and nature, and this is a process.

"In your relationships with one another, have the same mindset as Christ Jesus: Who, being in very nature God, did not consider equality with God something to be used to His own advantage; rather, He made Himself nothing by taking the very nature of a servant, being made in human likeness. And being found in appearance as a man, He humbled Himself by becoming obedient to death—even death on a cross! Therefore God exalted Him to the highest place and gave Him the name that is above every name"(Philippians 2:5-9).

THE MINDSET OF CHRIST

WHAT WAS JESUS' mindset like when He walked the earth? The Bible tells us that we are to have His same mindset. So what was it? Even though He was all God, He was all man, and as a man, Jesus emptied Himself of all His divine rights and therefore, used no power of His own to operate in, but depended only on the power of the Holy Spirit. All the miracles, signs and wonders that He did were done by the power of the Holy Spirit. He did not boast within Himself, but in God and His works. Jesus did not seek His own glory. (John 8:50) He said, *"I do nothing of myself...."* (John 5:30, 8:28) Jesus learned to operate in the Spirit, to yield to and humbly obey God. The Bible also tells us that He learned obedience through the things He suffered. (Heb. 5:8)

So with us, ministers of Christ, we are to have the same mindset as He did. Not in selfish ambition, choosing to make a name or reputation for ourselves, our ministries, or our church. It's not how *great* we are in the Kingdom, but rather if we are cultivating a heart of lowliness and humbleness of mind exalting Christ and serving each other with a pure heart. Jesus said if we are to be great in the Kingdom of God we are to be a servant to all. (Matt. 20: 26) Any work we do must be done through the power of the Holy Spirit. And so, any powerful movement of God is not because of us, but because of His working. To God be all the glory! It is His anointing

for His glory and we don't want to steal His glory. We can pray for greater anointing and for God to move, but ultimately it is God who does the work. We are to learn to obey Him in all things, and do all things without vain ambition, conceit, or striving to impress others. This is the mindset of Jesus.

JANUARY 31

"'Arise, and go down to the potter's house, and
there I will cause thee to hear My words.'
Then I went down to the potter's house, and,
behold, he wrought a work on the wheels.
And the vessel that he made of clay was marred in the hand of the potter:
so he made it again another vessel, as seemed good to the potter to make [it].
Then the word of the LORD came to me, saying,
'O house of Israel, cannot I do with you as this potter? Saith
the LORD. Behold, as the clay [is] in the potter's hand, so [are]
ye in Mine hand, O house of Israel.'"(Jeremiah 18:2-6).

THE POTTER'S TOUCH

VERSE: I'M SITTING on the Potter's wheel, waiting for my heart to heal. Why is it taking so long?

The Master has a special plan but I just don't understand—the days keep going on and on.

So I sing this song to Him of what I want to see, how much I want the Potter's will to be done in me.

Chorus: I want the Potter's touch upon my heart today—just the Potter's touch to mold this simple lump of clay. Upon the wheel of His grace, I will look into His face. I need the Potter's touch today.

Verse: I'm waiting now, cause I've tried so much, and I long for the Master's touch. His hand I want to feel.

Upon my heart He works away, until He sees a grand display upon the Potter's wheel.

Chorus: I want the Potter's touch upon my heart today—just the Potter's touch to mold this simple lump of clay. Upon the wheel of His grace, I will look into His face. I need the Potter's touch today.

Bridge: Make me; Lord, shape me—I am waiting here for You. Mold me, enfold me with Your Love.

Copyright 2013 Roxanne Eilers

FEBRUARY 1

"All your people will be righteous. They will possess their land forever, for I will plant them there with My own hands in order to bring Myself glory" (Isaiah 60:21).

YOU ARE PLANTED—NOW BLOOM

*D*ID YOU KNOW you were created for God to display His splendor through your life? Isaiah 60:21 says that we are the shoot He has planted. We are the skilled work of His hands for the display of His splendor. What does this mean? I believe God is telling us here that He planted within each of us a measure of faith that we can use in the place where He has planted us, and that is the place where you are right now. It is right in this particular place where God will shine through you and display the beauty, love and glory of His Son, Jesus Christ. So don't be in such a hurry to move away from where you are, at home, at work, in ministry… You've heard it said, *"Bloom where you are planted."* God is asking us to do just that.

FEBRUARY 2

*"But the Lord is faithful, and He will strengthen
you and protect you from the evil one"
(2 Thessalonians 3:3).*

HOPE IS REAL

*I*T'S BEEN A while since our beloved son, Joseph, was hit by a car and taken away up to heaven. A parent who has lost a child is the only one who can understand the pain, grief, anguish and emptiness that comes with this kind of loss. I have been in the depths of grief that at times, refused comfort but wallowed in its persistent pain. I have also felt the supernatural grace and strength of Our Lord Jesus sustaining me and pulling me out of myself and my pain over and over again. I have experienced His peace and even a happiness of knowing that I am His and that my Joseph was His also, and is safe with Him. I know that some of you are going through struggles right now—hardships, difficulties that could blow someone away. I know some of you are at your wits end, your pain and grief, your loss has been great and you don't know how you can go on at times. I know that some of you are in a battle of some kind every day—clinging to your faith in God, rehearsing His promises with tears in your eyes. Please be encouraged today. There is a God who cares about what you are experiencing right this minute. We don't have all the answers, but we have the One who can make things okay. Somehow, He knows how to make things work out for our good and for His glory as we release our trials to Him. Even in the midst of the fires He is there to shelter and deliver. Keep steady. Keep worshiping God and obeying what He says in the Bible. In the Gospel of John, Jesus' words are so compelling and powerful when He says, *"Did I not tell you that if you believe, you will see the glory of God?"* (John 11:40) Keep believing and sooner or later you will see His glory a little bit clearer. You will worship Him a little bit longer and love Him a little bit deeper.

February 3

"I am the LORD, the God of all mankind. Is anything too hard for Me" (Jeremiah 32:27)?

Powerless Over the Situation

*T*HERE ARE TIMES when circumstances come into our lives that we have absolutely no control over. We cannot manipulate, change or rearrange what's going on. We feel powerless over not being able to make things okay. This is the time when God is saying to us to completely release it to Him. He is big enough to take care of the whole matter. We are not God. God is God and He is able to do what we cannot do. He is able to accomplish His will. At these times, especially, we must let it go from our hands to His hands. He will show us moment by moment what steps to take next. He is aware of all the struggle, worry and fear you are experiencing. Release it to Him and rest in His peace.

FEBRUARY 4

"And who knows but that you have come to your royal position for such a time as this" (Esther 4:14)?

REVEALING WHO YOU ARE

*I*N THE BOOK of Esther, we are told that King Xerxes was looking for a wife, and Esther, Mordecai's cousin, was one of the candidates. As she goes through the process of the preparations, Mordecai forbids her to reveal her nationality and family background. Later, after she is made Queen, the perfect time comes to her where she should reveal this information. She was brought to that place and position by God for just a time as that. And because she walked in wisdom over this thing she saved her people from death.

Sometimes, we as Christians, need to wait on the Lord for wisdom when to reveal our faith, to whom and where. There is an appointed time to share our faith and we never have to feel driven or afraid. God may be preparing the situation or person to receive His truth. And He will bring you to a particular place and give you a certain position, in order for you to share the gospel and who you are in Christ. Pray for wisdom. God will guide. Be ready!

FEBRUARY 5

"Moses answered, 'What if they do not believe me or listen to me and say, The LORD did not appear to you?' Then the LORD said to him, 'What is that in your hand?' 'A staff,' he replied. The LORD said, 'Throw it on the ground.' Moses threw it on the ground and it became a snake, and he ran from it. Then the LORD said to him, 'Reach out your hand and take it by the tail.' So Moses reached out and took hold of the snake and it turned back into a staff in his hand. 'This,' said the LORD, 'is so that they may believe that the LORD, the God of their fathers—the God of Abraham, the God of Isaac and the God of Jacob—has appeared to you'"(Exodus 4:1-5).

WHAT IS IN YOUR HAND?

OSES USED THE staff that was in his hand to become a serpent and to part the Red Sea. David used the sling that was in his hand to slay Goliath. The little widow at Zarephath used what was left of her oil and flour to feed Elijah. Jesus used a few fish and loaves to feed over five thousand people. As I have studied God's Word and walked with Him for over 40 years, I have come to realize and understand that God wants us to use what we have at our disposal to the utmost before He entrusts more to us. He doesn't want us to make excuses why we cannot do what He asks us to. We are to utilize what He has put in our hand. He will bring the increase. He will accomplish the miracle.

It is not what you have in your hand, but what you are doing with it.

It is not how much you possess, but how obedient you are with what God has given you.

FEBRUARY 6

"After washing their feet, He put on His robe again and sat down and asked, 'Do you understand what I was doing? You call Me Teacher and Lord, and you are right, because that's what I am. And since I, your Lord and Teacher, have washed your feet, you ought to wash each other's feet. I have given you an example to follow. Do as I have done to you'" (John 13:12-15 NLT).

A SERVANT'S HEART

JESUS SAID IF you want to be great in His Kingdom you must become the servant of all. We must be willing to serve in humility of spirit and lowliness of mind, for Jesus humbled Himself and came to serve. Ministry is just that—serving others, being the Lord's hands, feet and voice. Sometimes we get the wrong idea of leadership, and we are tempted to want to sit at the head place at the table, but this cannot be. The first must be last to function in God's Kingdom. We are all servants to one another and also to those who need Jesus.

"Now to Him who is able to do immeasurably more than all we ask or imagine, according to His power that is at work within us, to Him be glory in the church and in Christ Jesus throughout all generations, for ever and ever! Amen" (Ephesians 3:20-21).

THE ANSWER IS COMING

HAVE YOU BEEN praying and praying and praying about something, and it seems you are not receiving an answer? Don't be fooled by what you feel or what you see with your eyes, or even what you think is happening. God is at work on what you have been praying about and the answer is on its way. Never doubt that God is answering your prayer. He may answer it in a way you never even imagined. You might be looking down one fixed avenue where you think He will work, but God may have another from where He will answer you. And remember God is able not just to do what you ask or even think, but He is able to do EXCEEDINGLY, ABUNDANTLY, ABOVE all that you ask or even think!

February 8

*"He that dwells in the secret place of the most High
shall abide under the shadow of the Almighty"*
(Psalm 91:1).

The Secret Place

*T*HERE IS A place where we can find God that is called the *secret place* or the *"secret of God's tabernacle"* where we cannot be moved by trouble or trial. It is the place where we "dwell under the shadow of the Almighty." Hannah Whitall Smith says that this secret place wherein dwells the presence of God, is the safest fortress to be in; it is safer than "a thousand Gibraltars." Trials will still come into our lives, but they cannot disturb the soul in that secret place with God (Smith 1956). And friends, it takes faith to enter into this quiet place where strength and hope can be found.

So we enter in by faith. We meet with God by believing He is there to meet with us—we meet with God with our spirit and through our mind. Andrew Murray speaks about "practicing the presence of Christ." He makes reference to this practice as a person who *lives* in Christ—abides and stays in Christ (Payne 1989). When we abide in Christ we live in Him and He in us, and it is a practicing of His presence that can become our daily habit in our quiet time with Him.

Taken from *Hope in a Season of Suffering* by Roxanne Eilers

FEBRUARY 9

"If you are faithful in the little things, you will be faithful in the large ones" (Luke 16:10 NLT).

BE FAITHFUL

GOD IS THE one who is truly faithful, completely faithful in His character and person. The Bible says that He is faithful even when we are faithless (2 Tim. 3:13). God calls us to be faithful in our walk with Him. If we are faithful in the little things that we are given to do, we will be given larger things to accomplish. Sometimes it is difficult and boring to keep doing the little things that stare up into our faces, the everyday mundane things. But if we do them with honor and joy unto the Lord, and if we are faithful to serve in those small areas, God will bring into our lives assignments that require more faithfulness, more prayer and He knows He can trust us to do them. So be faithful right there where you are planted, and allow God to build the fruit of faithfulness into your life, and you will grow up into your next assignment from God!

FEBRUARY 10

*"In all this you greatly rejoice, though now for a little while you may
have had to suffer grief in all kinds of trials. These have come so that
the proven genuineness of your faith—of greater worth than gold,
which perishes even though refined by fire—may result in praise,
glory and honor when Jesus Christ is revealed"(1 Peter 1:6-7).*

THE TEST

*T*HERE COMES A time in every Christian believer's life when
everything he has learned and known is tested. The Bible is not
just a book full of wishful thinking and encouraging words.
These words must be tested in order for us to experience that they are true
and trustworthy. *"Every word of God is tested; He is a shield to those who
take refuge in Him." (NASB) Proverbs 30:5*

*"As for God, His way is perfect! The word of the Lord is
tested and tried; He is a shield to all those who take refuge
and put their trust in Him." (AMPC) Psalm 18:30*

The Bible says that God is our strength. Now will I make this my own
personal word and by faith walk in it, or will I just keep acknowledging it,
but fail to really get a hold of it? Do we really believe what God tells us? If
we do, it will be tested in us by fiery trials. Our faith must be tried through
difficulties so that the Word of God and His ways have become woven into
the very fiber of our souls and spirits.

God's Word has been tried and proven—it must now be tried and proven
in us through our faith.

February 11

"Then came Jesus forth, wearing the crown of thorns, and the purple robe. And Pilate saith unto them, Behold the man" (John 19:5)!

Behold This Man

Verse: Behold this man, who hung on a cross for me.
Why did He die? It was to set the captives free.
He stretched out His arms and He looked up to heaven—
Cried to His Father, *"Father, forgive them."* Behold this man. Behold this man.

Chorus: He is the King who came to save us! He is the Lamb, the Lord of Glory. He is the One who lifts up the burdened and the weary—He is the Shepherd of love and mercy. Behold this man, Behold this man.

Verse: Behold this man, the nations will bow down before Him.
He will rule and reign when He comes to the earth again.
Now His arms are outstretched and He looks down from heaven—
Giving praise to the Father for we are His children. Behold this man. Behold this man.

Chorus: He is the King who came to save us! He is the Lamb, the Lord of Glory. He is the One who lifts up the burdened and the weary—He is the Shepherd of love and mercy. Behold this man, Behold this man.

© by Roxanne Coutts Eilers 2013

FEBRUARY 12

"For this reason I say to you, do not be worried about your life, as to what you will eat or what you will drink; nor for your body, as to what you will put on. Is not life more than food, and the body more than clothing? Look at the birds of the air, that they do not sow, nor reap nor gather into barns, and yet your Heavenly Father feeds them. Are you not worth much more than they? And who of you by being worried can add a single hour to his life? And why are you worried about clothing? Observe how the lilies of the field grow; they do not toil nor do they spin, yet I say to you that not even Solomon in all his glory clothed himself like one of these. But if God so clothes the grass of the field, which is alive today and tomorrow is thrown into the furnace, will He not much more clothe you? You of little faith! Do not worry then, saying, 'What will we eat?' or 'What will we drink?' or 'What will we wear for clothing?' For the Gentiles eagerly seek all these things; for your Heavenly Father knows that you need all these things. But seek first His Kingdom and His righteousness, and all these things will be added to you"(Matthew 6:25-33).

LILIES AND SPARROWS

*L*OOK AT THE lilies of the field and the birds of the air. Your Heavenly Father takes good care of them. The lilies are beautifully clothed in gay array; they parade their delicate colors. The birds of the air are plump with worms and bugs, meat, fruit and seeds. They are very well fed. Both bow before the Father who made them and takes good care of them. His eye is always upon them, every tiny bud and open flower, every little baby sparrow and the regal eagle who swoops down on its prey.

Now how about you? You are the very apple of God's eye, His treasured possession and deeply loved by Him. The Bible tells us that He cares for you, and the very thoughts He thinks towards you are greater in number than the sands of the sea. If the Father takes care of the lilies and the sparrow how much more will He provide and take care of you, His own child?

Take heart! God is your refuge and strength. Your God will come and

bless you. He will give you all you need, for He is the God who provides. Just let go and lean back into His arms and trust Him as He sets a table before you. You are much greater and much more important to Him than lilies and sparrows. Take heart!

FEBRUARY 13

"How precious to me are Your thoughts, God! How vast is the sum of them! Were I to count them, they would outnumber the grains of sand—when I awake, I am still with You"(Psalm 139:17-18).

A NOTE FROM JESUS

"GOOD MORNING," JESUS says. *"My eye is upon you this day to guide and direct your steps into My ways and paths. Don't be afraid to do that thing that you may find difficult at the moment. My grace will be, and is, sufficient to carry you through. I speak words of encouragement and life to you today. I have set My love upon you and I am looking forward with joy to meet with you. It is in our meeting that you will find increased joy and strength. You are in My thoughts continually throughout this day. I love you."*

FEBRUARY 14

"Then those who feared the Lord spoke with one another. The Lord paid attention and heard them, and a book of remembrance was written before Him of those who feared the Lord and esteemed His name" (Malachi 3:16).

GOD HEARS

WE ARE OF those who fear and reverence the Lord, and what do we speak to one another about? You see, God is always listening to our conversations we have when we meet with each other. He desires that our words be seasoned with grace and truth. How easy at times it is to speak negatively of others, but God hears us. When we choose to set a guard over our lips and carefully choose our words, the Lord hears and those things we say that are precious to Him, He has written down in a Book of Remembrance. Perhaps He goes back at times to reread something we said that filled His heart with joy. When we get together with each other let us remember to reverence the Lord and speak as if He were present and listening, because He is. He is eager to hear us speak of our love for Him and others—to talk of His wonders and great deeds He has done.

FEBRUARY 15

"A psalm of David. My heart is confident in You, O God; no wonder I can sing Your praises with all my heart! Wake up, lyre and harp! I will wake the dawn with my song. I will thank You, LORD, among all the people. I will sing Your praises among the nations. For Your unfailing love is higher than the heavens. Your faithfulness reaches to the clouds. Be exalted, O God, above the highest heavens. May Your glory shine over all the earth"(Psalm 108:1-5 NLT).

PSALM 108:1-5

O GOD, MY HEART is unshakable! It is holding firmly and securely to Your Word. With everything that is within me—with my entire being I will declare Your praises in song. I say, *"Wake up my guitar!"* I will play upon it early in the morning. I will play with all my might to You, Lord. When I am gathered together with Your people I will shout Your praises! Whenever I travel throughout the land, even to other foreign lands, I will sing and play upon my guitar. I will sing about Your great compassions and Your truth that go on and on forever. Be lifted up O God, far above all creation and the whole universe to the highest heavens! Let Your glory hover over the entire earth.

Let this day be filled with praises to the Lord. Sing to Him in song and thank Him for all His blessings He has showered on you!

FEBRUARY 16

"Do not be anxious about anything, but in every situation, by prayer and petition, with thanksgiving, present your requests to God. And the peace of God, which transcends all understanding, will guard your hearts and your minds in Christ Jesus" (Philippians 4:6-7).

PEACE INSTEAD OF WORRY

ARE YOU FEELING anxious or overly concerned about something? God says not to worry about anything, but in every situation pray and bring your petitions before Him. Then give Him thanks that He has heard and that He is doing something about your situation. How will you know that you are trusting Him? You will know, if you have His peace filling your heart and mind. To keep His peace in your heart, *train* your mind to dwell on those things that are uplifting and positive. I believe there may be something positive in every circumstance we find ourselves in. Look to find what is good, and if you ask God to show you what that is, He will. Is He teaching you something about Himself? Is a person coming closer to receiving Christ because of what you are going through? Are you in a place where you have to turn to God and depend upon Him more than ever?

Be at peace and trust your Heavenly Father to take care of your concerns.

FEBRUARY 17

"My eyes stay open through the watches of the night, that I may meditate on Your promises" (Psalm 119:148).

GOD AT NIGHT

*D*ID YOU KNOW that God often visits His children in the night seasons? It is then that the world is quiet and our hearts are more transparent and open to God's Spirit. In the night God tests our hearts and brings to our attention areas that He desires to work on. The Lord gives us counsel in the night. He uses our heart as a lamp to instruct us in ways we should go, and at times it is in these very moments that He shows us hidden things, things to come, and where He wants to take us (Ps. 16:7). God desires us to meditate and ponder upon His Word through the night watches. He may awaken us with a scripture (Ps 119:148). Sometimes we are startled and awakened with a fearful feeling. We sense warfare going on in the spiritual realm. At these times we need to call on the name of Jesus and claim His power over all the power of the enemy. God can speak to us in the night in a dream, in a vision, while we are deep in sleep. He opens our spiritual ears and gives us instruction to follow (Job 33:14-16). Our spirit is very much awake at night and longs to fellowship with God (Is. 26:9). God also gives us songs in the night—songs of praise and ministry to His body (Job 35:10). You will find that if you ask God to wake you in the night so you can spend time with Him, He will. Listen to God in the night seasons and when you wake, see if God confirms what He has shown you.

FEBRUARY 18

> *"Without weakening in his faith, he faced the fact that his body
> was as good as dead—since he was about a hundred years old—
> and that Sarah's womb was also dead. Yet he did not waver through
> unbelief regarding the promise of God, but was strengthened in
> his faith and gave glory to God, being fully persuaded that God
> had power to do what He had promised"(Romans 4:19-21).*

GOD'S PROMISES ARE SURE

THE OLDER WE get the more we can see how swiftly time goes by. We may find ourselves still hoping for unfulfilled dreams and wondering how they will ever come to pass. We look at our age and may feel anxious that the years have flown by and the promises the Lord has given to us are still unfulfilled. We ask *"When?"*

In the Bible, Abraham surely must have felt this way when he was waiting for a son to be born to him from his wife Sarah. It appeared all hope was gone because Sarah was way passed her child bearing years (Genesis 15:1-6). But God knew what He was doing and waited until their faith was at a pleasing point, and then performed a miraculous conception and birth with bringing Isaac into their lives. Abraham's faith was steady and sure as he held on to God's promises with all that was in him.

I believe this story of Abraham's and Sarah's faith is an example for us to follow and imitate. We are to hold on to God's promises no matter what it looks like, how long it takes, or how old we are. The Bible tells us in Psalm 39:5 & 7 *"Indeed, You have made my days as a handbreath, and my age is as nothing before You…And now, Lord, what do I wait for? My hope is in You."*

Never give up on what God has highlighted and illumined in His Word for you. Hold steady for He is faithful who promised (1Cor.1:9).

FEBRUARY 19

"Whom have I in heaven but You? And earth has nothing I desire besides You"(Psalm 73:25).

JESUS SAID

JESUS SAID I am with you always-
Therefore I am never alone.
Jesus said My grace is sufficient for you-
Therefore I will make it through.
Jesus said let not your heart be troubled; neither be afraid-
Therefore I can have peace of heart and mind.
Jesus said follow Me-
Therefore I have direction.
Jesus said seek first the Kingdom of God and everything else will be added unto you-
Therefore my needs are always met.
Jesus said whoever comes to Me I will never cast out-
Therefore I am fully accepted.
Jesus said the one who believes in Me has eternal life-
Therefore I am eternally secure in Him.

"Lord, please show me Your glory"(Exodus 33:18).
"...[this trouble] has come for the glory of God, that the
Son of God may be glorified in it"(John 11:4).

THEN GIVE HIM ALL THE GLORY!

GOD WILL SHOW you the way through your situation. Be still and listen for His voice and instructions. Don't be in a hurry or act in haste, or out of fear and anxiety. God knows what is going on and He has the solution. Inquire of Him and then wait on His move. He will show forth His glory in His own way and time. You will not drown nor be over taken by your circumstance. Rest in His loving care and watch what He does. Stand in awe and then, give Him all the glory! Give Him all the glory!

FEBRUARY 21

"Jesus stepped into a boat, crossed over and came to His own town. Some men brought to Him a paralyzed man, lying on a mat. When Jesus saw their faith, He said to the man, 'Take heart, son; your sins are forgiven'"(Matthew 9:1-2).

DO YOU HAVE IT?

*I*N MATTHEW 9 there is the story of the paralytic. There were "some men who brought Jesus a paralyzed man lying on a mat"—Jesus was looking for something from these men. He was looking to see if they had the key that would unlock the door to His healing virtue. Did they have it? Jesus saw it. He saw their faith and their faith moved Jesus to perform the miraculous for them. The paralyzed man was forgiven for his sins and healed physically.

Do you have it? Will your faith unlock the door to God's power to move in behalf of whatever you are praying about? Jesus is looking for the key. God tells us in the Book of Hebrews that faith pleases Him. So have faith. Everyone has a measure of faith and can increase it through meditating upon, hearing and reading God's Word.

February 22

*"...for, Everyone who calls on the name of the
Lord will be saved"(Romans 10:13).*

Salvation

To *"Call on the name of the Lord"* means to cry out for aide, to fall at His feet in adoration, acknowledging Him to be Lord and make the "Decision." It is the decision that connects us to God's Spirit. It is the decision to believe in the Son of the Living God, and cry out for His mercy upon our sinful soul. It's the humbling of the heart to receive and embrace the truth. This decision brings about the holy re-birth within our spirits—-the uniting of our spirits with the Holy Spirit.

I believe that God eagerly searches for that one tiny speck of light that generates faith, that one itty bitty seed of repentance, that small turning of the heart to God, and He grabs hold on to it bringing the unredeemed to redemption, and into His Kingdom.

FEBRUARY 23

*"He has made everything beautiful in its time. He has also
set eternity in the human heart; yet no one can fathom what
God has done from beginning to end"(Ecclesiastes 3:11).*

THE BEAUTY OF RESTORATION

GOD GAVE ME a promise that He, Himself, would restore to my
life what the locusts had eaten, all the years that seemed endless with suffering. God began to bring people, books, music and
other agents into my life to bring about my healing and wholeness. Different
pieces of the puzzle, that seemed to be missing, were slowly being uncovered
and began to fit into place. Slowly, faith began to replace fear, and joyful
expectation began to replace the dark depression.

I have experienced so much freedom, and my heart overflows with
thanksgiving to the Lord, who does all things well. The Bible tells us there is
a particular time that God has for us to become beautiful in an area that we
have been struggling with. We must also not forget that healing is a journey
and continual process.

God is in the business, of not only allowing us to be torn down, but also
building us up and restoring us. In Ecclesiastes 3:3 we are told that there
is a *"time to tear down and a time to build."* God has to build on a good
foundation, so we may find ourselves being stripped down to bare root in
an area of our lives. God has to build what He desires in us so that we can
serve Him fully, being filled with joy, and bringing Him glory. As a new creation in Christ, our spirit has been made brand new, but our mind has to be
transformed. This is part of the restoring process. I have found restoration
has three main ingredients. *The Working of the Holy Spirit, Knowing and
Obeying God's Word, the Bible, and the Passing of Time.*
.—TAKEN FROM MY BOOK *HOPE IN A SEASON OF SUFFERING* ©2018

FEBRUARY 24

"'Does Job fear God for nothing?' Satan replied. 'Have You not put a hedge around him and his household and everything he has? You have blessed the work of his hands, so that his flocks and herds are spread throughout the land'"(Job 1:9-10).

THE HEDGE

*I*N PSALM 121 verse 5, it says, *"The Lord is your keeper… "* This word "keeper" in the Hebrew language is *Shamar* which means "to hedge about, guard, protect, attend to, keep, preserve and watch" (Strong's 8104). God places a supernatural hedge about us; even Satan knows God has set this hedge around His people in Job 1:9-10. God shelters us with His hedge. It protects us from evil. I believe there are *four* components that make up this hedge.

Psalm 34:7 tells us it is the angel of the Lord who encamps around us to deliver us. Then in Psalm 139:4-5 the Lord hems us in all around by the Holy Spirit. I also believe our faith and obedience to God keep that hedge up around us. So the hedge is God's mighty angels, His own embracing Holy Spirit, His protecting and preserving hand and our faith and obedience.

The only way something can touch us is if He lifts His hand and allows it to pass through to us, for His own purpose and glory, and for our good and growth. In Exodus 33:14 God says He will send His presence with us to help us face whatever comes into our lives, and He will give us rest. Our God will never leave us, nor forsake us. He is our true helper.

FEBRUARY 25

"I keep my eyes always on the LORD. With Him at my right hand, I will not be shaken"(Psalm 16:8).

UNSHAKABLE FAITH IN AN UNSHAKABLE GOD

BECAUSE GOD IS my Rock—my solid unmovable Rock and my full Salvation, because He is my Protector and Shield, and He is the Place I can run to in times of distress, I declare that I will never be shaken in my faith. I will not waver or doubt when trials come against me, but I will stand firm and steadfast, for I know whom I have believed in, and I am persuaded that He is able to keep and strengthen me with His might in my inward man. I will not be moved.

"This is what the LORD says—
He who made a way through the sea,
a path through the mighty waters, who drew out the chariots and horses, the
army and reinforcements together, and they lay there, never to rise again,
extinguished, snuffed out like a wick:
'Forget the former things; do not dwell on the past.
See, I am doing a new thing!
Now it springs up; do you not perceive it?
I am making a way in the wilderness and streams in
the wasteland. The wild animals honor Me,
the jackals and the owls, because I provide water in
the wilderness and streams in the wasteland,
to give drink to My people, My chosen,
the people I formed for Myself that they may
proclaim My praise'"(Isaiah 43:16-21).

GOD WILL MAKE A WAY

WHEN MOSES AND the Children of Israel were shut up with their backs against the Red Sea, it appeared in the natural that there was no way they were going to survive the Egyptian army that was coming against them. If they fled to the sea they would surely drown. Where could they go? They were terrified and felt paralyzed. But God tells Moses to instruct the Children of Israel to go forward. God made a *way* in the Sea. He made a *path* through the mighty waters. He wanted His people to go on ahead and forget the former things they had been through. God was doing a new thing right before their very eyes, so that His people, He had formed for Himself, would see His mighty works and declare His praise.

Today, God is calling you to go forward as He makes a *way* in your sea of impossibilities. He is carving out a *path* with each step you take. He calls you to forget where you have been, and to look forward to the new things He is going to do, and is already doing, in your life and in the lives of your

loved ones. He will even make a road in your wilderness and rivers in the desert. He will supply your needs when all around you is dry and parched. You will hear Him say to you, *"This is the way, walk in it."* Whenever you turn to the right or to the left you will be guided by God's Holy Spirit and protected by His angels. So go forward as God shows you the way. He will make a *way* where there is no way.

The Children of Israel miraculously passed through the Red Sea and arrived safely on the other side giving glory to God for His awesome works. Can you give glory to God in advance for His powerful deliverance in your life?

FEBRUARY 27

"When we arrived in Macedonia, there was no rest for us. We faced conflict from every direction, with battles on the outside and fear on the inside" (2 Corinthians 7:5 NLT).

WE ARE HUMAN

IN THIS PASSAGE, Paul is confessing to the Corinthians the trouble he was struggling with. He said there was trouble everywhere he turned. Outside of him and around him were conflicts going on. He, and those who were with him, were being extremely pressured and persecuted. His soul felt trapped in a tight place he didn't like. The strife he encountered grieved his heart. He then confesses that he battled with fears within himself.

When we think of Paul we might imagine him as super human and not vulnerable to feeling the weaknesses of the soul and flesh. On the contrary, he was just a human being as we are, and he had to turn to God to give him strength, deliverance and comfort in his afflictions. God did bring Paul the comfort he sought. Paul says that God comforts the downcast. When we are feeling so very human and vulnerable, weak, weary and afraid, God does not condemn or judge us, but rather gathers us up into His arms of mercy and grace. He will continue to be there for us each time we encounter weak and fearful moments in our lives.

FEBRUARY 28

"If only you had paid attention to My commands, your peace would have been like a river, your righteousness like the waves of the sea"(Isaiah 48:18).

CHOOSE TO OBEY

IN ALL OUR dealings with God, we have choices to make. When He asks of us obedience, we must choose to obey and go His way. All through the Bible are accounts of men and women who have had to make these same choices. Choices to embrace God's plan and purpose, to say yes to suffering, and no to pleasures of sin, to pray and not to faint, to trust instead of doubt....The choices to give ear to God's commands, to His Word, and to do what He says.

God promises if we choose to obey Him, He will give us peace of mind and spirit—a quiet and contented heart—right in the middle of the grueling storm. Ought we not to make the wise choice of obedience today, tomorrow, and always?

MARCH 1

"Paul and Timothy, bond-servants of Christ Jesus, to all the saints in Christ Jesus who are in Philippi, including the overseers and deacons:" (Philippians 1:1 NASB).

DOULOS—BONDSERVANT

IT IS AMAZING to me that Jesus, who is God, took on the form of a bondservant. *"He took on the likeness of men, and He humbled Himself and became obedient to the point of death, even the death of the cross" (Phil. 2:6-8)*. Jesus served His disciples and washed their feet. He said it was an example for them to follow—to serve others in the spirit of humility (John 13). God calls Jesus, His Servant whom He has chosen; His beloved in whom He is well pleased (Matt. 12:18). In Mark 9:35 Jesus tells His disciples that if they want to be first, they are to be last of all and servant of all. The Bible calls us bondservants of Jesus Christ. The Greek word for "bondservant" is *Doulos*, and it is someone who belongs to another and has no rights of their own. We choose to submit to the authority and rulership of our Savior, Jesus. It is said that this title "bondservant" is used with highest dignity in the New Testament *(HelpsBible.com)*.

Jesus gave up all His heavenly rights when He came to earth and committed Himself completely to the Father. Whatever the Father said, Jesus did. So if the Son of God took on the life of being a bondservant to the Father, He knows how to help us to be a bondservant also.

A bondservant serves with a cheerful heart and seeks the interests of others. A bondservant seeks the welfare of others and does what his Lord tells him to. We are asked to give up all our earthly rights and to submit our will to God. A bondservant places others in the prominent seat and esteems them instead of self. He is not self-centered or seeking recognition and glory for himself. He only seeks to bring God the glory.

Are we truly living our lives as bondservants of the Lord? Are we washing

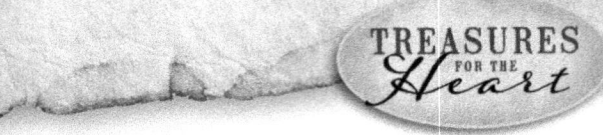
the feet of another? Are we humbling our hearts and do we strive to walk in a lowly spirit?

I want a bondservant's heart. O God, give me this mindset that was also in Christ Jesus.

March 2

"The LORD is my shepherd, I lack nothing.
He makes me lie down in green pastures, He leads me
beside quiet waters, He refreshes my soul. He guides
me along the right paths for His name's sake.
Even though I walk through the darkest valley, I will fear
no evil, for You are with me; Your rod and Your staff, they
comfort me. You prepare a table before me in the presence of my
enemies. You anoint my head with oil; my cup overflows.
Surely Your goodness and love will follow me all the days of my life,
and I will dwell in the house of the LORD forever"(Psalm 23).

The Voice of a Sheep—Psalm 23

LORD, YOU ARE my Shepherd and You take care of all my needs—

When I am weary and tired, You show me where the green, luscious pasture is so that I can rest and renew my strength. Your hand takes mine, and You gently lead me to the places where I will have peace and quietness for my soul—Your presence refreshes me.

And when I am taking a wrong path, You quickly guide me with Your rod and staff back on to the right road for Your own glory and honor, Lord.

I won't tremble or be terrified when I step into the valley of great darkness and death because You are right there next to me—my eyes are *fixed* on You because You will bring me through to the other side. You are my greatest comfort.

Right in the middle of my trials and tribulations, You serve me the spiritual food that I need to keep going on, and You pour out Your Holy Spirit all over me like oil. You anoint me to serve You! How happy I am!

I am convinced that I will experience Your goodness and faithful love every day that I have breath, and when this life is over, I will live with You, my Shepherd, forever and ever and ever. Amen.

MARCH 3

*"Wait for the LORD; be strong and take heart
and wait for the LORD" (Psalm 27:14).*

WALLED IN—NO WAY OUT

DO YOU EVER feel frustrated and discouraged that you have come to a wall that won't come down, or you find that every door is shut? You've prayed and God seems silent. You've come to a standstill. What are you to do? Keep doing what you are doing—keep steady, unmovable, because sooner or later that mountain will come down or a door will open for you. These times of waiting and seeming detours are designed by God for you. Don't move or try to propel yourself ahead. Wait for God. Just wait and try to be patient. Keep tilling the soil, or planting those seeds, or watering, because the harvest will come. God will personally open that door and escort you through!

MARCH 4

"This is the day that the Lord has made let us rejoice and be glad in it" (Psalm 118:24).

THIS IS THE DAY!

ODAY IS THE day that God has made and created just for you and me to be happy in. We can *learn* to be content in our day and have a thankful heart, however our day may be. Look for the good in the world and in people. Look for the beauty and glory of the Lord in His creation and in His works. Look for that promising rainbow and that peek of sun through the clouds. Be content within yourself and with who God has made you, and is making you to be. Rejoice in the work of His hands in your life! Be thankful for family and friends and those who cheer you on in life. Live in the present, and adore God who makes all things possible for you. Take hold of His promises, because not one word of His will fail without being completed. Stretch out your arms to the heavens and worship the King who is worthy to be adored. Be glad you are blessed with this day of your life.

MARCH 5

*(Speaking of Abraham) "...who contrary to hope,
in hope believed...."(Romans 4:18).*

KEEP BELIEVING

*W*HEN YOU ARE believing God for something, and He has given you a promise in your heart through His Word, you must keep holding on to it tenaciously. Do not flinch in your belief, because God looks for faith that is alive and active to honor. Will we really believe God to do the impossible for us? Will we really believe God to save that loved one or friend? Rescue that son or daughter in trouble? Supply groceries? Give you that needed car? Heal that constant infirmity? Direct your steps in a matter? Supply your rent money? Deliver you from that fear? Reconcile a troubled relationship?

Keep thanking God for what He has already done and will do. Have persistent faith. Faith can be stretched and faith can grow, so when all seems to be contrary to what you are believing for, then that is the time to really hold firm to your faith.

"The Word of God is living and active..."(Hebrews 4:12).
"So is My word that goes out from My mouth; it will not
return to Me empty, but will accomplish what I desire and
achieve the purpose for which it was sent"(Isaiah 55:11).
"God watches over His word to perform it"(Jeremiah 1:12).

God's Words

God's words are found in the Holy Bible, and it is astonishing what I found out about them. Listen to this. When the Bible tells us the Word of God is *living* it means it is full of the life of God—*Zoe* life (the life of God, in the Greek). God's words are no ordinary words. They are alive because they are God-breathed. God's very pulsating life fills His holy Word, and that is why we can say, *"He sent His Word and healed them."* The Word does something within the physical body, mind and spirit of a person. Other books with words are just that, words on a page that only come alive through our imagination. However, God's words are already alive, and breathe life into those who take them in. Jesus said the words that He spoke, they were spirit and they were life (John 6:63). They have the capability of continuing to speak and operate in the spiritual realm as they are spoken forth. There is power in the Word of God to bring something out of nothing.

Not only is God's Word living, it is active. This word in the Greek is *energace* which has the meaning of being productive with a result, effective (it works) operative—full of energy—energizing (Strong's Greek 1756). Wow! God's Word is a living, working entity in itself, and wherever it is sent it performs its mission and transforms, heals, delivers, saves, teaches, enlightens, encourages, comforts, directs...etc. It makes itself known through our voices and written form throughout the world, and in the heart of man. The Word of God energizes us spiritually. It is no ordinary Word. That is why we are urged to take it in and confess it out loud. It is pounding and resounding with life and power. The Word of

God, spiritually and literally, feeds our spirit man, makes it strong and then renews our minds.

MARCH 7

A LESSON RELEARNED

WHEN I AWOKE this morning, I felt quite under the weather. Before I knew it, foreboding thoughts began to crowd their way into my mind. I felt weak and vulnerable to fear and doubt. Later that morning I went to the store, still feeling apathetic and dragging. My faith seemed to be hiding somewhere. It appeared to be fluctuating, and I felt shaken a bit. Then as I chose an item on the shelf, the Lord spoke to me in a clear way, *"Faith has nothing ever to do with how you feel. It has everything to do with obedience and choice."* I realized then what was going on. It was an attack of the enemy on my faith. I stood my ground and even though my feelings were still trying to dominate my being, I rested in the solid fact that I had chosen to have faith. I had chosen to believe. I was at peace and rejoiced in the lesson I was reminded of again. I chose to obey the Lord and chose faith over feelings.

"So we fix our eyes not on what is seen, but on what is unseen, since what is seen is temporary, but what is unseen is eternal"(2 Corinthians 4:18).

HEAVEN

HEAVEN IS A real place. We sometimes are so caught up in this age that we don't give much thought to our beautiful future home where we will one day come to live. Heaven is like earth in that it is a country, a city where people live and accomplish their dreams. We will walk in God's love and anointing with no earthly body that will dim this experience. We will have a glorified body and we will be with our loved ones forever enjoying all that God has prepared for us. Heaven is not a place where we just float around on a cloud looking like an angel. No. God has created a spectacular place for us. The world cannot begin to fathom the glories of heaven because they do not have the Spirit of God who could reveal some of these glories to them. Sometimes God will reveal some of the secrets of the life beyond to some, in order for them to share with us some of the wonders that await us. We can even taste heaven at times here on earth. As a Christian believer we are called to be aware of this other world so that we do not lose sight of what really is important in this life. God and people are most important. Even the saints of old kept their spiritual eyes fixed upon a heavenly city to keep them walking in hope.

"This is what the LORD says—your Redeemer, the Holy One of Israel: 'I am the LORD your God, who teaches you what is best for you, who directs you in the way you should go'"(Isaiah 48:17).

THE IMPOSSIBLE PLACE

*I*F YOU ARE in a tight spot—I mean a place where at times it seems everything appears to be closing in on you. That spot where there seems to be no answers; the place where the battle is on and you feel backed up in a corner—the impossible place. You are right where you should be at this time in your life. If you have given your heart to Jesus Christ and you believe on Him, you have become a child of God. Nothing is by chance when it comes to God and His dealings with His children. You are in the right place, so remember these things: God will always sustain you. He will always deliver you and bring you out of the valley. He hasn't forgotten you, and your case lies open continually before Him. He is watching your heart and every time you choose faith, to trust in Him and rely on His goodness and love. Take heart! You are right where you need to be at this time in your life.

MARCH 10

"Beloved, think it not strange concerning the fiery trial which is to try you, as though some strange thing happened unto you"(1 Peter 4:12).

ENCOURAGE YOUR SOUL

*T*HERE COMES A time in every Christian believer's life when his faith is tried to the uttermost. All securities and sureties are taken away. It appears that there is no hope in sight. At these times we must take hold of the Lord and His Word and determine to rely solely on Him for the outcome. He is the Creator of all, and is more than able to take care of our particular matters. Release it into His hands because *"Shall not the Judge of the earth do what is right?"* (Gen.18:25). He is always good, and works all for His purpose and plan, and He will fulfill and perfect that which concerns you. Look not at the things which you hear, see or feel. Look only to God for His way is perfect. Take heart and encourage your soul in your God.

"In Judah is God known: His name is great in Israel" (Psalm 76:1).

IN PRAISE GOD IS KNOWN

*T*HE NAME *JUDAH* means praise, so we can say it is in our times of praise that God reveals Himself to us. God has been nudging me about spending more time worshiping and praising Him. He is worthy of all our praise. Remember, if we do not praise Him, the rocks will cry out declaring His goodness and greatness. I believe something mystical happens when we join our spirit with God through praise. We can sense His presence, and the Holy Spirit will bring joy to our heart, bearing witness with our spirit that we indeed belong to God, and we are His beloved child. Through worship the Lord will reveal His majesty and glory to us. We can see this in the spiritual realm within our heart and mind. The more we glimpse His loveliness, the more we want to praise Him.

Now what about when we don't feel like praising God? The Bible says that in these times we are to offer up the sacrifice of praise to Him continually; this is the fruit of our lips—we have to say something audible to God. We thank Him for His wonders, His mighty acts, for who He is, and all that He has done for us (Heb. 13:15). Doing this refocuses our spiritual eyes on spiritual matters and opens our spirit up for joy. We praise even if we are feeling down because God is worthy of our praise. Many times during praise people are healed, answers to problems are given, deliverances happen. I believe this happens because we get our eyes off of ourselves, and this frees up our faith to be expressed before a mighty, worthy God.

Right now I am going to praise the Lord in my prayer closet. I need a fresh revelation of His presence to touch my life and sustain me for the day.

MARCH 12

"Continue to remember those in prison as if you were together with them in prison, and those who are mistreated as if you yourselves were suffering" (Hebrews 13:3).

URGENT PRAYER FOR THE PERSECUTED

DEAR FATHER, OUR hearts go out to all of those who are being severely persecuted and killed for their faith. Please intervene and make a way where there is no way for them to escape to safety. Shield them, deliver them, have mercy on them, O God. Hold back the hand of the wicked who seek to torture and destroy the innocent. Fight on the behalf of Your people, O God. Let them have a supernatural encounter with You and Your sustaining presence with them. Lead them out, Dear Lord. Lead them to safety. Send Your angels to assist in protection and deliverance. Show Yourself strong on behalf of these dear people. We stand in faith agreeing and believing that You will move in a powerful way confounding the enemy and rescuing Your people. Thank You, Father, for hearing our cries. We ask this in Jesus' Powerful, Mighty Name. Amen.

MARCH 13

*"For the weapons of our warfare are not carnal but mighty in God
for pulling down strongholds, casting down arguments and every
high thing that exalts itself against the knowledge of God, bringing
every thought into captivity to the obedience of Christ, and being
ready to punish all disobedience" (2 Corinthians 10:4-6).*

PULLING DOWN STRONGHOLDS

GOD HAS GIVEN us all we need to pull down the strongholds in our life. What is a stronghold and how do we pull it down? Strongholds are the places in our thoughts where we do not have the peace of Christ reigning. Instead there is fear, worry, guilt, shame, lust, and unforgiveness, lurking and each one takes us captive. Where there is a stronghold the enemy can come in and harass and oppress and confuse. Strongholds are those things in our lives that are opposite of what God says. For instance, I may have a stronghold of fear of what others think of me. This fear can be so strong that it holds me back from allowing Christ's nature to rule and increase in that area. My motivation for doing things is driven by the fear of not being accepted and of being rejected. It is a stronghold when it rules us and we are its slave. Now God has given us weapons whereby we can pull down these strongholds. The main weapons we can use are the Name of Jesus, and the Word of God. We have authority in the Name of Jesus to resist the devil's lies and to break his power off of our lives. When we choose to take and believe God's Word instead of the lie behind the fear, Christ is being formed in us in that area, and where Christ reigns, the stronghold must come down and peace will rule. Every thought must be brought captive to obeying and believing Jesus. We must have the praises and Word of God on our lips and allow His nature to dominate our heart.

MARCH 14

"But Zion said, 'The Lord has forsaken me, the Lord has forgotten me.' Can a mother forget the baby at her breast and have no compassion on the child she has borne? Though she may forget, I will not forget you"(Isaiah 49:14-15)!

GOD WILL NOT FORGET YOU

*H*AVE YOU EVER said, *"The Lord has forsaken me; the Lord has forgotten all about me and my circumstance?"* It looks that way at times doesn't it? The trial we keep battling seems to go on and on with no end in sight. We've prayed, fasted, done all we could do, yet the wall we are up against appears to remain the same. Where is God? Why doesn't He do something?

One day when I was at Vanguard University, responding to an altar call in chapel, I felt my heart was broken. I was sobbing and crying out to the Lord about how hard the situation was that I was struggling with. I felt alone and hopeless. How long would I have to suffer so much? Then from within my inner most being, the Holy Spirit spoke to me, it was almost like an audible voice. It was today's scripture that I heard spoken to me. I felt enveloped in God's presence. I'll never forget it. He told me He would never forget me. That meant that He still knew what I was going through, and He still had everything under control. He was there all the time.

Remember, when you feel alone and doubts are assailing you, that God *can't* forget you. You are constantly before His eyes.

MARCH 15

"My God, whom I praise, do not remain silent"(Psalm 109:1).

THE SILENCE OF GOD

$\mathcal{I}$N PSALM 13, David talks about how he feels forgotten by God—forsaken—that God is hiding His face from him in his time of deep dark trouble. Most of us have felt this way at one time or another. It is the loneliness in the dark night of the soul when we can't feel or sense God with us. It is when the heavens seem brass and our prayers appear to go unanswered. Is God silent at these times?

In Hebrews 13:5-6 we are told that God will never leave us nor forsake us—that means never, so He is ever with us. However, God does allow these periods known as the dark night of the soul to encourage and stretch us to go deeper with Him, to grow our faith, to examine ourselves and confess known sin, to come to know God in a more intimate way. But if we will listen, God is still speaking to us through the felt silences. Even in the silence God is communicating with our hearts. He has never gone anywhere, nor will He. He has not ceased to answer our prayers. He is just allowing a slight delay for our benefit and growth. Praise Him in the silence and listen to what He is saying to you. Even the silence speaks.

MARCH 16

"For sin shall no longer be your master, because you are not under the law, but under grace"(Romans 6:14).

SPIRITUALLY OVERCOME STUBBORN SINS

1. RECOGNIZE IT IS sin and not pleasing to God. Also recognize it is Satan working to bring you down and back into bondage.

2. Confess your sin and apply the blood of the Lamb—meet Jesus at the feet of the cross.

3. Consider your sin and old nature crucified with Christ on that cross.

4. Accept that the new nature has risen and is ruling over the old nature. Position yourself spiritually with this truth.

5. Now turn away from everything that is associated with that sin. Hate the sin and flee from it. If you still desire it, it will stay and you will remain trapped. Even in this, ask God to take away the desire for this sin.

6. Praise God for the cleansing blood of His Son that has made you pure and spotless before Him.

7. Now go forth in victory, empowered by the Holy Spirit, holding high the shield of faith.

8. When the enemy brings it before you again tell him you are washed by the blood of the Living Lamb and will have nothing to do with the way of that sin. You are dead to the effects of that sin.

9. Leave old memories and feelings behind as you replace them with new and healthy ones; gradually the old memories with their feelings will lose their grip and fade in the back ground.

10. If you cannot do this yourself, seek out other mature believers who can show you the way and hold you up in prayer. Seek out someone you can trust and share with.

11. Don't linger on the nature of the sin and its consequences. Keep moving forward accepting your lot and learning from your mistakes.

MARCH 17

"Submit yourselves, then, to God. Resist the devil, and he will flee from you. Come near to God and He will come near to you. Wash your hands, you sinners, and purify your hearts, you double-minded"(James 4:7-8).

CHRISTIAN LIVING

FIRST, GIVE YOURSELF to God without reservation; then you can combat the devil who works against you, by firmly withstanding his evil darts of fear and doubt. Stand your ground. Know that you have authority over him and his cohorts. Oppose all he is and stands for, and when he sees that he can't get to you and cause you to be discouraged, alarmed or waver in your faith, he will run from you because he fears the authority and power you have in Jesus' Name.

Come into the presence of the Lord with complete confidence. Open up your heart to Him, for He is always ready to receive all who you are. His heart yearns over you as a father his child. Ask Him to wash away the wrong choices you have made and where your heart has gone astray from His ways. By His blood He will make you clean and pure. Seek Him with a teachable and pliable heart, and He will lift you up and place you where you will prosper and flourish—a place where you will bear much fruit.

*"The righteous will flourish like a palm tree, they will grow like
a cedar of Lebanon; planted in the house of the LORD, they
will flourish in the courts of our God" (Psalm 92:12-13).*

FIVE STEPS TO FLOURISHING SPIRITUALLY IN THE SUMMER

THIS SUMMER YOU will need springs of water and streams in the desert to flourish spiritually. Where do we find these springs and streams? The first place to look is in the Word of God. Nourish your soul and spirit on every word that proceeds out of the mouth of God. His words are like honey to the lips. Read, study and meditate upon them. Plan to do a little study on a subject or topic, using online commentaries and helps (biblehub.com).

Next, spend time in the Lord's presence soaking in the Holy Spirit who is water to the soul. Jesus said that if we come to Him, out of our bellies will flow rivers of living water—this is the Holy Spirit filling, baptizing us afresh, and empowering us to live for God.

Then grow your faith in an area of your life that needs it. Find all the scriptures on that subject and meditate upon them. Allow them to transform your heart and your thinking. Choose to trust God in a bigger way, and believe for greater things to be accomplished in your life and in the lives of your loved ones. God will answer.

Fourthly, pray. Increase your prayer life and pray in the Holy Spirit. Purposely include God in your thoughts all through the day. Pray with a friend. Along with prayer, worship God with songs of praise and be thankful. Look for things to thank God for, and cultivate a heart of gratitude.

Finally, spend time fellowshipping with God's people. There is power when we corporately gather to worship God together. Our faith is strengthened and renewed.

These are your springs of water and streams in the desert. Let this be a time of renewal and revival in your heart to the Lord. These steps will

prepare you for the next season in your life. They will fortify you so that you will not grow weary and parched from the heat of the trials that come your way. You will be a well-watered garden flourishing in the Lord.

MARCH 19

"For God, who commanded the light to shine out of darkness, hath shined in our hearts, to give the light of the knowledge of the glory of God in the face of Jesus Christ" (2 Corinthians 4:6 KJB).

COMMAND THE LIGHT!

I BELIEVE THAT WHEN we encounter a person, place or circumstance of darkness and sin, we can command the light of God to expose the truth. God's light is His Word. He says His Word is a lamp unto our feet and a light unto our path. Whenever there is darkness, if light is held up to it, the light will make things that are unseen to be seen. I believe God can open our spiritual eyes to people, places and circumstances as we speak His Word over them. We can say, *"Let there be light in this dark situation!"* God can direct us what to do about what is uncovered by His light. Even in prayer we can declare the Word over a person or ourselves. An example of this is, if a person is being tormented by fear and guilt, we can speak over them the Word of God. Perhaps we can declare, *"Where the Spirit of the Lord is, there is liberty."*—that could be liberty from any spiritual oppression or bondage of any kind. We can ask the Lord to expose what may be the cause or source of the oppression. He can, and will, give us light on what is going on in that person's life and what we can do about it. Therefore, we can pray more effectively. Remember, the light shines in the darkness, and the darkness can never snuff out the light!

MARCH 20

"It is written: 'I believed; therefore I have spoken.' Since we have that same spirit of faith, we also believe and therefore speak" (2 Corinthians 4:13).

BELIEVE AND SPEAK

WHEN WE ENCOUNTER God's Word, we must understand that His words are spirit and they are life. They are living and powerful. In the Greek it says that they are full of energy and they are producing a result whenever they are read or spoken. When they are spoken, they produce transformation. Speaking God's Word audibly is powerful for the believer. What we believe, that we will speak. *"As a man thinks, so is he."* What are you believing?

I believe that the victorious Christian life can be attainable as Paul says, in 1 Corinthians 15:57, *"Thanks be to God who gives us the victory through our Lord Jesus Christ."* One of these ways to walk in victory is to declare the Word of God over yourself, over others, and over situations. You are not merely speaking ordinary human words, but you are speaking out the empowered, living Word of God Almighty. I challenge you to find portions of God's Word that encourage your heart and to speak them out. I frequently say, *"Thank You, Father, that the blood of Jesus Christ cleanses me from all sin; I am the righteousness of God in Christ Jesus; I am acceptable to God; I have been given the right to be called a child of God."*

It's exciting to see the Word cause transformation in our lives as we speak it forth confirming what God has already told us. We are in agreement with God.

MARCH 21

"As the Scriptures say, 'People are like grass; their beauty is like a flower in the field. The grass withers and the flower fades. But the word of the Lord remains forever '" (1 Peter 1:24-25 NLT).

TEMPORAL AND ETERNAL

I LOOKED OVER AT the freshly mowed lawn in my neighbor's front yard—the grasses were green, strong and flourishing. Then I remembered the scripture in 1 Peter 1:24 that says every human being on this earth is like the grass. And all the great and noble things we do are compared to the flowers in the grass. The grass will last for a short time, and then wither and burn up under the hot sun. The flowers will dry up and fall away. So temporal are we, in our tents of flesh, so very weak, and our life is but a fleeting breath—a puff of wind that dissipates in a second. Even all our wonderful accomplishments and feats of glory, fame and successes are forgotten in a flash, and come to nothing before God. What does this all mean to us? It is teaching us that we need to be eternal minded and seek after the things that will last. The things we see with our eyes in this world are temporal, but the things we can't see, like the Spirit, faith, eternal life, our heavenly city, heavenly inheritance and God transforming our hearts, these things will last forever. Therefore we must turn our focus to seek the face of God and His ways, and not get caught up and overwhelmed in the circumstances we may find ourselves in here on earth. The Lord will help us handle them; He will take care of it. Let us seek to build His kingdom, and purpose in our hearts to wholly follow Him, for our reward is great in heaven.

MARCH 22

A SHORT STORY
THE RICH YOUNG RULER

Mark 10:17-27

ONE DAY A young man who was rich came up to Jesus and asked Him how he could go to heaven and live forever. The man had called Jesus "Good Teacher." Jesus addresses that first by asking him a question. Jesus always sought of ways to prompt people to think and ponder upon their own lives and motives. Jesus asked him why he called Him "Good." Only God is good Jesus told him. *Are you saying I am God? Do you really believe this?* He began to move this young man closer to a right decision for his life. Then Jesus tells him that he needed to keep the commandments. The young rich ruler asked Him which ones? Jesus proceeded to recite some of the Ten Commandments to him. The young man quickly, without hesitation, said, *"Oh, those commandments. I have kept them since I was a child."* Now Jesus may have been thinking, *sure you have.* You see Jesus knows what is in the hearts of men. He knew what was in this man's heart. Jesus knew the scripture that says there is none that does good—no not one; and all our best deeds are but as a dirty rag in God's sight. God wants perfection which no man can live up to, for all have sinned, and fallen short of the glory of God. God looks on the heart, so Jesus told this man if you want to be perfect you need to heed what I tell you. Jesus brought up to the rich young ruler the fact that he was lacking and began to tell him what he needed to do, thus drawing him closer to making that life changing decision.

Jesus aims straight for the heart and pierces it with the light of His truth. He tells him to go and sell all his riches and give to the poor, then to come, take up his cross and follow Him. There it was! The invitation to eternal life—the way to heaven. Letting go of things that hold on to and control

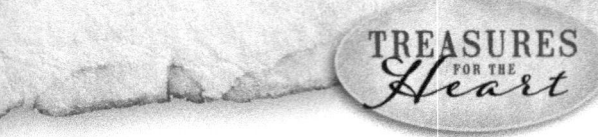

the heart and embracing the Son of God completely by faith, following Him wherever He goes. Following His ways, His words, His life. Come to the Savior and be saved from your sins. The young man became very sad because his heart was revealed and it said, *I can't, or I won't. I love my possessions. They have my heart, and I am not willing to let them go and follow You.*

He did not like it either when Jesus mentioned for him to take up his cross—this meant self-denial and humility. The young ruler went away without eternal life for he chose this life's riches over the eternal treasure. Jesus' disciples could not believe it when Jesus told them that a rich man (someone who loves and trusts in his riches and possessions and forgets God) has a very hard time getting into heaven. The disciples were stunned by Jesus' words and asked Him who then can be saved if a man of nobility and means cannot make it? Jesus looked lovingly at them and said with a twinkle in His eye, *"A man can never save himself, but God can save a man."* God can draw a person's heart to Himself and when that person chooses to trust wholly in the Son of God, Jesus, that person will be saved and his sins washed away; his home is in heaven and he receives the gift of eternal life.

If this little story touched your heart and you want to go to heaven when you die, and you want to follow Christ, here on earth. Pray this simple prayer of faith with me.

> *Dear Father, I believe that You love me and that You sent Jesus to die on the cross for my sins. I believe He was buried and rose again on the third day. I am sorry for my sins and turn from them to serve You all the days of my life. Please come and save me I ask in Jesus Name, Amen.*

Man prays
God saves
Now go and live for Him

MARCH 23

"And He said, 'Go forth, and stand upon the mount before the LORD.'
And, behold, the LORD passed by, and a great and strong wind rent
the mountains, and brake in pieces the rocks before the LORD; but
the LORD was not in the wind: and after the wind an earthquake;
but the LORD was not in the earthquake: And after the earthquake
a fire; but the LORD was not in the fire: and after the fire a still
small voice. And it was so, when Elijah heard it, that he wrapped
his face in his mantle, and went out, and stood in the entering in
of the cave. And, behold, there came a voice unto him, and said,
'What doest thou here, Elijah'" (1 Kings 19: 11-13 KJV)?

LISTEN FOR GOD

IN THE OLD Testament when Elijah, the prophet of the Lord, was feeling very discouraged and afraid, God planned to reveal Himself to him and encourage him. The Lord told Elijah to go out and stand on the mountain ledge before Him. Elijah was in a cave where he had spent the night. He was running away from his situation and problems, feeling alone and in despair. His hope had drained away, and if he ever needed a strong and hopeful word from the Lord it was now. So God was about to pass by Elijah and all of a sudden a very great and strong wind swept into the mountain and it broke some of the mountain—rocks went flying. Elijah looked, but the Lord did not reveal Himself in that mighty wind. It was just a phenomenon of nature. After that, came a rumbling earthquake that shook Elijah and the mountain. Elijah paid attention but did not hear or discern the Lord in the earthquake. Then Elijah looked up and saw a burning fire that just appeared. He didn't see nor hear God in the fire. He didn't hear God in all of these powerful manifestations of nature.

Yes, God had spoken to Moses in the fiery bush, and with thundering and earthquakes He made His power known. Even in the wind He spoke to Job out of the whirl wind, but He was going to speak to Elijah in a different way this day.

Elijah heard a still small voice and knew at once it was Him, the Lord God. So out of great respect He wrapped his face in his mantle and stood outside the cave. The Lord then proceeded to give Elijah instructions to follow that would take care of his concerns. Elijah was comforted and reassured by God that he indeed had been doing what was right and that God had everything under His control.

Likewise, know that our God desires and seeks to comfort and encourage you in your time of feeling discouraged and over-whelmed, and when He meets you it will be in a way He knows you will recognize His voice and person. When He does meet you, do whatever He tells you to.

MARCH 24

"You, LORD, are my lamp; the LORD turns my darkness into light.
With Your help I can advance against a troop; with my God I can scale
a wall. As for God, His way is perfect: The LORD's word is flawless;
He shields all who take refuge in Him"(2 Samuel 22:29-31).

A DECLARATION OF POSITIVE FAITH

*L*ORD, YOU ARE the One who brings the light of hope to my
dark days. Your Word and Your Holy Spirit illumine my spirit
and soul so I can see beyond the shadows of my life. No matter
what I am facing I know and am confident, that I can handle it and that it will
not prevail against me.

No matter if a host of problems and difficult situations come at me, I
will be able to escape in God and His presence; He will give me the grace
to be able to bear up victoriously. None of these things will move me. My
faith will support me, the angels will assist me, and God will provide for me
out of His abundance. The Lord's way is always the best way for me to take.
I have relied on His promises for they have always proved to be true and
effective in my life. My trust is in God alone because He clothes me with
spiritual armor and gives me the sword of the Spirit wherewith I am able to
extinguish the flaming arrows of the enemy.

MARCH 25

"Those who sow with tears will reap with songs of joy. Those who go out weeping, carrying seed to sow, will return with songs of joy, carrying sheaves with them" (Psalm 126:5-6).

PRAY, SOW, REAP

At THE TIME I became a new born Christian follower of Christ my heart was overwhelmed and burdened with the spiritual state of all the members of my family. I knew they needed to give their lives to Jesus Christ so they could walk in the light of His life and have lasting hope. I wept over them in prayer and shared the Lord with them whenever I could. One night when I was sitting outside on the steps crying and feeling grieved over my loved ones, the pages of my open Bible blew with a little gust of wind. It blew open to a particular scripture. It was God's doing in order to give me hope for my family. I didn't know yet the Scriptures, nor God's promises that I could hold to and rest in. I wiped my eyes and under the porch light I read what was opened before me.

"Those who sow in tears shall reap in joy. He who continually goes forth weeping, bearing seed for sowing, shall doubtless come again with rejoicing bringing his sheaves with him."

Wow! God spoke directly to my weary heart.

When I earnestly pray for my loved ones, I will, without a doubt, see them come into the Kingdom of God because my heart has been broken over them, and I have sown the living seed of God's Word into their hearts. Surely with confidence I will jump for joy as one by one they come into the Kingdom of God! And this is what has been happening over the years! Thank you, Jesus!

"As for me, I will always have hope;
I will praise You more and more"(Psalm 71:14).

ENOUGH, LORD!

AVE YOU BEEN going through a season of difficulty that has lasted longer than you had thought or even imagined? God still asks you to have hope and to trust in His love for you. So often when there seems to be no relief in a particular difficulty we are experiencing, our heart can grow overwhelmed, exhausted, bitter, discouraged, and dim.

Job, in the Bible, had terrible trials that appeared to go on and on—one thing after another. He cried out, groaned and complained. It wasn't fair that he should lose all his children, health and possessions. Where was God? Job, however, says that even though God had allowed him to be overrun by calamity and suffering, he would still trust Him to do what was good and right in his life. God was still good and still loved Job. Later, God did deliver Job and gave him relief from his suffering.

God will also deliver you—He hears your cries of anguish. In some way, He will come to your rescue and will give you relief in your pain and suffering. Look for these intervals and seasons of rest and rebuilding, and be sure to thank God for His tender care over you.

May God strengthen and encourage your heart and soul today. May He ease your burden and bring you joy even in the midst of your difficulty. Look to Him and you will never be disappointed. Remember, just because He doesn't answer you according to how you think He should, doesn't mean He's forgotten you. He has a purpose and a plan, and you are a huge part of it. Look for the good and the lovely, and wait for your God.

MARCH 27

"In all your ways acknowledge Him and He shall direct your paths"(Proverbs 3:6).

GUIDE ME, LORD

ID YOU KNOW one of God's jobs is to direct our steps and guide our life? Over and over in the Scriptures we are promised that God will lead us and guide us in our everyday living. Oh, how we need His eye upon our decisions and choices! I believe if we take our options and ways to the Lord and discuss them with Him, He will direct our path and show us which road to go down. We can take a way we think could be profitable, and if it isn't where we should be, I am confident that the Lord will open or close the doors and confirm His will to us through His Word, the witness of the Holy Spirit, through circumstances, and other believers.

I recall choosing to go through an open door that looked promising, but it was only as I was experiencing living out that choice that I realized it wasn't right for me. God dealt with my heart and mind and clearly showed me this was not His will for me. Circumstances didn't turn out the way I expected. So I obeyed Him and changed directions to another avenue that, after some praying and planning, I came to the conclusion that this was not His plan for me either. So He led me to just wait.

Sometimes the Lord has us in the position of waiting until certain things fall into place and our hearts have been prepared for our next assignment. Learn to listen to God's still small voice and stay in the Word of God, for it is a lamp unto our feet and a light unto our path. Pray with others about the matter and share your heart and plans with someone you trust. You can be sure that the Holy Spirit will guide you into all the truth and teach you all things. At times He asks us to walk on through, to wait, or to make a detour.

MARCH 28

"Again I say, don't get involved in foolish, ignorant arguments that only start fights. A servant of the Lord must not quarrel but must be kind to everyone, be able to teach, and be patient with difficult people"(2 Timothy 2:23-24 NLT).

ARGUE GOD'S WAY

OW EASY IT is to get into an argument with those we love when we disagree on a matter. Sometimes we respond in anger and we yell and carry on, our lips spewing out words that can hurt. Sometimes we respond in tears and try to manipulate the other to feel sorry for us. Other times we don't talk at all but stew and ignore the issue and the person. Disagreements will always come into our relationships, so it is best to learn how to respond the way God says to.

First of all, we are not to have anything to do with *"stupid and foolish arguments; they only produce quarrels."* Weigh out what is important to confront and talk about and what is not. It is not wrong to argue a matter because we may have different thoughts on a subject than the other person. *"Arguing is reasoning based on facts; quarreling is wrangling angrily over personal preferences using facts or not."* Quarreling includes loud shouts that lead to anger. When we argue we are trying to get the other person to change their view (alphadictionary.com).

When the Bible calls our arguments "foolish" or "stupid" it means they lead to nothing but contention and strife—there is no *problem solving* being done. God says when we disagree we must be kind, able to show the other person our side in love and not to be resentful. It is the foolish person who is hot-tempered, but a man who is patient and understanding calms down a quarrel.

So be kind and don't press buttons that will trigger anger in the other person; listen and answer in a spirit of meekness. Choose to remove yourself from a situation of abuse whether emotional or physical. Face and talk about differences and always work to *problem solve*. If it lies within you,

avoid strife and quarrelling—just remove yourself if it starts up. Do not sin when you are angry, but exercise self-control which is the fruit of the Holy Spirit, and choose a godly response.

MARCH 29

*"When the angel of the LORD appeared to Gideon, he said,
'The LORD is with you, mighty warrior'"(Judges 6:12).*

GOD BELIEVES IN YOU

*G*IDEON, IN THE Book of Judges, in the Old Testament, was minding his business threshing wheat when the Angel of the Lord came and spoke to him. He said to him, *"The Lord is with you, you mighty man of valor!"* The Lord saw greatness in this man, Gideon, even though he was from the weakest and least of the Israelite clans. God called this man "mighty." This word has the meaning of someone "fitted to withstand a forcible assault-well fortified" (biblehub.com). God saw Gideon as someone who could lead His people, the nation of Israel, to fight the Midianites in battle. God was going to use Gideon and his army in a powerful way. He also referred to Gideon as "a man of valor." The definition of "valor" in the *Free Merriam Webster Dictionary* is "strength of mind or spirit that enables a person to encounter danger with firmness—personal bravery." God knew Gideon and what pressures and fires he could withstand, and He assured him that he had what it would take to carry out the assignment he was called to. And God proved His words true. Gideon went out to war with only 300 men to fight the Midianites who were as "numerous as locusts." One hundred and twenty thousand of the Midianite men and more were slain that day. Gideon was a mighty man of Valor, and the Lord was with him to give him victory.

Now, God sees who you are. He calls you, *"Oh mighty man and mighty woman of Valor!"* He has set a task before you this day that seems impossible; however, God sees that you are capable of doing all He has asked you to do because He has created you with everything you need to face and conquer your difficulties. Plus the Lord is with you empowering you with His strength, might and Holy Spirit. You can stand whatever comes your way—no matter how rough or painful it might seem. You have strength of mind and spirit—you can do all things through Christ who empowers you.

He adds His inexhaustible strength to whatever strength you already have, and you can soar upward to victory. God believes in you and your ableness to accomplish what He has set before you. Now go forth mighty man and mighty woman of Valor and conquer in Jesus Name! Win that battle for the Lord!

MARCH 30

"For if you remain silent at this time, relief and deliverance for the Jews will arise from another place, but you and your father's family will perish. And who knows but that you have come to your royal position for such a time as this" (Esther 4:14)?

WHY, LORD?

*a*RE YOU STRUGGLING with a difficult situation that presses upon you? You may be asking, Why, Lord? Why can't an answer be found for the situation—a problem solved—the burden lifted? You have prayed, believed and sought God's deliverance and intervention in this thing, but it continues to wear upon your emotions and take away your strength. *Why, Lord? Why was this difficulty allowed to touch, interrupt and rearrange my life?* Then God says to you, *"It is not always about you, My child, but often times it is more about what I am working to accomplish in those around you—those closest to you."* Are we willing to suffer for the sake of someone else so God can save them, change them, heal them, and draw them to Himself?

Why, Lord?

Why not? Can we say it is okay, because God is ultimately in control and is sovereignly at work? Can we say, *"Yes, Lord, I will be the one You need—send me? I will trust Your will and plan as it unfolds before me. I will be an instrument of Your mercy and grace."*

Perhaps if we completely surrender to the Lord in our matter of concern, we will find peace and learn to be content with how things are being changed and rearranged in our lives.

Look around at those in your life and ask God if what you are experiencing today has anything to do with their lives being formed.

Circumstances were altered in Queen Esther's life, in the Bible, and it wasn't all about her, but about the deliverance God was bringing to His people. He had raised up Esther for such a time as this.

MARCH 31

"So do not worry, saying, 'What shall we eat?' or 'What shall we drink?' or 'What shall we wear?' For the pagans run after all these things, and your Heavenly Father knows that you need them. But seek first His Kingdom and His righteousness, and all these things will be given to you as well" (Matthew 6:31-34).

LEAN DAYS

MANY ARE GOING through lean days—financial struggles right now. Don't be too surprised that your faith is being tested through your finances. Will you trust God when it appears you cannot make ends meet, when you are short on your rent, when your food supply has gone down or when you are getting behind on your bills? God wants us to live out our faith in our daily lives. The Bible tells us that our Heavenly Father knows what we have need of before we even ask Him. Rather than make money our number one aim, God desires us to seek after Him and His Kingdom—give Him first priority in our lives.

Again, He tells us if we set our heart on Him, He will add to us what we need for living. He will supply our needs, but don't forget He has a specific time for His answers and a specific way that He has planned to bring provision to us. We must stretch our faith and not be filled with worry. We must pray and rely on God to come through for us. We must learn to be content in whatever state we find ourselves in, but that doesn't mean we are to do nothing. God will direct our steps on how to increase our finances and stretch our budget.

Keep steady during lean days for God is faithful. Be just as grateful in lean days as in days of fatness. God is always concerned with our heart's attitude whenever we go through trials. How will we respond?

APRIL 1

"You can be completely confident of this very thing that He who started a good work in you will keep on working until the very day Jesus returns" (Phil.1:6 Eilers' paraphrase).

WHAT IS GOING ON IN MY LIFE?

O YOU EVER wonder what God is doing in your life? Things just don't seem to make sense and you are questioning the direction your life is heading. God seems to be doing His own thing and hasn't let you in on it yet. You have no idea what is going on with you and the circumstances that have come into your life. Others appear to hear God clearly—what is wrong with you and your spiritual walk, that God seems silent and far away? You pray and read the Bible, but it is as if there is a wall up, and you are being tempted to doubt that God has it all in His hand and that He knows exactly what He is doing.

Don't fret, my friend, you've done nothing wrong, and God hasn't given up on you or abandoned you. He is still as near to you as your own heartbeat and dearly loves you. He is fine tuning you to serve Him in an even greater capacity. He is teaching you to live by faith and not feelings, for feelings have nothing to do with faith; faith has everything to do with choice and obedience.

Keep steady. God will reveal what He is doing when He is ready. Just keep walking by faith doing what is set before you to do, seeking the face of God. Things will get clearer, and you will see that God was carefully and skillfully working in you so that you bear much fruit.

APRIL 2

"Yours, LORD, is the greatness and the power and the glory and the majesty and the splendor, for everything in heaven and earth is Yours. Yours, LORD, is the kingdom; You are exalted as head over all. Wealth and honor come from You; You are the ruler of all things. In Your hands are strength and power to exalt and give strength to all. Now, our God, we give You thanks, and praise Your glorious name"(1 Chronicles 29:11-13).

GOD'S SOVEREIGNTY

SINCE GOD IS infinite in power, wisdom, love, goodness and mercy, He has a divine design for all things. He never asks us to understand, nor even try to understand, the events that come into our lives. Sometimes He will show us what He is doing; other times He does not. His ways are incomprehensible to our finite reasoning and mental abilities. But we know that He is our refuge and "underneath are the everlasting arms."

It is comforting to have the knowledge that the Lord's hand is governing over everyone and everything. Our trials never come to us by accident, neither are they flung on us by Satan without God's knowledge, but God has *"ordained and ordered them"* for His purposes. 1 Thessalonians 3:3 tells us that we are appointed to afflictions. Remember that God is our wise Father and He never allows us to shed tears without a merciful and loving reason that is beyond us.

When we truly accept the sovereignty of God and His control over all, we can enter into a peace that passes all understanding. We do well to leave what He deems best up to Him. God is never wrong, never makes mistakes, and never fails us.

There is something to note here, and that is, that God did not create man's wickedness, for man makes that choice himself. God made man upright in the garden and they chose to sin. Sin is the built in result for disobedience. Even though the devil is the author of all evil, he cannot do as he pleases. Even he must come under the governing power of God. We must remember that God allows only what will be for our spiritual good, and will

not permit us to be touched by any type of calamity, except that it be ultimately for His eternal purpose.

Only prayer can influence God to change a decree, and it is prayer that can help usher in God's will upon the earth. Prayer is a powerful tool. It can be used to bring healing and comfort. We can pray for the direction and protection of our leaders, the unsaved in the world and so forth; and it is our responsibility to exercise this action on behalf of loved ones, ourselves and others. The outcome is then left in the hands of the sovereign, righteous Lord.

—Taken from *Living Lessons(2020)* by Roxanne Eilers

"Wait for the Lord and be of good courage and He shall strengthen thine heart; wait, I say, for the Lord"(Psalm 27:14).

Wait For the Lord

THE BIBLE TALKS a lot about waiting on God, and for God. Let us look at some verses that tell us what happens when we wait on the Lord.

Isaiah 40:31—When we wait for the Lord our strength is renewed and we are revived.

Psalm 27:13-14—He will show you His goodness.

Lamentations 3:25—The Lord is good to those who wait for Him.

Psalm 130:5-6—Our hope in His Word is increased.

Psalm 37:34—A reward for waiting on God is that He will lift you up and bless you.

Psalm 40:1-7—Wait patiently because the Lord hears your cry. He will draw you up out of your pit. He will secure your ways. He will cause you to sing for joy because of His faithfulness.

"Wait" in the original Hebrew means to *"stretch—the tension of enduring"* (Strong's 6960). Our faith is being stretched, our endurance and perseverance is being increased.

What are we waiting for? We are waiting for God to show up in our circumstance and to do something about it for us. God, however, also asks us to wait and that, patiently, for His move. And at His appointed time He will move and show His goodness in the land of the living.

APRIL 4

"By faith the people passed through the Red Sea
as on dry land" (Hebrews 11:29).

SHUT IN TO FAITH

*L*ORD, MY BACK is up against a wall—I've come to the end of myself and my resources. I am facing my Red Sea. I am shut in to faith. What can I do? Where can I go?

When the Children of Israel were up against their Red Sea, they were overwhelmed and terrified for the Egyptian army was closing in on them from the other side. Moses told them, *"Do not be afraid. Stand firm and you will see the deliverance the Lord will bring you today."* God told Moses what to do and he lifted his staff over the Red Sea. A miracle happened! The sea began to part right down the middle and the Israelites went through on dry ground. God made a way where there was no way. Hebrews 11:29 tells us about the people's attitude as they began to go forward through the Red Sea. It says it was their faith in what God could do that made a way through the Red Sea. Oh, at first they were angry and afraid, but Moses got them back into faith and a miracle happened.

Are you experiencing a Red Sea in your life right now? Do not be afraid, stand firm in your faith and you will see what God can do.

Oh, Lord I don't know what to do but my eyes are on You!
(2 Chronicles 20:12).

APRIL 5

"The Son is the image of the invisible God, the firstborn over all creation. For in Him all things were created: things in heaven and on earth, visible and invisible, whether thrones or powers or rulers or authorities; all things have been created through Him and for Him. He is before all things, and in Him all things hold together. And He is the head of the body, the church; He is the beginning and the firstborn from among the dead, so that in everything He might have the supremacy. For God was pleased to have all His fullness dwell in Him"(Colossians 1:15-19).

CHRIST/NEW AGE

*D*O NOT BE influenced or moved by the religion of this age—mainly the New Age Movement. Basically the belief held, is that everything and everyone is united as one; man is on the brink of a new era which elevates human achievement and ability. This will end all war and bring unification around the globe. Everyone will have what they need as the resources of the world are redistributed. The earth environment is of utmost importance. But there is a rejection of who God is, as He is identified in His Son, Jesus Christ. Jesus is just a good role model to follow, but then. so are the other teachers in the other religions.

This New Age Movement is not something that just surfaced though. It has been around since man fell into sin. It holds to *monism* in which everything is one and "interrelated, interdependent and interpenetrating." We are gods ourselves for everything is God. However, they do not believe in a personal God as the Christians do. They believe God is a force, light or energy, which needs to be ignited inside each of us.

In light of all this, we are to be aware of what's happening in our world and hold the truth and light of Christ even higher, that being, His "all-supremacy, all-sufficiency" and the complete embodiment of all who God is, and ever will be. Christ is the sole creator and upholder who sustains everything in the universe. He is the only one worthy of all glory, praise and allegiance, for He is sovereign God. He is the only mediator between God

and man, and He is coming a second time to rule and reign on earth. We do not need New Age sprinkled on and mingled with Christ. It is Christ *alone* who redeemed us from our sins and gives us life forever!

(BIBLE.ORG)

APRIL 6

*"And pray in the Spirit on all occasions with all kinds of prayers
and requests. With this in mind, be alert and always keep
on praying for all the Lord's people"(Ephesians 6:18).*

A Prayer for You

MY PRAYER FOR you today is that God would graciously answer that desired request you've been diligently praying about. I pray He will bring you a swift and speedy answer and reveal His power and glory to you. I pray you won't lose heart as you wait for His reply to your prayer. May God encourage your spirit, calm your heart, steady your purpose and give you hope you can hold on to. I pray you will give thanks to the Lord even if you haven't seen anything happening yet. May you clothe yourself with peace and steadfastness, and keep your confession strong according to what God's Word says.

When the manifestation for your request comes, be sure to give God glory and tell someone about His awesome deeds!

"The Lord will perfect that which concerns me" (Psalm 138:8).

APRIL 7

"Wisdom is more precious than rubies; nothing you desire can compare with her"(Proverbs 3:15 NLT).

WORDS OF WISDOM

THIS PART OF your life will be even better and greater than the first part.

Never give up on your dreams.

Dream Big!

No matter how old you are keep growing and learning new things.

Enjoy your days and seize the moment—live in the moment, feel the moment.

Really love and tell those you love, that you love them.

Fall more in love with Jesus, your Savior.

Grow your faith stronger.

Take care of your body, mind and spirit.

Love who you are and accept yourself just as you are—this includes every little sag, line and wrinkle, weakness and mistakes.

Grow old gracefully and graciously, and be the best you can at every age.

APRIL 8

*"I will also meditate on all Your work; and talk of Your deeds.
Your way, O God, is in the sanctuary. Who is so great a God as
our God? You are the God who does wonders; You have declared
Your strength among the peoples"(Psalm 77:12-14).
"Then Simon himself also believed; and when he was
baptized he continued with Philip, and was amazed, seeing
the miracles and signs which were done"(Acts 8:13).*

GOD OF WONDERS

GOD WORKED WONDERS in the Old Testament, healed the sick, raised the dead, provided food where there was no food, did miracles and signs so all could see His great power and might, and put their faith in Him. Jesus worked miracles in the New Testament, healed the sick, opened blind eyes, raised the dead, did supernatural acts back when He was walking this earth. He did these wonders to show His Lordship and prove He was the Son of the Living God, so people could see and believe. Why would that all change today?

God hasn't changed. He is still the worker of miracles. He still heals the sick and opens blind eyes. He still raises the dead and does awesome signs and wonders to witness that He is alive, and offers eternal life to all who will come to Him in faith. He says, *"I am the Lord; I change not."* Therefore expect signs, wonders and healings to be evident in your ministry. You have not, because you ask not. You have not, because you believe not.

*"And they went forth, and preached everywhere, the Lord
working with them, and confirming the word with signs following" (Mark 16:20).*

APRIL 9

"Let us hold tightly without wavering to the hope we affirm, for God can be trusted to keep His promise"(Hebrews 10:23).

YOU STOOD FAITHFUL

*Y*OU HAVE STOOD firm even when times were difficult and trying. You did not turn your heart away from Me when you couldn't make sense of things. You kept faith when all was contrary to faith. You persevered in hope even when there was no hope in sight. You sought my light when it was dark all around you.

Now I will make you like a strong green tree whose roots reach deep down into My soil of love and grace. You will have times of refreshing and you will have confidence whenever tough times come. I will always take care of you and your needs for I am your God.

> *"But blessed is the one who trusts in the LORD, whose confidence is in Him. They will be like a tree planted by the water that sends out its roots by the stream. It does not fear when heat comes; its leaves are always green. It has no worries in a year of drought and never fails to bear fruit" (Jeremiah 17:7-8).*

APRIL 10

*"And therefore will the LORD wait, that He may be gracious
unto you, and therefore will He be exalted, that He may
have mercy upon you: for the LORD is a God of judgment:
blessed are all they that wait for Him"(Isaiah 30:18 KJV).*

YOUR GOD WILL COME

*T*HEREFORE, THE LORD who created you, will hold back the manifestation of the answer to your prayer; He will allow it to be delayed for a bit, but don't let this concern you or cause you to doubt Him in any way, because when the time is right He will be quick to usher in the answer to your request. He will give command to His angels to act on your behalf, as they are ministers to assist you in your needs. You will see God's goodness to you through the works of His hands. And you will lift Him up with praise and thanksgiving for His tender mercies to you. For your God is always fair and can be trusted to handle your affairs and the matters and petitions that weigh heavily on your heart. So keep on waiting for Him because He is faithful, and your God will come and will not delay.

APRIL 11

"Overhearing what they said, Jesus told him, 'Don't be afraid; just believe'"(Mark 5:36).

JUST BELIEVE

I AM LONGING FOR you to believe Me—just to believe who I am, and what I am capable of doing in your life and in the world around you. You have been asking Me for things to happen in your life, yet you won't fully believe Me, that I am taking you there. Don't stop believing because it takes time for the invisible to show up in the natural or physical realm. If you could only see how busy My angels are as they are carrying out My commands. Some of these commands include you and your circumstances, you and your prayers. Listen closely to My Spirit and My Word and you will have more confidence to believe and not waver on your requests.

Do you remember the story of Jairus' daughter who was sick? Jairus came to Me and earnestly pleaded with Me to come and lay My hands on his daughter to heal her. I went with him, but on the way there was a woman who was believing Me to heal her of internal bleeding. She was instantly healed when she touched My robe. I told her that her faith had brought healing to her. What happened is her faith connected to My healing power and the miracle happened. In the meantime, Jairus' daughter had died, but we kept walking to his house, and I told him these words that I am telling you today, *"Do not be afraid; just believe."* When I got to his house I took the little girl by the hand and healed her. I will do miraculous works for you also if you believe Me to. (Mark 5:21-43)

APRIL 12

"Are not two sparrows sold for a penny? And not one of them will fall to the ground apart from your Father. But even the hairs of your head are all numbered"(Matthew 10:29-30 English Standard Version).

STAY IN FAITH

LOOK FOR GOD'S hand at work in every circumstance and happening around you. Look expectantly for His glory to be manifested in certain areas of your life. Stay in faith. Stay in hope and consider Him faithful who promised. Speak like God speaks calling into existence those things that are not yet manifested. Look for their manifestation. Walk in wisdom. Stay in faith, receive by faith. Be unmovable and tenacious for what you are believing God to do. Don't give up so easily just because you can't see anything happening right this minute. Stay in faith no matter how long it takes. Stay in faith. Great faith doesn't happen overnight—it is a constant cultivation of the heart. A determination to believe. So stay in faith.

APRIL 13

"Truly He is my rock and my salvation; He is my fortress, I will never be shaken"(Psalm 62:2).

LEAN ON THE ROCK

*P*SALM 62:1-8—-O MY soul, let down your defenses and walls before God; be yourself before God with a transparent heart. Hope awaits you as you find what you have been searching for in God. God is your unmovable Rock. He is the one who mightily saves you. He is the place you can go to whenever you are fearful, worried, weary or needy. And because He is so great, you need not be thrown off course, nor feel unsteady in your way, for you can depend wholly on God. He is the one who gives you life and places your feet secure on the high places. Such a powerful God is He; you can hide away in Him. Now I will tell everyone to trust and rely on Him always, all the time through every season of life. We can be honest before Him and pour out our hearts to Him—He is a safe place. We can be real with Him because He knows us already so perfectly and completely and He so loves us.

APRIL 14

"...making the most of every opportunity, because
the days are evil"(Ephesians 5:16).

PROPHETIC WORD

I HAVE SET BEFORE the Church a door of opportunity, and it is wide open; however, there will come a time in the future when that door will not be open as wide. There will be animosity and rivalry over what My Word says. You will be My voice, My teacher, to teach the people what My will is. I am not willing that any should perish but that all will come to repentance. The time is coming when those who preach in My Name will rise up in a powerful way, and they will take a sure stand over what is ungodly. This stand will mark them and they will bring glory to My Name. Those who stand up for righteousness are like the stars that shine in a dark place. Hurry, for the time has become shortened—men will continue to be evil and seek their own ways, but you must take My Word to the people. Test all things and hold to only what is true.

APRIL 15

"Our God, will You not judge them? For we have no power to face this vast army that is attacking us. We do not know what to do, but our eyes are on You" (2 Chronicles 20:12).

WE DON'T KNOW WHAT TO DO

*I*N THIS STORY, King Jehoshaphat had a great multitude of enemies who were coming to fight against him. Jehoshaphat was afraid for his people and himself, but he knew God. So the first thing he did was, he set himself to seek the Lord. He proclaimed a fast among all the people to ask help from the Lord. King Jehoshaphat prayed, and he called on God in this situation where he saw no solution. He humbly admitted *"we have no power against this great multitude that is coming against us, nor do we know what to do."*

Do you feel you are up against an enemy of some kind—a situation or circumstance too big for you to handle and you do not know what to do? Well, say what Jehoshaphat said to the Lord. He said, *"...we do not know what to do, BUT OUR EYES ARE UPON YOU."* Fix your eyes on Jesus for He will direct you to the solution.

This story ends with God's Spirit coming upon Jahaziel, a Levite, who declared the Word of the Lord to Jehoshaphat and the people. Listen to what he said because this word is for you.

> * "Do not be afraid nor dismayed because of this great *multitude [or these insurmountable problems you are facing]* for the battle is not yours but God's...position *[yourself]* stand still and see the salvation of the Lord...and go out against them *[do what the Lord shows you to do]* for He is with you." And so they went out praising God! When they began to praise the Lord, He set ambushes against their enemies and their enemies were defeated!

So go out now praising God and He will work mightily on your behalf! Glory!

*(Author's brackets and additional wording added for clearer understanding of the passage.)

APRIL 16

"My grace will sustain you, for I have called you to live this Christian life and to glorify Me through My Son, Jesus Christ. You are suffering right now, but don't lose heart or perspective because it won't last forever, for the time will come when you will grow in spiritual maturity and you will find your faith made secure and permanent, strengthened and settled. You will be firmly fixed and immovable as you hold on to your hope in Me" (1 Peter 5:10-11 Eilers' paraphrase).

FIRMLY FIXED

THERE WAS A season in my life when I was really battling with my faith, having questions and doubts. My emotions were like a yo-yo. I had faith one day, and the next day I wavered. Because I was experiencing difficult emotional struggles, I wondered if I would ever be steadfast in my faith the way I really wanted to be. I strove and prayed, and one day I found the scripture in 1 Peter 5:10-11 that deeply encouraged my heart and gave me confidence. It was an anchor when the waves were threatening to pull me out to sea. God spoke to me. And down through the years this is exactly what happened! Through the seasons of suffering and trial, and through the good times of blessing, my faith has become immovable and solid. Praise God!

"Rejoice greatly, Daughter Zion! Shout, Daughter Jerusalem! See, your King comes to you, righteous and victorious, lowly and riding on a donkey, on a colt, the foal of a donkey" (Zechariah 9:9).

PALM SUNDAY

*J*ESUS ENTERED INTO Jerusalem on a colt of a donkey, and He fulfilled the prophecy concerning Himself at this time in Zechariah 9:9. The people were full of excitement that day and were giving Jesus praise and adulation! They were looking at Him as Messiah and King of the Jews, but they were waiting for Him to deliver them out from under the rule of the Roman Empire and to set up His kingdom! They shouted "Hosanna! Hosanna!" which means "Save now." They were laying their garments and palm branches on the road for Jesus to pass over. This was their custom when a king entered the city or a warrior who had had a victory. Jesus was seen as a King at this time. But it wasn't long before these same people who gave praise to Jesus would shout out, "Crucify Him! Crucify Him!" There are four points I'd like to point out from this story.

1. Recognize who Jesus is. He is Messiah and Savior. The people appeared to believe in who Jesus was, but they didn't have a true trusting faith in Him. He is Lord and King. Is He Lord of your life and are you worshiping Him as King?

2. Jesus always did the Father's will. Even though it meant praise for just a day, while coming through Jerusalem on a donkey, and then suffering and death at the hands of those same people, He fulfilled the plan that the Father had assigned for Him. Jesus' greatest challenge became His greatest victory! And so we are called to do the same for our greatest challenge will become our greatest victory!

3. Keep loyal to Jesus—keep steady in your allegiance to Him. The people in Jerusalem that day seemed to stand by Jesus, but their hearts did not love Him. They were fickle and were swayed with what others thought

or believed. No matter what the world does or says we need to keep our faith loyal to Jesus.

4. Finally, take Jesus as an example of leadership. Jesus did not come on a horse shouting war on His enemies. He did not wear fancy clothes, or gold or silver. He came on a donkey, meek, lowly, humble and gentle. How are we in our positions of authority? Husbands and wives, Parents and children, teachers and students…etc.

APRIL 18

"This is what the Lord says, Your Redeemer, the Holy One of Israel:
'I am the Lord Your God, who teaches you what is best for you;
who directs you in the way you should go'" (Isaiah 48: 17-18).

IS GOD IN YOUR PLANS?

WHEN GOD IS in what we have set out to do, He will show us how to accomplish our goal. He will teach us how to prosper. The Holy Spirit will reveal things about our situation to us, so we can decide what moves to make. We are partners with the Holy Spirit as we work together to accomplish what He has called us to. God is the one who instructs us on what is the best way to take, by directing our hearts and minds by His Word and His Spirit. Seek His face in your plans, and He will establish your steps; He knows just what people and resources you need in order for you to get the job done. He will cause you to succeed when you completely put Him first in a matter, and take Him as your spiritual partner in your decision making.

Prayer: Dear Lord, please guide me in my decisions and plans for my future. Teach me what is best for me, and lead me in Your ways. Open my eyes to what You are doing in and around me. Help me to hear Your heart and mind. In Jesus Name, Amen.

APRIL 19

"Take the helmet of salvation and the sword of the Spirit,
which is the Word of God"(Ephesians 6:17).

THE HELMET OF SALVATION

WHEN WE SEEK to get closer to the Lord and experience intimacy with Him, there is going to be a fight with Satan. He abhors us being close to God and will do all he can to pull us away. The chief way he works on us is through our minds, our thoughts. He can whisper lies to us, and trick us into believing they are from our own hearts. Beloved, they are not. He will accuse us of sin and pile false guilt upon our consciences. He will cause us to doubt God and ourselves. He is the author of all lies and must be resisted. If something doesn't bring you nearer to God, but places a barrier between you, resist it immediately. You are forever God's beloved child and He desires your love and fellowship. The fiery darts of the enemy are aimed straight for the mind, so guard your mind with the Helmet of Salvation.

The Helmet of Salvation is *knowing* who you are in Christ—you are saved and delivered from the Law of sin and death. You are secure in the love of God and in your position with Him in the heavenly places. Know who you are and what power God has given to you to overcome all the power of the enemy, and nothing shall in anywise harm you spiritually or emotionally. The mind protected with the Helmet of Salvation is a sound mind, unafraid and trusting God.

Remember, we overcome Satan with the blood of the Lamb. We can ask the Lord to cover our thoughts and hearts with His blood and to dissolve all strongholds. We, also working with Him, cast down all imaginations (thoughts that are contrary to God) and bringing every thought captive to the obedience of Christ.

APRIL 20

"Let us not become weary in doing good, for at the proper time we will reap a harvest if we do not give up"(Ephesians 6:17).

THE ASSIGNMENT

*T*HERE WILL BE times when God tells you, *"Sometimes, My child the assignment I give you, or what I ask you to bear up under, will not be an easy one. It will be difficult and demand all of your energy and commitment. You will feel drained, exhausted from the struggle against evil. The assignment will always be a very important one though. Each time you complete one of these assignments, I want you to be sure to know that a huge transformation is taking place in you, as well as in the lives you have influenced by My love and holiness. Your reward in heaven is weighty and you have made Me, very proud of you. I honor your courage and persistence in serving Me. Your life with Me will never be dull or boring but it will always be adventurous and fruitful."*

APRIL 21

"Then the word of the Lord came to him saying…" (1 Kings 17:2).

THE WORD OF THE LORD

HERE WAS A great drought in the land and the word of the Lord came to Elijah. God instructed Elijah where to go for provisions. He was to get away to a brook where there was plenty of water, and it was here, that ravens would come daily to bring him meat and bread. So during this time of drought Elijah was completely taken care of.

After a while the word of the Lord came to Elijah, again telling him to leave the place where he was and to move on to a new location where his needs would be met, for the brook had dried up and the ravens had stopped coming. So he did, and God supplied.

We need the word of the Lord to come to us in our time of need to show us what to do next and where to go. The word of the Lord will come in an appointed time. Don't lose heart. Don't grow anxious or discouraged. Don't be in a haste.

APRIL 22

"When you go through deep waters, I will be with you. When you go through rivers of difficulty, you will not drown. When you walk through the fire of oppression, you will not be burned up; the flames will not consume you"(Isaiah 43:2 NLT).

CATCH ME, DADDY!

SOMETIMES GOD TAKES us to the very edge of something before He comes through with the answer. Sometimes He asks us to step off the edge and trust Him to catch us. He wants us to develop strong faith muscles because all things are possible to him who believes.

This reminds me of when I was a child and my own daddy was teaching me to swim. He would call to me to come to him and I would swim like crazy, a few feet from the edge of the pool, reaching for his big arms to catch me. However, Daddy, in his wisdom, knew I could go just a little bit further still and would back up a little, while calling me to himself. Then just in time, he would grab my little hands and draw me up into his arms. A few times of that was enough for the day.

God is like that! So when you find yourself being stretched to go a little further in your faith, believing Him, know that He is just backing up a bit calling you to Himself, and He will draw you up into His arms.

APRIL 23

"But blessed is the one who trusts in the LORD, whose confidence is in Him. They will be like a tree planted by the water that sends out its roots by the stream. It does not fear when heat comes; its leaves are always green. It has no worries in a year of drought and never fails to bear fruit" (Jeremiah 17:7-8).

HOW TO BE BLESSED

*D*O YOU WANT to be blessed? Then put your trust and confidence in the Lord. How will you be blessed? Jeremiah 17 says that you will grow like a tree that always has its roots stretched out by the cool streams of water, and even if hard times of affliction come like the burning heat, your leaves will always be green. You will be spiritually healthy and thrive in your walk with God. You won't be full of anxiety even if everyone around you seems to be panicking, lacking and in drought. Because your trust in the Lord is unmovable, you will bear fruit all year round, regardless of what the weather is like!

APRIL 24

"The next day John saw Jesus coming toward him and said, 'Look, the Lamb of God, who takes away the sin of the world'" (John 1:29).

LAMB OF GOD

WHEN I AM thinking, praying or referring to Jesus Christ I often use the title of Lamb of God. Today I am thinking about the Lamb that was slain for us. In the Old Testament when the Passover was instituted, a lamb was slain and the blood smeared on the door posts. This was needed in order for God to pass over and not judge those individuals and their families inside the home. This is a picture of the Lamb of God being slain and taking the punishment for all mankind. When the sacrifices of lambs and other animals were brought in to be sacrificed to the Lord, the animal was to be innocent and unblemished. It was brought and sacrificed in order to take the place of the person's sin. Again, this was a type of the Lamb of God to come, who was innocent and without sin, who took our place and died in our stead. The Old Testament was pointing to the Lamb of God that was coming into the world. Finally, in the New Testament, we hear John the Baptist introducing Jesus to his disciples and saying, *"Behold the Lamb of God who takes away the sin of the world"* (John 1:29). On the cross we can hear the last cry of the Lamb of God as He is being slain, when Jesus cries out, *"It is finished. Into Your hands I commend My Spirit."* The Lamb of God was the final sacrifice for all men for all time.

Thank You, Sweet Lamb of God for giving Your life for me—
Thank You, for Your sacrifice on the cross at Calvary.
Underneath Your blood I am covered—no more blame—
The Innocent for the guilty—took away all of my stains.

"And they have defeated him [Satan] by the blood of the
Lamb and by their testimony" (Revelation 12:11).

MY CONFESSION

*D*ON'T EVER CHANGE your confession of faith. Keep it steady and in line with the Word of God. *"My God is always good, always wise, always wants the best for me. My God will come through for me. My God can be completely trusted and relied upon. I will not be disappointed when I trust His ways. I will be unshakable in my faith. I will serve my God no matter what happens in my situation and in my life. My allegiance to Him is unmovable. I declare before all of heaven and all of earth that I am His child and He deals well with me. He blesses me abundantly and makes me a blessing to others. I will forever love and trust my God. "*

APRIL 26

"So please don't lose heart because of my trials here. I am suffering for you, so you should feel honored. When I think of all this, I fall to my knees and pray to the Father, the Creator of everything in heaven and on earth. I pray that from His glorious, unlimited resources He will empower you with inner strength through His Spirit"(Ephesians 3:13-16 NLT).

A HOLY PRAYER

I BOW BEFORE GOD in Jesus Christ in whose name, through faith in His name, we all have become one great spiritual family, both in heaven and on earth. I ask that according to His glorious riches that He would pour His mighty Spirit into your heart and life so that you may increase in your faith in Christ—that you become like a sturdy, flourishing green tree whose roots grow down deep into the good soil of God's love, so that you may be able to grasp and appropriate with all your spiritual brothers and sisters, the enormous, tremendous, ardent, unrelenting love that Christ has for you—such love that goes deeper than the deepest depth, wider than the widest measure, longer than what can ever be measured in length, and higher than the expanse between earth and heaven. This love goes beyond what you can ever take in, and surpasses every, and all your idea and understanding of what love is.

I pray that God would keep on filling you up with His strength, His breath, His Spirit, His presence, His life and His transforming power.

And now I know that He will do all this and exceedingly much more, because He is able to do far beyond what you can ever imagine according to His Spirit that daily energizes and empowers you. To Him be the highest glory and praise forever and ever. Amen. (Eilers' paraphrase)

"Surely it was for my benefit that I suffered such anguish. In Your love You kept me from the pit of destruction; You have put all my sins behind Your back"(Isaiah 38:17).

THERE IS BENEFIT IN SUFFERING

C AN WE SAY it was for our benefit that we have suffered such pain in our lives? When we are in such a state of anguish, can we find some comfort in the words *"it is for my benefit?"* At the time it can't possibly seem for our good, or our blessing; yet God says it is.

God knows what He is skillfully working in us during the season of suffering. Not only is He doing something wonderful in our hearts and lives, He has other purposes in mind that will touch and bring healing and provision for others.

In Genesis, chapter 50:19-21, Joseph's statement to his brothers, who had so cruelly mistreated him, is astounding. He can finally see what benefit came from his terrible anguish of heart and years of testing. He says, *"Don't be afraid. Am I in the place of God? You intended to harm me, but God intended it for good to accomplish what is now being done the saving of many lives."* So, likewise, allow your hearts to be comforted with the knowledge that benefit will follow suffering if we love God and trust in Him.

APRIL 28

"You have heard of the perseverance of Job and seen the end intended by the Lord—that the Lord is very compassionate and merciful" James 5:11

HANG ON FOR THE RIDE

SOMETIMES OUR DAYS can feel like we are on a roller coaster frantically hanging on throughout the ride. We go up the structure, around, down, upside down—we are all over the place. You know it's at these times that God asks us to hang on and go with the ride. Ride the waves—don't fight against them, for resistance will break you. Flow and go wherever God takes you over one hill or down a steep mountain. Make it a journey that is full of expectancy and lessons. Sooner or later your roller coaster will come to a halt, your wave will bring you in ashore, and you will be able to look back and see where God has brought you from. Ride with, go with the flow. Don't get frantic—easy now your time of victory is right around the bend.

APRIL 29

"Even in darkness light dawns for the upright, for those who are gracious and compassionate and righteous. Good will come to those who are generous and lend freely, who conduct their affairs with justice. Surely the righteous will never be shaken; they will be remembered forever. They will have no fear of bad news; their hearts are steadfast, trusting in the LORD. Their hearts are secure, they will have no fear; in the end they will look in triumph on their foes"(Psalm 112:4-8).

TO THE UPRIGHT IN HEART

To THOSE WHO live lives that are clean and holy, always choosing to do the right thing and to please God, this is for you. Even though your days be troubled by trial and suffering, hope will assuredly arise in your midst, light will be shed upon your lot, and you will know what to do. God is gracious to you and like a father his child, He has true compassion for what you are going through. He is full of holiness and uprightness.

May God send good people into your life to deal graciously with you—who will lend you a hand in your time of need. May you also be that good person who also lifts up the needy and who continually seeks counsel in your life from God. You will never be shaken in your foundation of faith. God keeps you in His thoughts and heart forever. You will not tremble or be anxious over the negative voices that try to discourage you. Your heart, my beloved, is unshakable because you have made up your mind to place all your confidence in the Lord your God. Your faith has grown strong through the testings, and your roots go way deep down into God's love and care for you. Remember who you are in Christ and don't give into fear. God gives you mighty victory over all the enemy's tactics.

April 30

"You, my brothers, were called to be free. But do not use your freedom to indulge the sinful nature; rather, serve one another in love" (Galatians 5:13).

Our Freedom in Christ

THE LOAD OF sin has been lifted from us and we are released from its bondage! We are free to obey God and walk in the Spirit, but the Bible warns us that we can also go back to living a life of sin, *"as a dog returns to its own vomit"* if we use our freedom carelessly and forget who brought us out of the yoke of slavery.

Just as Christ forgave us when we came to Him, He continues to wash us daily as we come before Him with our failures and when we miss His mark of righteousness. But if we allow little sins to creep in, unconfessed, and if we allow the world to entice us to live carnally, if we allow our hearts to drift away from our first love in Christ, we could find ourselves back under the noose of "guilt and shame, having forgotten that we were purged from our old sins." So we will not use our freedom of forgiveness and redemption to do as we please, but we will strive to do God's will and "serve one another in love." *Stand firm, then, and do not let yourselves be burdened again by a yoke of slavery (Galatians 5:1).*

MAY 1

"...and the people all tried to touch Him, because power was coming from Him and healing them all"(Luke 6:19).

HIS HANDS ALSO HEAL

HE LORD HAS brought to my attention some specific truths that He opened my eyes to. I understood them before with my intellect, but now I am grasping them with my heart. It is with the heart man believes and has faith. These truths are such: Jesus bore our sin in His own body so we would be free from the bondage and power of sin in our lives. He also bore our sicknesses and infirmities so that we would be free of its power and hold on our lives. What does this mean?

It means that we, as children of God, need to walk in our healing, and not allow the enemy to steal it from us through unbelief and fearful symptoms. I believe it means that our physical healing was provided for by Jesus, and we need to appropriate it to whatever area we have infirmity. Does God want to heal us? Absolutely! We see this in Jesus' ministry. *All* who came to Him He healed. So why can't we get our healing? I believe there are three main reasons.

First, we don't persevere in believing God. Sometimes it takes years. Are we willing to believe Him for as long as it takes to become a reality and to continue to thank Him for bearing our sickness so we don't have to bear it?

Next, we just plain don't ever hear it preached from the pulpit so our faith isn't built up to believe as we should. Finally, we just don't think God heals today because we have doctors we can go to.

Why isn't every believer healed? Well I'm not God; you'll have to ask Him when you get to heaven. I do know this that He is sovereign and has His plans and secrets we will never know this side of heaven. What are we to do then with these scriptures on healing?

We are to apply them to ourselves and do whatever God tells us in order

for healing to come. Whether we go to the doctor and take medicine, quit smoking, exercise more, eat better. Just keep on believing God for wholeness.

To *"save"* in the Greek means to "make whole." God desires us to be whole. If you have been struggling with an on-going illness, never lose heart. Get these scriptures down into your heart and remember Jesus healed a man who had his infirmity for 38 years (Jn.5:5). Never give up believing God wants you well. Accept your lot and don't be in denial concerning your illness, but continually build your faith and see what God will do!

Healing scriptures:

Isaiah 53:4-5; Matt. 8:16-17; 1 Peter 2:24; Psalm 107:20; Prov.3:7-8; Ex. 15:26; Psalm 103:3; Ex.23:25; Psalm 118:17, 147:3; James 5:15; Psalm 30:2; Jer .33:6; Matt. 4:23, 8:13, 9:35, 10:1, 12:22, 14:14; Luke 6:19.

MAY 2

"...until Christ is formed in you"(Galatians 4:19).

CHRIST FORMED IN YOU

*I*S CHRIST BEING formed in you? Are you responding to your everyday challenges the way Jesus would? If you come up against a situation where you are tempted to respond out of fear and doubt choose to respond and react as Christ would. Deal with this thing with confidence, wisdom and soundness of mind. Don't lose your temper or slip into a state of anxious thinking. Look upon Christ and allow His life to be formed in you. Resist all intimidation and shrinking from steady faith. Encourage and nurture victorious living and a champion's attitude. Don't allow yourself to be brought down to a fleshy response towards your problems, but a spiritual response. Be led and empowered by the Spirit and bring victory out of defeating circumstances. Allow Christ to be formed in you.

"…but one thing I do: forgetting what lies behind and reaching forward to what lies ahead"(Philippians 3:13).

ACCOMPLISH IT!

WHAT HAVE YOU wanted to do all your life but have been too afraid to launch out? God does not give us a spirit of intimidation. God has given us everything we need to achieve all that He has called us to be and do.

God places a certain specific desire in our hearts to accomplish a dream, and He is the only one who can lead you and show you how to bring it to its fullness. Don't be afraid to launch out when God calls you to take your next step. Don't half realize your dreams. You have to go beyond your comfort zone to accomplish your dreams God has placed in your heart. You must. It is a fact in this life. Step forward toward and embrace change, discipline, instruction, hard times, and all that God allows to touch your life. Resist all the negative voices and dark thoughts that are determined to stunt your growth. Reach out for God in Christ Jesus and fulfill your great calling in Him. Accomplish it!

MAY 4

*"My sheep hear My voice, and I know them, and
they follow Me" (John 10:27 NASV).*

GOD'S VOICE

HOW CAN YOU hear from God? First of all you want to daily live a pure and holy life, seeking after things that have to do with right living. Then you can look for God to speak personally to you. However, sometimes God will speak to us even when we are not living right, and it usually is a warning to us or a calling us back to Himself.

1. *God speaks to us through the inward Witness, that is, the Holy Spirit. It is an unction, a knowing, a perceiving, a discernment, a peace—velvety feeling, a prompting, a red flag or green flag.*

2. *God speaks to us through His Word, the Bible. A scripture will become illumined to us by the Holy Spirit and it will always go hand in hand with the inward Witness. The inward Witness always agrees with the Word.*

3. *Outward circumstances are a third way God leads. Doors are opened or closed. If open then we are to pray for further leading and confirmation from the Holy Spirit.*

4. *God uses other believers in our lives to lead us. They will usually* confirm *what God has already been speaking to us about.*

The more intimate we become with God, the greater our sensitivity to His voice, and the clearer we will hear it.

MAY 5

"For we are His workmanship created in Christ Jesus for good works, which God prepared beforehand that we should walk in them"(Ephesians 2:10).

HE SPEAKS YOUR LANGUAGE

*P*ETER AND ANDREW were casting a net into the lake, for they were fishermen. *"Come, follow Me,"* Jesus said, *"and I will make you fishers of men."* At once they left their nets and followed Him (Matt.4:18-20).

It is interesting to know that Jesus uses us just where we are at, and what we are doing at that time in our life, to mold and make us into His disciple who can reach the lost. He called Peter and Andrew to be "fishers of men" and He spoke their fisherman language which they understood. So He speaks your language, whatever that is, wherever you have come from. He relates to you and uses your skills, abilities and things that you have learned to form you into a fit worker in His fields. But we are to follow Him, to tread in His footsteps, walk where He walks, and He will be the one who will do the "making" in our lives.

MAY 6

"And say to Archippus, 'Be sure to carry out the ministry the Lord gave you'" (Colossians 4:17 NLT).

FULFILL YOUR DIVINE DESTINY

HESE DAYS I really believe that God wants us to focus on living and running the race He's given us in this life. There is so much to do before the Lord returns. We are to be busy with His work and allow the fruit of the Spirit to be cultivated in our lives. God has a specific plan that He has ordained just for you that only you can fulfill. You will have a life changing influence on certain people and you will grab some away from the fires of hell.

Don't ever underestimate your life and the way God has made you. You are wonderfully designed to do the works God has created you for. I know you may be going through some very uncomfortable struggles at times—I say, allow these difficulties to be stepping stones to a greater, richer, fuller life in the Spirit. Ask God to show you how to do this. Ask God to bring the people and things you need into your life to help you to live victoriously.

MAY 7

"Blessed are those whose strength is in You, whose hearts are set on pilgrimage. As they pass through the Valley of Baka, they make it a place of springs; the autumn rains also cover it with pools. They go from strength to strength, till each appears before God in Zion" (Psalm 84:5-7).

COME THROUGH THE VALLEY

WE GO FROM strength to strength. We go from having one victory through a dark valley to another, and then another, all the while developing inward godly character and becoming a brighter light for Jesus. Can you say with me, *"There is no darkness in me, and I won't stay in any type of darkness but will learn how to bring the light and power of God into it—thus extinguishing it?"*

Come up hither out of the valley, and do what God has called and prepared for you to do. Remember you walk THROUGH the valley. It is God's will that you come through whatever trials you are experiencing today. Run your race fixing your spiritual eyes on God and fulfill your God-given destiny!

MAY 8

*"Let the saints be joyful in glory: let them sing aloud upon their beds.
Let the high praises of God be in their mouth, and a two-edged sword in
their hand; To execute vengeance upon the heathen, and punishments
upon the people; To bind their kings with chains, and their nobles with
fetters of iron; To execute upon them the judgment written: this honor
have all His saints. Praise ye the LORD."(Psalm 149:5-9 KNV).*

WEAPONS OF OUR WARFARE

SOMETHING SUPERNATURAL HAPPENS in the spiritual realm
every time a believer praises and worships the Lord. Psalm 149
gives us a peek into this realm and what happens. This psalm
starts out with singing to the Lord, rejoicing in Him, dancing before Him
and praising Him with instruments. These are all ways to praise Him. Then
in verse 6 it says, *"Let the high praises of God be in their mouth!"* We enter
into these high praises when we come into the throne room and worship God
in unbroken praise, beholding His glory and gazing at His awesome radiant
beauty. God takes our worship up into high praises. These praises are similar
to what the angels do before the throne of God day and night. This kind of
praise carries with it a two-edged sword—it is a weapon against the enemy.

In verses 7-9 we are told what this weapon of praise does. It brings about
God's justice on the nations and judgments on the peoples who are against
Him. It binds up Satan with spiritual chains and the demons with fetters
of spiritual iron. It is excruciating for them to hear us give all our adoration
to the Lord.

Finally, it brings about judgment that torments the enemy and his
cohorts. All saints have access to this weapon, and it is to be used especially
when we encounter dark situations. Just ask the Lord to receive your praise
and allow it to ascend into His very presence in the throne room—the angels
will join in with you and spiritually there is glorious warfare taking place.

MAY 9

*"Take delight in the LORD, and He will give you
the desires of your heart" (Psalm 37:4).
"The Scripture says, 'Whoever believes in Him will not be
disappointed'" (Romans 10:11 Good News Translation).*

DREAM BIG!

I'D RATHER TAKE the risk to dream big, expect big, and look for the best, and then be disappointed, than not to ever have dreamed at all, expected or believed or looked for the best in situations and in people. Dreams have an excellent opportunity to become a thriving reality when we walk with God, walk in faith and obedience to His Word. God is a God who dreams big and expects big, and the answers and works He does in accordance to our faith, are big! We are to be God-thinkers and imagine what we can do and what we can accomplish for Christ with His ability working in us. Even our failures can be turned into stepping stones to higher ground. Dare to dream outside the box. God always calls us to things that are way beyond our own ability and that require faith that can be stretched—even to the limits.

MAY 10

"Yet the LORD longs to be gracious to you; therefore He will rise up to show you compassion. For the LORD is a God of justice. Blessed are all who wait for Him"(Isaiah 30:18).

YOUR GOD WILL WAIT

THEREFORE THE LORD will wait to answer your request. He will hold off on showing Himself mighty on your behalf. He will hold tight and allow more time to pass by. Why? So that He may give more divine grace to you, so that you can stand in unwavering faith, so you can stand and persevere in hope. So that His mercy and goodness will be heaped upon your life and on your particular situation. And then when the answer finally arrives, you will greatly exalt Him for His glory and mighty works! Remember, God is always fair with His dealings in your life and will not delay any longer than needed. And you therefore, will be blessed richly, if you can learn to wait with joy for God's timing.

MAY 11

"Though He slay me, yet will I hope in Him..."(Job 13:15).

TIRED OF THE TESTINGS AND TRIAL?

AS YOUR FAITH been tested to its limit lately? Do you feel you cannot hold on a second longer? Are you beginning to wonder if God has passed you by? Are you having doubts that your prayers are mere words that are bouncing off the wall and onto the floor?

Be of good cheer! You're just about ready to the point of breakthrough, not breakdown. So here's what you do: dig your heels of faith firmly in the ground of God's love and grace. Set your heart and eyes back on your powerful God. The God of the impossible! Be aware of what's going on—the truth of the matter is that your faith is being tested and made to be stronger.

The enemy is jabbing you in areas where he knows you're weak. God is equipping you to pass on and through. There is a great cloud of witnesses who are cheering you on.

So, you must take up the impenetrable shield of faith to put out every fiery dart of the wicked. Speak the truth of what God's Word says—don't focus on how you are *feeling* at the moment. His Word says that He will never let you down and that He cares deeply about what you are going through. Keep persistent in your prayers, for prayer works!

Now rest, and wait on God for His next move. He will not tarry a moment too long. Don't give up! Never give up! You will make it through your valley.

MAY 12

"I am the LORD, the God of all mankind. Is anything too hard for Me" (Jeremiah 32:27)?

NEED A SOLUTION TO YOUR PROBLEM?

WHEN YOUR PARTICULAR circumstance contradicts all you believe in, doubts and questionings will continually arise in your heart. And there appears to be no resolution or answer to your problem. Your reserves feel spent, and you are wondering how much longer you will have to deal with your situation. Trouble and anxiety are no strangers to you.

I say to you this day, listen and you will hear your God saying, *"Is Anything too hard for Me?"*

It's not too difficult for God to handle and figure out what's going on. He can handle that loved one who you're struggling with. He can handle your financial burdens. He can handle your stubborn illness. He is big enough to handle that broken relationship, that new and challenging endeavor, an uncertain future and unsolvable problems. God is able. He's got it.

So rest now in this promise of assurance, and ask the Lord to give you fresh grace and wisdom for each day. He is faithful to guide you through. He will bring solutions from sources you never imagined.

May 13

*"I will instruct you and teach you in the way you should go; I
will counsel you with My loving eye on you" (Psalm 32:8).*

Something Familiar, Something New

WHEN GOD WANTS to teach us something unknown about Himself, ourselves, other people or things, we may encounter new trials of sorts—or we may find ourselves treading in unfamiliar waters. When He wants to reinforce a lesson or a truth in or to us, we may find ourselves battling the same old agitating difficulties and challenges we thought we had already learned and squeezed every ounce of lesson out from the thing.

God allows us to be tested to make sure it is not just head knowledge we are acquiring, but that each thing gleaned has been burned and impressed indelibly into our spirit. Much of the time we will spend our days and moments walking on the well-trodden paths of adversity. Each victory we make or lesson we embrace and allow to become ours, prepares us for the new uncharted experiences that God wants to take us through.

So are you in a repeat lesson or in a fresh learning season? If it is a repeat lesson respond with all that you have already learned—rest instead of strive, trust instead of doubt or wonder. Do not shy away from stepping out into the great unknown and the unfamiliar, because Jesus has already been there and He will take you through. You will use all the things you have learned through past tests and trials, and then you will discover some new ways of becoming victorious. So, enjoy the journey of your spiritual growth.

MAY 14

"That's why I work and struggle so hard, depending on Christ's mighty power that works within me"(Colossians 1:29).

GOD ABILITY

*I*N THE 6TH chapter of Ephesians, Paul tells us about the armor of God and the schemes of the enemy. But before he goes into describing the devil and the armor we are to put on, he talks of our position in Christ. He says to *"Be strong in the Lord and in His mighty Power."* If we can wrap our minds around this we would never fear Satan and we would be true over-comers.

When we become born again God plants within our hearts His dynamite power, His ability, His energy. We have God-Ability overflowing within us and just waiting to be used. And how do we use this God-Ability? First, we yield to the Holy Spirit. Then we walk it out by faith. Everything we receive from God is through faith. We believe we have it and that it is working in and through us to defeat the enemy in the Name of Jesus! The devil trembles at the Name of Jesus when we use it and he flees in terror. Use your God-Ability, your God-Power that comes through the Holy Spirit working mightily within you.

MAY 15

"In addition to all this, take up the shield of faith, with which you can extinguish all the flaming arrows of the evil one"(Ephesians 6:16).

THE SHIELD OF FAITH

*D*ID YOU KNOW that back in the days of the apostles the Roman soldiers would soak their shields (that were made of three sheets of wood glued together and covered with canvas and leather) in water. Why? Because the arrows that were shot at them had their tips wrapped in cloth and soaked in a flammable liquid so that when they hit their target they would explode into flames. So then when the fiery arrows of the enemy would fly at them the Roman soldiers held up a shield that was sure to put them out because it was soaked with water. Now if their shield was dry you know what happened don't you? It burned up. How does this apply to our Shield of Faith that we are to take up?

Water represents the Word of God, and the Word of God is Jesus, so we are to be soaked in the Word of God and Jesus. We will put out those fiery darts of the evil one! Our faith increases as we feed on the Word of God and our trust and confidence in Him also grows. Faith, is believing God to be, and to do all He said! If we become spiritually dry we can become burned by the devil's darts. Therefore, hold up that shield of Faith that is soaked in the Word and Jesus and march on into Victory.

"Finally, brothers and sisters, whatever is true, whatever is noble, whatever is right, whatever is pure, whatever is lovely, whatever is admirable—if anything is excellent or praiseworthy—think about such things"(Philippians 4:8).

WHAT IS THE HELMET OF SALVATION?

WE ALL KNOW that a helmet protects the head which contains the brain, the control center that runs the entire body. Well, the Helmet of Salvation is an invisible, but real, helmet that protects the soul which includes mind, intellect, will and emotions. Our soul directs our spiritual life through the choices that we make and the thoughts we think. Satan loves to attack our soul with blows of discouragement and fear, and make us doubt God's love and care for us, even questioning our own salvation at times. So we need to take the Helmet of Salvation and put it on. But what is the Helmet of Salvation?

It is having security in our salvation and hope for the future. Let me explain. Our salvation has three aspects to it. First one is that we are freed from the *penalty* of sin, we have escaped spiritual death and the fires of hell through our faith in the death, burial and resurrection of Jesus. This is a one-time deal. We become a child of God and are *born-again* of the Spirit and are sealed by the Holy Spirit. We are secure in Him. We are saved.

Next aspect is that of *sanctification,* this is a fancy word for God working with us, to work out our own salvation, transforming us to be more like Jesus. It is a process which will last until we see the Lord face to face. He also teaches us how to walk in victory over sin's domination.

The last aspect of our salvation is future—our *glorification.* We will receive new spiritual bodies and rule and reign with Christ forever. This hope gives us strength to go through the trials we encounter here on earth.

So how do we apply the Helmet of Salvation? We put it on through using our mind, or imagination, our intellect and will. We have a *mindset* that we

are **absolutely secure in our salvation in Christ, once and for all time**. We work agreeably with God when He puts His finger on things that need to be changed in our life. And we look forward to the glory of our new body free of pain and fear, and also we anticipate our home in heaven with Jesus.

MAY 17

"The weapons we fight with are not the weapons of the world. On the contrary, they have divine power to demolish strongholds. We demolish arguments and every pretension that sets itself up against the knowledge of God, and we take captive every thought to make it obedient to Christ" (2 Corinthians 10:4-5).

STRONGHOLDS AND OUR SPIRITUAL WEAPONS

SOMETIMES WE BUILD up strongholds in our emotions and mind and we don't realize what's happening. A stronghold starts in the emotions and mind. A wall is first built, and if the behavior and mindset is continued in that built the wall, then our spirit becomes weakened so the enemy can come in and build a stronghold.

We build up walls that we are not even aware of, and if it is not knocked down, a strong hold is built. An example of a wall and a stronghold is thus: wall of unforgiveness = stronghold of bitterness; wall of anger = stronghold of rage; wall of sinful behavior = stronghold of addiction; wall of disobedience to God = stronghold of spiritual blindness.

The good news is if we have built up walls and if the enemy has built strongholds, they can be torn down and demolished through our mighty powerful spiritual weapons. We break the power of the enemy in the name of Jesus, and break the *spiritual* stronghold. Once that is broken, and this is immediately done, we must deal with the walls and strongholds in the *emotional* realm—sometimes even in the *physical* realm with our bodies.

The Word of God and Prayer are two very effective weapons; they are our battering rams that break down walls and strongholds. This is a process sometimes, and many times we need assistance from other believers to help us change our behavior and mindset that have gotten us into the stronghold in the first place. Some other spiritual weapons we can use are: The Name of Jesus, The Blood of Jesus, which Satan is reminded of his total defeat; Praise also silences the enemy and stops his maneuvers. Prayer and faith together are also vital and powerfully effective.

MAY 18

"For I know the plans that I have toward you, says the Lord, plans of peace and not of evil to give you an expected end"(Jeremiah 29:11).

GOD'S PLANS

THIS VERSE WAS first spoken to Jeremiah the prophet by the Lord for the Children of Israel. They had been carried away to Babylon into captivity by King Nebuchadnezzar, and they were taken from their beloved homeland in Israel, Jerusalem. The temple of the Lord had been demolished, and the walls of the city torn down and broken. Here they were in a foreign land and they felt hopeless and in despair. They feared they would never ever see their homeland again. But the Lord remembered them and sent them a good word by Jeremiah. He gave them an encouraging word of hope!

God explained to the Children of Israel that He knew all about the plans He had in store for them and their loved ones. He assured them the plans He was leading them into were plans to bless and increase them, plans for restoration and wholeness, plans with the end result of peace. He also wanted them to be aware that He was never the one to bring evil upon them, rather He would always turn around for good what was meant for evil to them. Yes, He would allow suffering and trial only for an outcome of victory and blessing.

Tribulations would come to them for that is the way of life and growth, but no matter how adverse circumstances became, God would always work it for their good if they would trust Him. He wanted to give them hope! This captivity into Babylon had stripped away their hope and the Lord wanted to restore hope back to them again! Indeed He would bring them back to their beloved land.

And you and me? This promise is for us also. Have you been wrestling with something so adverse and hard in your life that you are beginning to feel hopeless? Look up. God's plans for you include all that you are going through for He knows the outcome will be good. Trust Him.

MAY 19

"Therefore, I urge you, brothers and sisters, in view of God's mercy, to offer your bodies as a living sacrifice, holy and pleasing to God—this is your true and proper worship" (Romans 12:1).

GIVE ME A LIFE THAT IS LOVE

DEAR GOD, GIVE me a heart that loves mercy. Give me eyes that see the beauty in everything around me. Give me a mind that reflects on Your words. Give me lips that gently heal with their words. Give me wisdom when I enter trial and difficulty. Give me hands that gently guide those who are stumbling in the dark. Give me feet that will go to those places where hearts are in need of encouragement. Give me a spirit that adores and worships You. Then give me a voice to ever sing Your praise. Now, Lord, I give You all that I am, holy and pleasing to You.

"'Have faith in God,' Jesus answered. 'Truly I tell you, if anyone says to this mountain, Go, throw yourself into the sea, and does not doubt in their heart but believes that what they say will happen, it will be done for them. Therefore I tell you, whatever you ask for in prayer, believe that you have received it, and it will be yours'" (Mark 11:22-24).

FEAR NOT, ONLY BELIEVE

IN YOUR PARTICULAR situation it is important that you look at it through the eyes of faith and not fear. Jesus said, *"Fear not, only believe."* He also said that *"all things are possible to him that believes."* And then *"If you would believe, you would see the glory of God."* Do you want to see God move in your case? Do you want to see His glory and hand at work for you? Then believe. This means resting instead of fretting; it is choosing to put your faith over on the believing side and see your circumstance not with you alone by yourself, but with God at the wheel. I believe you will see what God can do and you will be talking about it to friends and loved ones. It will make you stand in awe of One so wise, great, good and loving.

May 21

"Yet he did not waver through unbelief regarding the promise of God, but was strengthened in his faith and gave glory to God" (Romans 4:20).

Faith Again

*I*F YOU REALLY believe that God has answered what you have been praying about you will thank Him in advance of seeing it. Faith is already having the thing that you have requested from the Lord, through the eye of faith, and you are already rejoicing in it! The manifestation will come after you have persevered in steady unwavering faith in a God who does the impossible.

One time God told me that we were going to have a child and we needed a bigger place. This had been my prayer also. When we found a house that would do, I saw it inside my spirit and laughed with joy!!! I knew it was ours. And I thanked God for a baby also. I saw him in my spirit. Within a frame of God's time we bought the house, and a month later I became pregnant with our son, Joseph.

Faith takes hold of the promise of God and runs with it, being fully persuaded that what He has promised He is able to perform. What is it you need from God right now? Ask in faith, keep asking until your faith is firm, and you've received the answer already in your heart before ever seeing it. If you would believe, you would see God's answer.

MAY 22

"Praise the LORD. Praise God in His sanctuary; praise Him in His mighty heavens. Praise Him for His acts of power; praise Him for His surpassing greatness. Praise Him with the sounding of the trumpet, praise Him with the harp and lyre"(Psalm 150:1-3).

PRAISE HIM!

*a*LL THROUGH THE Scripture we are exhorted to give praise to the Lord. How easy it is to give praise when we feel good and when things are going well for us. Thank you, Jesus! Praise comes easy when we feel the anointing of God on us, and the joy of the Holy Spirit. But how about when we are feeling dry, discouraged, down, lonely, battling pain or grief? When we don't feel God at all? Heb. 13:15 tells us that we are to then, *"continually offer to God a sacrifice of praise."* The first part of that verse is the secret to how we can turn our perspective Godward. *"Through Jesus, therefore let us continually offer up . . . "* We can do all things through Christ's strength. And then praise to God is to be a continuous practice in our lives, not just when we are up to it. Sometimes it definitely is a "sacrifice of praise," and is difficult to lift up our voices in praise to His name. I have found if I am feeling worn, weary or discouraged, I can go to the praise psalms and obediently say them to the Lord, and because of my obedience the Lord meets me where I am and ministers to me. We are to praise God for who He is, what He has done, and for what He is going to do. Do you remember that praise song we used to sing back in the 80's? *"We bring the sacrifice of praise into the house of the Lord. (2x) And we offer up to You the sacrifices of thanksgiving and we offer up to You the sacrifices of praise."* Praise psalms to say: Psalms 145,146,147,148,149,150.

MAY 23

"Many are the plans in a person's heart, but it is the LORD's purpose that prevails" (Proverbs 19:21).

PREPARATION FOR SERVING HIM

*D*ON'T BE DISCOURAGED about where you are at and what's happening right now in your life. God has every detail planned and is carefully developing and preparing you for His service, always for His service. He uses the assignment you are in right now to grow you up to be ready for your next assignment. I know how difficult it is to think nothing's going on important in your life, and that God seems awfully quiet. But let me assure you that He is very much actively involved with you and His plan for you. Use your time wisely and enjoy your special unique journey with God. He is teaching you how to bear much fruit wherever you are and that your fruit will remain. Remember what you always wanted to do for God— the dreams He set in your heart? Well He's faithfully fulfilling them. Trust in His love for you. Trust His guidance and rejoice in His ever abiding presence.

Life isn't always fair, but God is always fair. We may not always see this apparent in this life but nevertheless God never makes a mistake with or in your life.

MAY 24

*"I can do all things through the strength that Christ pours
on and through me" (Phil. 4:13). (Eilers' paraphrase)
"... for your Father knows exactly what you need
even before you ask Him" (Matthew 6:8)!*

HE KNOWS

I AM DETERMINED TO rely on the Lord for all my needs. And I will strive to have a happy heart, lifting praise and thanksgiving to my God because His love for me is so strong and consistent. His eyes see everything I am struggling with, those things that are causing me much worry and concern. He knows the state of my heart and mind. He knows the unsteadiness I feel. But He has given me this time and all the room I need, in order to grow and spread my wings of faith. I will grow strong in Him, and cultivate a heart that is content in whatever circumstance I find myself in.

MAY 25

"I will remember the deeds of the LORD; yes, I will remember Your miracles of long ago. I will consider all Your works and meditate on all Your mighty deeds" (Psalm 77:11-12).

REMEMBER YOUR GOD

SO WHEN THINGS aren't going so well for you and doubts and worry seem to be swirling around in your mind, do what the Psalmist did in Psalm 77:11-20. He says, *"I will remember who God is and what He has done. I will remember the miracles He performed for His people long ago—like the crossing of the Red Sea. What a mighty act of God!"* As I think upon these awesome works, my faith is encouraged, because I know if God could make a way where there was no way then, in that day, He can do the same for me today. I will meditate on how He has answered my prayers in the past. This builds up my hope, and I remember that He is able to display His power in my life and in the lives around me. He is Lord over all situations and circumstances. I will ponder upon His guiding presence through every storm. I may not always see which way He's taking me, but this I know, He will gently lead me as a Shepherd His flock, and I will find myself in the place where all things are possible with Him.

MAY 26

"Give thanks to the LORD, for He is good; His love endures forever. Let the redeemed of the LORD tell their story—those He redeemed from the hand of the foe, those He gathered from the lands, from east and west, from north and south" (Psalm 107:1-3).

HAPPY DAY TO YOU!

GOOD MORNING WORLD! God's got it all in His hand. I can skip out the door to work and know that He's carrying my load of concerns. I can smile and be kind because I know He loves me and is kind to me. Whatever comes my way today, I can deal with it because I have what I need in Christ. My strength, my joy, my wisdom, my protection, my provision, my peace….

Today is a good day to be alive! Thank You, Jesus for this awesome gift of life! Lift up those who are bent over with worry, fear and dismay. Gently lift their eyes to Yours so they can see Your care and love for them. They matter to You.

"Casting all your care on Him for He cares for you" (1 Peter 5:7).

"By faith Abraham, when called to go to a place he would later receive as his inheritance, obeyed and went, even though he did not know where he was going" (Hebrews 11:8).

MOVING ON

CHORUS: I'M MOVING on, I'm moving on to the place that I belong
Heaven knows this road I'm on
I'm moving on, I'm moving on
Verse: Dear Jesus, I've been waiting here singing the same old song
Until I heard You loud and clear, *My child it's time to move on*
Verse: Don't know where You're taking me, but I know You care
Won't let this be shaking me cause I know You are taking me there
Chorus: I'm moving on, I'm moving on to the place that I belong
Heaven knows this road I'm on
I'm moving on, I'm moving on © 2014

MAY 28

*"This is the day the LORD has made. We will rejoice
and be glad in it" (Psalm 118:24 NLT).
"So don't worry about tomorrow, for tomorrow will bring its own
worries. Today's trouble is enough for today" (Matthew 6:34 NLT).*

THE PRESENT

W E CAN PLAN for the future, but we cannot live there. We can reminisce over the past, but we cannot live there either. We must capture and live in the present—for it is in the present that we have what we need, grace for that moment, strength and guidance. It is in the present that God calls us to live with Him.

MAY 29

"My children, with whom I am again in labor until Christ is formed in you" (Galatians 4:19 New American Standard 1977).

GIVE ME YOUR HEART, O GOD

O YOU KNOW what is really beautiful and fills me with great happiness? It is when I see my heart becoming more like Jesus' heart. It's when I see my heart loving more like Jesus. It's when I see my heart becoming more confident in the Father's love and security.

Look and see—if you do something with love attached, this is Jesus' heart being developed in you.

When you see yourself acting in love and faith—rejoice because Christ's heart is being formed in you!

Oh God, let me see Your heart for everything. Give me Your heart even if it means breaking mine.

MAY 30

"...and the earth was without form and void and darkness was on the face of the deep, and the Spirit of God hovered over the waters. Then God said, 'Let there be light and there was light'" (Genesis 1:2-3).

LET THERE BE LIGHT

*A*s I was on my walk today the Lord showed me that when we are in the pits and darkness covers what light we had, and when we feel empty of strength because we are tired of dealing with the same impossible things, if we let God be God, we will see something wonderful happen. We can pray that the Holy Spirit of God would come and hover over our problem and as He hovers over it, He is creating something new. The Father will then declare from heaven that the way be made clear to you, and He will light your path. But remember between the hovering and the declaring must be a soul that *waiteth patiently* as possible.

MAY 31

*"LORD my God, I called to You for help, and
You healed me." (Psalm 30:2).*

GRIEF

I FEEL LIKE I'M floundering in the waters of the deep sea. Lord,
I want to hurry this process, but I can't. I don't want to feel this
pain in my soul, but I must—and I will with your help. I've
watched these waves of grief as they come and go, and I know they ebb and
flow. The ebb sucks me back, back until I feel I will not get back to shore. Then
the flow throws me forward casting me back on the shore. I am left breathless
and exhausted. How can I go on?

Somehow with Your help Lord, I will survive these tidal waves of grief—
You told me I would, if I keep going through them holding on to my hope
in You. They will become more manageable.

But when, Lord, when?

JUNE 1

"And so we know and rely on the love God has for us. God is love.
Whoever lives in love lives in God, and God in them" (1 John 4:16).

GOD'S COMFORTING LOVE

I AM FINDING THAT the more I am able to sit still, even for a little bit, and think upon God and His love for me, I can see my troubles in a healthier way. They don't consume me—they are manageable.

I think of God and His love—it is a real thing—God is real, not just a force out there. His love is real and as tangible as a mother's to her child.

The Bible tells us that God is Love and that He is spirit. Jesus Christ is all of who God is, manifested in a body. God is a person not a force. He is not the universe—He *created* the universe and all things. God shows us what His love is like when He says that even though we were sinners and breaking His laws, He gave us His only beloved Son, Jesus, to die on the cross to pay the penalty for the sin we should have to pay for. Jesus, His Son, paid our debt. We just have to receive this wonderful gift by faith.

The greatest love a person shows is when they give their life for another. Jesus did this for us. He also rose again from the dead and promises that those who believe in Him will also be raised from the dead at the last day.

This Love of God is poured out into our empty hearts by His sweet gentle Holy Spirit. He wraps us in His love. Daddy to child. His feelings of affection for us are deep and true.

God is real. He is a personal God, and He has revealed His love to us through His Son, Jesus.

I know and rely on His love.

JUNE 2

"...and provide for those who grieve in Zion—to bestow on them a crown of beauty instead of ashes, the oil of joy instead of mourning, and a garment of praise instead of a spirit of despair. They will be called oaks of righteousness, a planting of the LORD for the display of His splendor" (Isaiah 61:3).

PSALM FOR THE DOWNHEARTED

OUR GOD COMFORTS all of us who mourn. He gives peace and relief to those who struggle with grief and sorrow in their hearts. And those things that once caused the fires to go out in our souls, reducing our hopes to ashes, He turns around and develops a fragrant kind of beauty that flows out of us to others who are also hurting.

Our God lifts our spirit of heaviness and fills us with worship and praise to His name.

And why will He perform such wonderful deeds for us? To secure our faith in Him, to be unmovable as an aged oak tree, so that all those who touch our world in some way will stand amazed when they see that it is God's hand that has delivered and blessed us when we were distressed, and thereby give Him the glory He deserves.

JUNE 3

"But one thing I do: Forgetting what is behind and straining toward what is ahead, I press on toward the goal to win the prize for which God has called me heavenward in Christ Jesus" (Philippians 3:13-14).

HEADED FOR HIGHER GROUND

WHEN GOD MOVES, then it is time for us to move. God may want to bring us to a new level of faith in our Christian walk with Him. Can we step out in the areas He is asking us to and grow our roots of faith a little deeper in His love and in His Word? God may ask us to come out of our comfort zone and experience new adventures with Him. Does He want to use us to pray for others in a more powerful way with a stronger faith and anointing? Does He want you to speak out on issues of morality that can influence our world? Move when God moves. Go places with Him you never thought possible. Believe for those finances, for that complete healing, for the salvation of that loved one or a deliverance from bondage. Believe God will use you in a more powerful and effective way in this day and time in history. God wants us to leave behind a godly legacy for others to be encouraged by. You are one of the great cloud of witnesses here on earth to cheer the weary on in the faith. So move when God moves.

June 4

"O Lord, You have examined my heart and know
everything about me"(Psalm 139:1 NLT).

God Knows You

*H*AVE YOU EVER been so anxious you couldn't sleep at night? So many issues pressing in on your heart and questions that seem unanswered, and you are worn out praying and waiting for solutions. At times you wonder if God has your number and sees your situation. Not only does God have your number, He knows you so well and sees exactly where you are at in your life. He not only knows you, but has studied your weaknesses and strengths. He knows your physical and emotional struggles. He understands why you think the way you do and He loves you. He is patiently molding your character, and even though it is painful, He knows all about it and is doing everything He can to bring His purpose to fruition in and around you.

He has never abandoned you. He has the answers and the solutions which He will reveal in His own time. Take heart and know that God is personally taking your case seriously and He will do something. It comforts me to know that He knows my story, my life, and my story's ending. He knows yours too. So will you pray this prayer with me from King David?

"Search me, O God, and know my heart; test me and know
my anxious thoughts. Point out anything in me that offends
You and lead me along the path of everlasting life" (Psalm
139:23-24 NLT).

JUNE 5

"Pure and undefiled Religion before God is this: to visit orphans and widows in their trouble and to keep oneself unspotted from the world" (James 1:27).

WHICH IS THE TRUE RELIGION?

*S*OME MAY ASK, *"Which Religion is the true Religion"* or *"Do they all lead us to God?"*

What is Religion? Religion is something someone is dedicated to in order to reach out and get in touch with God. The Bible tells us in James 1:27, that if our Religion is true, living and life-changing, we will care about the needy and reach out to those who are unable to provide for themselves—it is looking beyond ourselves to others.

This is the first part of a true Religion. The second, is to live a pure and holy life putting off all manner of sinful behavior. We can indeed help those in need, but how can our Religion keep us living a holy life separated unto God? How can any man be absolutely clean and pure before God? I believe the only true Religion that can allow us to do this is the Christian faith.

Why? Because Jesus Christ took all our sins on the cross and forgave us from breaking God's laws and not living up to His commandments. Remember, if you break one commandment, you are guilty of all. But if we accept and receive the sacrifice of Jesus offered for us on the cross, we will be washed by His blood, set apart for Him, and made positionally holy before God. Then we are empowered by His Holy Spirit to choose to live a pure life and put off sinful behaviors.

No other Religion offers us this gift of total forgiveness, redemption and grace to live a righteous life for we, in our own power, can never be completely good. We are prone to sin and our hearts are desperately wicked. Only God, in Jesus Christ, can enter our heart and cleanse it, transform it, and then conform it to His own image.

Which is the true Religion? All Religions are *man's* efforts to reach

God—only in Christianity does *God* reach down to man. I believe the Religion of the Bible is the true Religion. I believe this because the Bible says it is, and I have found it to be true in my own life. God really is real and alive and He has shown Himself to me through His Son, Jesus Christ. God did for us what we could never do for ourselves. He redeemed us from our sins, freed us from the domain of the devil, and gives us a transformed heart to live a good life. All we have to do is to believe it and receive it, walk in it and live it!

JUNE 6

"...but understand what the Lord's will is" (Ephesians 5:17 NIV).

UNDERSTAND GOD'S WILL

WE ARE TOLD in this passage not to be unwise, but wise concerning God's will for us. We are told not to just know His will, but to also understand it. We can know lots of information about God's requirements, but if we have it in our hearts we will live it. And we do have it engraved spiritually upon our hearts. We need only to tap into the source.

Understand why He wants us to live a particular way. It is for our good.

The verses following Ephesians 5:17 give us some ideas of God's will for us. We are not to be drunk on wine, but be filled with the Spirit, because the Spirit will empower us to do God's will. The Spirit is the one who will teach us how to tap into God's will. Then let God's words flow out of your lips to edify others and to praise Him. Give thanks to the Lord for leading you in the truth and giving you power to obey Him. Be humble, for the humble can hear God's heart. Be submissive to one another. God may be speaking to you through someone in the Body. Be open and listen with wisdom. Understand His will for you and live a happy and abundant life.

JUNE 7

"I am the vine, you are the branches. If you abide in Me and I in you, you will bear much fruit; apart from Me you can do nothing" (John 15:5).

ABIDE IN THE VINE

*I*N THIS VERSE Jesus is telling us a truth that must be heeded. As one of the branches of the Lord, we are to abide in Him, for if we fail to, we will wither and die and bear no fruit at all. That word "abide" in the Greek is *parameno* which means to remain in a close working partnership, to remain close beside, alongside, and to continue to abide.

We have an intimate partnership with Jesus in our Christian walk. He urges us to keep walking alongside Him and to move as He moves, and go where He goes, to do what He does. If we continue in our close relationship with Him we will bear, not a few grapes, but much fruit! What is the fruit? I believe He is talking here about the fruit of the Holy Spirit as found in Galatians 5. He is also referring to bringing souls into the Kingdom, and then the fruit of encouraging and building up the members of His body. Do you exemplify these fruits?

If your fruit is little then you must spend more time in the Vine. Spiritually speaking, we can do nothing in the spiritual realm without Christ's power and direction guiding our lives. To bear much beautiful fruit that others can eat of we must cling to and get our nourishment from the Holy Vine, Jesus. This is to be a continuing process, as we know, in watching a vineyard grow.

JUNE 8

"I have placed My rainbow in the clouds. It is the sign of My covenant with you and with all the earth. When I send clouds over the earth, the rainbow will appear in the clouds, I will remember My covenant between Me and you and all living creatures of every kind. Never again will the waters become a flood to destroy all life. Whenever the rainbow appears in the clouds, I will see it and remember the everlasting covenant between God and all living creatures of every kind on the earth" (Genesis 9:13-16).

THE RAINBOW

As I was walking and talking to the Lord about the promises that He's made to me, I suddenly looked up and saw a small part of a rainbow peeking out of big billowy clouds. I said *"Wow! Beautiful! Lord, what does that mean to me today?"* He answered and said, *"It is a reminder that I will fulfill all My good promises to you and your family. I have made My covenant of love with you and I am your God forever."* I was awed by my God.

The rainbow is not just the outward promise of yesterday from the Old Testament, but it is fresh and new in our day for each of us. It keeps echoing the great faithfulness of our God. His promises to us are always yes and amen.

JUNE 9

"But He said to me, 'My grace is sufficient for you, for My power is made perfect in weakness.' Therefore I will boast all the more gladly about my weaknesses, so that Christ's power may rest on me" (2 Corinthians 12:9).

A THOUGHT ON SUFFERING

OMETHING SUPERNATURAL IS going on when we suffer—we are not only becoming more like Christ, but Christ's very power can be witnessed in our lives as we trust in Him. *"He is our refuge and our strength, our very present help in trouble" (Psalm 46:1).* If we call on Him, He will answer us and supply us with whatever we are lacking, in order that we might be able to stand and survive spiritually and emotionally.

He will also give us a way of escape so that we will be able to bear up under our trial. God tells us in *1 Corinthians 10:13, "No temptation has overtaken you except what is common to mankind. And God is faithful; He will not let you be tempted beyond what you can bear. But when you are tempted, He will also provide a way out so that you can endure it."*

He will always show us how to keep on going and to make it through, so leave yourself and your situation as clay in the Potter's hand and watch God work! Hold on to your hope!

*"I have put My words in your mouth and covered you
with the shadow of My hand" (Isaiah 51:16).*

ROAR LIKE A LION

*D*ON'T BE AFRAID to speak the words that God has put burning in your heart. Our world desperately needs to hear what is on the heart of God. As we yield ourselves to Him, He will entrust us with specific words He wants us to share. How will they know truth unless someone speaks it forth? You may lose those you thought were your friends because you speak out for the truth and for godliness. Keep speaking out. Never stop. Be bold. Be persistent, like Paul the Apostle. They tried to shut him up so many times. Do not fear, for God has placed His hand over your life and protected you to be able to speak His Word. Whosoever strikes back at you will find it will come back to them. Roar like a lion! Be harmless as a dove. Be wise as a serpent and speak the Word.

JUNE 11

"God's way is perfect. All the LORD's promises prove true. He is a shield for all who look to Him for protection" (Psalm 18:30).

THE HARD PLACE

*I*T IS NOT a secret to God where you have been placed at this time. It is not a surprise to Him what you are struggling through at this time in your life. All suffering is custom designed for our good and benefit. God does not ask us to understand all of the things that are taking place in us and around us—however, sometimes if we ask Him, He will reveal to us some truths of what He is doing.

I know this, that God is *for* us. He is the place where we can hide and find peace of mind even in the storm. We "learn" how to do this however, and unfortunately we learn while we are in deep suffering. Paul, the apostle, said that he learned to be content in whatever state he was in. I am sure there was a time when he was angry with his lot, or frustrated and despondent over not having everything the way he thought he should have it. Paul knew what it was like to hunger, thirst, be without, endure beatings, tribulations of all kinds. I'm sure he complained and told God it was all too much, even more than he thought he could bear. God kept on loving him and gave him some answers, like saying, *"My Grace is sufficient for You."* And, *"I am faithful to give you a way to manage and survive when you think you cannot" (2 Corinthians 12:8-10; 1 Corinthians 10:13).*

But one day there came a time when Paul could look back and say, *"I have learned!"* He knew what kind of mindset he needed to make it through. It was not one of self-pity, but one of quiet trust in a God who can be trusted.

And you? Are you in that place of "learning" to be content? Your steps are ordered by the Lord and He delights in your way. Hang on to Him and allow Him to do His gracious work in your life—and after you have done the will of God, you will receive the promise (Hebrews 10:36). Keep looking up!

JUNE 12

"...since what may be known about God is plain to them, because God has made it plain to them. For since the creation of the world God's invisible qualities—His eternal power and divine nature— have been clearly seen, being understood from what has been made, so that people are without excuse" (Romans 1:19-20).

GOD HAS MADE HIMSELF KNOWN

THE FOOL SAYS, *"There is no God."*

God has made Himself known through His beautiful creation! His signature is written all over His awesome handiwork! Then to get to know Him personally and on a deeper level, He has even given us His wonderful Word—the Bible. Those who say there is no God have no excuse because He has made Himself known. The Heavens declare the Glory of God and the earth displays His handiwork! He tells us if we search for Him with all of our heart, we will find Him. He is always ready to make Himself found and known to us.

JUNE 13

"And because you belong to Him, the power of the life-giving Spirit has freed you from the power of sin that leads to death" (Romans 8:2 NLT).

TEMPTATION

OW CAN WE make it through trying temptations? First of all, know that God never tempts us; the tempter is Satan. Matt. 4:1 tells us that it was Satan who tempted Jesus in the wilderness.

What happens in the temptation process? James 1:13-15 tells us that each person is tempted when they are led away by their own lust and enticed. Eve, in the garden, saw the fruit of the tree, and was drawn away by her own lustful desire to be as wise as God and she was enticed. At this point, however, sin has not yet been born. A person can turn away at this point. But if that lust has been nurtured within the mind and the heart and has not been resisted, it is conceived and gives birth to the *act* of sin, and sin, if it is allowed to dominate the soul and spirit, will bring destruction and death. Eve had set her eyes upon the fruit and thought about it. Then she ate it and disobeyed God. This threw all of mankind into a state of sin which can only be broken through coming to the person of Jesus Christ.

How can we be strong enough to resist temptation? Jesus told His disciples in Mark 14:38 to watch and pray that you enter not into temptation, for the spirit is willing to be obedient but the flesh is weak. So we are to be on guard with what is happening around and inside of us, and we are to pray for strength to resist.

Hebrews 12:4 says that in our struggle against sin we have not yet resisted to the point of shedding our blood. Jesus shed great drops of blood in the Garden of Gethsemane when He was praying against the temptation to avoid going to the cross. 1 Cor.10:13 says that there is no temptation that we will experience, except what someone, somewhere at some time, has experienced in some way. It is nothing new. However, God is faithful and He will

not let you be tempted beyond your point of endurance and resisting. You can bear the testing of the temptation. If you will look and discern, God has made a way out so you can endure it.

Joseph, in the Old Testament, was tempted to sleep with Potiphar's wife, but he found the way to escape was to run out of the room. For some of us it is using the Word of God to battle with, or it is leaving in a situation, or perhaps praying for deliverance, or taking yourself out of temptation's way. Listen to the lead of the Holy Spirit.

We can also pray that we will not be led into temptation. In the Lord's Prayer, *The Our Father*, God can allow us to be led into a place of temptation for His own purposes in refining us and Satan is the one who tempts us, but we can pray how Jesus instructed us to pray, *"Lead us not into temptation, but deliver us from the evil one, Amen."*

JUNE 14

"This is what the LORD says—your Redeemer, the Holy One of Israel: 'I am the LORD your God, who teaches you what is best for you, who directs you in the way you should go'" (Isaiah 48:17).

MY PLACE

WE THINK THAT we know what is best for our lives, and so we plan to go in that way, down that road. God wants us to be successful doesn't He? And this way, to my eye, appears to be a way where success can be accomplished. I want to be fruitful and like a green olive plant, a strong cedar tree that is lush and growing. I've asked the Lord to take me there—to this place where I can flourish. Then I find the doors closing before me and the direction is taking another turn. I am being led away from the green grasses and cool waters to the heat of the desert and wilderness. How can I grow in such a place as this, I ask? God tells me, *"I will teach you that this is what is best for you right now; I will direct you to where you will indeed flourish and grow under My eye and care. Because I love you, I will lead you."* Then God asks me to—go.

JUNE 15

*"If you keep yourself pure, you will be a special utensil for honorable use. Your life will be clean, and you will be ready for the Master to use you for every good work" (2 Timothy 2:21 NLT).
"No discipline seems pleasant at the time, but painful. Later on, however, it produces a harvest of righteousness and peace for those who have been trained by it" (Hebrews 12:11).*

PREPARATION AND TRAINING

*D*ON'T BE DISCOURAGED where you are at in your life; God is preparing and training you for future ministry. Every disappointment, every challenge, every grief and loss, every battle with physical or emotional pain is for your future preparation. God uses us just where we are at in our spiritual walk with Him, and yet He has future plans for us to fulfill which always include greater, bigger and more challenging works. Don't be discouraged because the desire of your heart has not been fulfilled—yet—God will give you the desires of your heart. In fact, He is getting you ready now, so that you will be able to handle the responsibility, pressures and demands that may come with your heart's desire. Trust Him because He knows what He is doing. Work alongside of Him and abide in Him. Move when He moves; wait when He pauses or stops and settles you in a certain place in your life. He wants to do work there. He is the Master Craftsman. Don't be stubborn, but do what He says and you will see results. Don't be discouraged because you are never too old for God to use you in ministry. Don't underestimate what God can do through your one solitary life. Remember everything Joseph, in the Old Testament, experienced in Egypt in Potiphar's house, and in prison—he was being prepared for a great position with great responsibility. Read Genesis chapters 37-47.

JUNE 16

"Then Jesus moved with compassion stretched out His
hand and touched him..."(Mark 1:41).

CALLED TO COMPASSION

YOU NEVER KNOW the battles that others go through—they hide the pain deep down inside their hearts for fear of being exposed, thus causing further hurt, or thought less of, or criticized. These brave souls have fought many battles in life and won many. They have also lost some of those battles. They are vulnerable and may be exhausted with the fight. Perhaps those times when you felt they have ignored you or acted distant were the very times when they were struggling just to hold on to life emotionally and spiritually. They felt they could take no chances of being judged or looked down upon.

As believers in Jesus Christ, we are called to "compassion." Compassion has no eyes for condemnation; compassion always sees the hurt and wants to help make things better.

These days walk a little lighter and be a little kinder and gentler with others, use kind words and do loving deeds—for you never know when you will need the same done for you. You too may one day need that steady hand of compassion to hold you up from the deep waters of trouble and lead you to peaceful resting places.

JUNE 17

"In this ye greatly rejoice, though now for a season (a little while) if need be, ye are in heaviness through manifold trials" (1 Peter 1:6 parentheses added).

A SEASON

GOD IS STILL God over the changing seasons of your life. Suffering will not last forever: there is an end to our suffering. You may be asking, *"How long will this pain go on? I can't take any more of this. It hurts too much. When will these clouds lift?"* The Bible tells us that suffering comes in seasons. It is a season in our life that comes if we need it to come.

Most of us need this "little while" or "season" of suffering in order to grow and become the beautiful person we were meant to be. Here is the good news—seasons change. We have winter, spring, summer and fall throughout the days of our lives.

Which season are you in right now? Ask God to show you what He is up to in your season of life. Journal it in your notebook. God is faithful to bring you through each season every time it comes around. I know! I have watched God at work in my own life.

God's Word tells us our affliction is but for a moment. We can stand anything one moment at a time. A moment is not forever. Our sufferings and unpleasant times will not last forever, and we *can* tolerate feeling uncomfortable for a period of time in order to achieve a higher gain in the future. God has a plan and a purpose, and He knows what is needed in this situation. God will answer our prayers and this season too shall pass.

Taken From *Hope in a Season of Suffering* (Eilers)

JUNE 18

"In all their suffering He also suffered, and He personally rescued them. In His love and mercy He redeemed them. He lifted them up and carried them through all the years" (Isaiah 63:9 NLT).

JESUS' VOICE IN TIME OF NEED

I CAN SEE THAT thorn that is pressing hard against your heart, dear child. I know what thorns feel like—I wore a crown of thorns pressed down upon My head one time, in time. I understand what pain feels like. I want you to know that I am with you in your pain.

I am searching deep down inside your heart to see if you have faith—even when you keep hurting and feeling pain. Do you still trust My ways? Will you still follow Me? I want you to remember that the plans I have for you are always for good. Everything I allow to touch your life, to come into your life, is designed only to ultimately bring about good for you and those you love.

I am not deaf—I am constantly listening for your voice. I know what you need, want and desire. Seek Me first, dear child, and you will begin to see some of what I am doing for you. Only one thing is needed.

Always remember sitting at My feet and breathing in My Life, learning from Me, being with Me will always keep your heart at peace—even in your pain. It is when you allow your trial to consume your life, and you lose sight of Me and My promises, that you begin to sink and lose hope. Abide in Me, and allow My words to really live in you. In this way you will be fruitful and live a life of victory.

JUNE 19

"Listen! The LORD's arm is not too weak to save you, nor is
His ear too deaf to hear you call" (Isaiah 59:1 NLT).

WHO DO YOU RUN TO?

*I*T IS INTERESTING to me, that when hard trouble comes our
way and barges into our predictable and familiar, comfortable
lifestyle, that we must draw back and consider our lot. We may
ask questions like: *Why is this happening? What should I do? What will
happen next? Who can help me?*

It is in those times when uninvited calamity hits us that we are forced to
examine our source of strength and help. And truly what we have believed
about our God comes to the front of the line. This thing is too big for you,
but not for God. The Bible tells us that *"All things are POSSIBLE with our
God."* Even that thing that threatens to crush you or drown you in the deep
waters of desperation.

In my short little life of 67 years I have come to learn that it is never an
option to run to the Lord and cry for help, but it is a *necessity*. I am always
amazed how I get to know Him a little better through every dark night I
have to pass through. Our intimacy grows.

My goal is to rely on Him completely at all times, convinced of His love
for me. It is my goal to find and do His will in every opportunity that comes
to me out of my "trial." I will live for God. My aim is heaven. My motivation
is out of love and neediness of heart.

Always Know God is your anchor of the soul and your absolute security
of heart and mind.

June 20

> *"He told them another parable: 'The Kingdom of Heaven is like a mustard seed, which a man took and planted in his field. Though it is the smallest of all seeds, yet when it grows, it is the largest of garden plants and becomes a tree, so that the birds come and perch in its branches'" (Matthew 13:31-32).*

INSIGNIFICANT TO GREAT

MATTHEW 13:31-33 TALKS about the mustard seed and leaven. In these two parables we see a contrast from small to large. The Kingdom of Heaven is compared to the mustard seed which is a tiny insignificant thing, which grows up to be one of the greatest and largest of garden plants—sometimes growing up to 10 feet tall and which houses the birds in its branches. The Scripture calls it a tree; such an exaggeration shows us that even if God's work begins so very small, in the end it will be huge, fruitful and mighty.

The Kingdom of Heaven will become so great it will house and gather in peoples of all nations. God's Kingdom started with just a small band of people, and when Christ returns, the Kingdom will be a mighty powerful Kingdom with countless souls because it is God's work.

Now the leaven is a very small thing, but when it is added to the flour it doubles and multiplies and brings forth much food to feed many. Again, God uses the meager little beginnings in our lives, and He will surprise us as we watch Him make something truly significant, useful, effective, influential, and powerful out of them. Remember something may start out very small and insignificant, but God always has growth and fruitfulness as the end result and product.

JUNE 21

"For the LORD is the great God, the great
King above all gods" (Psalm 95:3).

HAIL JESUS!

HAIL JESUS, FULL of grace and truth. You are Lord over me; blessed are You above all and blessed am I the fruit of Your righteousness. Holy Jesus, Son of God, You are interceding for me at the right hand of the Father, and You will continue up to the very hour when You welcome me home. Selah

Jesus Christ is the Lamb of God who is overflowing with grace and truth. He is the truth. Does He reign as Lord over your life and your will, over your plans and purposes? He is to be praised and blessed, for He is above all gods and above everything seen and unseen. Jesus is the holy One who was spotless and without blemish led to the cross to be slain for all sin for all time. And you are the very fruit of His resurrection from the dead—possessing the resurrection power of the Holy Spirit inside you. He dwells in the temple of the Holy of Holies which is your heart. Jesus is always praying for you, taking your case and cause before the Father. Jesus' prayers are always answered. Jesus' prayers will be with you all the days of your life and will bring you safely to your heavenly home. Amen.

JUNE 22

"Godly sorrow brings repentance that leads to salvation and leaves no regret, but worldly sorrow brings death" (2 Corinthians 7:10).

GODLY SORROW

WHENEVER SORROW GRIPS our hearts, whether from a loss or from feelings of regret over sinful behavior, if we humble ourselves in the midst of the grief, and if we allow God to use that sorrow to bring change within our heart, it will work salvation for us. However, when the world sorrows over loss or wrong doing, they have no hope without God. Hope and peace are not produced in them. Without God active in our lives, grief and sorrow can make us feel very hopeless and despairing. However, if we lean into God's plan and purpose for our lives, our sorrow and grief can become something He will work out for our good.

JUNE 23

"Trust in Him at all times, you people; pour out your hearts to Him, for God is our refuge" (Psalm 62:8).

A CONVERSATION WITH JESUS

Earlier:

Jesus: "I am here."

Me: "Oh, Jesus, I' m weary of heart."

Jesus: "I know."

Me: "I think I'll rest here a while."

Jesus: "That's good, My dear child, rest."

Later:

Me: "I'm here."

"Did You want to talk?"

Jesus: "My words are always glad to embrace you, child. How was your day?"

Me: "You were with me, so I walked in peace even though difficulties were strewn across my path."

Jesus: "Did you feel My strength child?"

Me: "Oh yes, and Your protecting hand covering me. I love You, Jesus. You are so good to me. Thank You, for Your surprises of love You show me every day!"

Jesus: "I've got so many blessings in store for the one I love."

"I've been thinking about us. I am so excited where I am bringing you in your walk with Me. I can see you experiencing My power and ability in a way you never have before. And this is so that the world will know that I have sent you and you are Mine. You will do the works of God, and many souls will believe on Me. Remember, I've planted My Holy Spirit in you, and He will teach you and guide you.

Our love is also growing more and more intimate as you take that time with Me alone. I so enjoy that time."

Me: "Jesus, I want to worship You right now! I lift up my voice in thanksgiving and praise for You are a good and merciful God! I love You so much!"

Jesus: "My love for you is always strong and full of passion—I am here for you. And where My love is there is an absence of fear. Please, dear one, walk in this truth—live it out in your life. Refuse to entertain fears of any kind. Peace I leave with you."

Me: "Thank You, Jesus."

JUNE 24

"Be perfect, therefore, as your Heavenly Father is perfect"(Matthew5:48).

CAN WE BE PERFECT?

*W*HAT DID JESUS mean when He said this? This is a hard saying if you take it for just what it says. How can we be perfect? We fail; we fall short every day? This is too high of a standard for us to reach if we are to be sinless. If we look at the verses before this verse, in Matt. 5:38-47, we can get some insight into what Jesus meant when He said to be perfect. In these verses Jesus talks about an "eye for an eye" but this is not to be so for His followers. If they are slapped on the right cheek they need to turn the other to him also. Then He talks about loving your enemies and doing good to those who hate you. Jesus goes on to say that it is easy to love those who love you and do good to them, but I say the world does this anyway. Then He says, *"Therefore you shall be perfect, just as your Father in heaven is perfect."*

Let us look at the Greek word for "perfect" and its full meaning. The word for "perfect" is *teleios* which means "complete in all its parts, completeness of Christian character, mature in spiritual growth, mental and moral character." I believe what Jesus is saying here is that we, as His followers, must do beyond what the world does. In doing this, we will show them how the Father's heart is, for He has mercy on the just and on the unjust. We too, are to show mercy and grace, forgiveness and kindness to all people, because this is what the Father does. We can indeed strive to mature in this standard of our Christian lives especially empowered by the Holy Spirit. So this does not mean to be sinless, but to have a true and consistent, good moral character in striving to be like Jesus.

JUNE 25

"And we know that God causes everything to work together for the good of those who love God and are called according to His purpose for them" (Romans 8:28 NLT).

WATCH, FOR THEY ARE OPPORTUNITIES!

2 CORINTHIANS 12 TALKS about Paul being given a thorn in the flesh that he asked God to take away—three times he asked. God's answer to Paul was, *"My grace is sufficient for you, for My power is made perfect in weakness."* Then, we see Paul's answer to all of this in verses 9-10. He said from then on instead of complaining about his plight, his weaknesses, insults, hardships, persecutions, difficulties, he would purpose to boast about them and what good they were working for him—not for themselves in themselves—but the opportunities they brought for God's power to be seen actively at work in his life. God did just tell Paul that His strength would never fail him, and that it was completely enough to sustain and carry him through all his trials.

This speaks to me that we, too, should take the mindset to get excited when times get tough because we can look for and anticipate the undeniable power of God at work. We delight in what all the "stuff" will eventually reveal—God's strength and sustaining ability being accomplished in our human lives! I have seen it for myself!

June 26

"For You created my inmost being; You knit me together in my mother's womb. I praise You because I am fearfully and wonderfully made; Your works are wonderful, I know that full well. My frame was not hidden from You when I was made in the secret place, when I was woven together in the depths of the earth" (Psalm 139:13-15).

When Does Life Really Begin?

How precious is the conception of life wrought by the hand of God. When does life begin you may ask? Life begins at the very onset of conception when the two become one—the sperm and the egg meet and join together to produce life. The writer of Psalm 139 says that God's eyes saw our substance being yet unformed. That means when we didn't have any flesh or bones, but we were something that God called wonderful and awesome.

It is God who forms our inward parts, our substance in our mother's womb. God's hands skillfully take part in forming us before we are born. How dare someone ask, *"Will she keep the baby?"* What? Do women have the choice to destroy what God does in holiness and love? The Hebrew language says that we are created in love. Life is always to be valued. They say, *"Oh, it's not a baby yet, just tissue and cells."* God says that He witnesses the tiny beginnings of a baby's life even before the baby begins to be formed and is but a group of multiplying cells. He breathes His Spirit into those precious cells of life and the inner person—the spirit of the little being begins. I wonder how many babies that have been aborted are in heaven right now being raised by God's saints?

The question is not, *"Will I keep the baby?"* but, *"Lord, prepare my body, mind and heart to accept this new life."* Every pregnancy is a miracle of God no matter how it may have come about. That baby has a right to live. Those doctors who perform the terrible act of abortion and the killing of innocent babies will be severely judged by God. *"Let me live!"* The babies cry out.

It may be painful for a mother to accept a pregnancy, but pregnancy

is the blessed consequence that God made to happen when the man and woman join together sexually. He had planned they would join together as man and wife inside the bond of marriage. We must be willing to take on what we have become responsible for.

> *"Oh God, please open the eyes and hearts of men and women all over the world to see that every life is a gift to be respected and allowed to live and grow."*

JUNE 27

"The LORD says, 'I will guide you along the best pathway for your life. I will advise you and watch over you'" (Psalm 32:8 NLT).

GOING DOWN AN UNPLANNED ROAD

ARE YOU GOING down a road that you didn't plan on? Is it a road you would rather not take? Don't lose heart because God knows all about it. At times God asks us to take detours that will lead us to the places we need to come to, and stop off at for a time, to learn some important things. Embrace your life; embrace God; embrace His plan and move on to where He is leading you. Enjoy the walk as much as you can, and let gratefulness, thanksgiving and praise be found on your lips because this heart attitude will help you get through anything you need to get through. Paul tells us to *"Rejoice in the Lord! Again I say Rejoice!"*

We are not to rejoice in the disappointments, discouragements, losses or griefs, but to rejoice in the Lord for what He is doing in our life, and in the lives of our loved ones through these trials. Rejoice in the Lord for His constant love and care over you. Go in the direction that God takes you because He is wiser than you and sees the end result.

> *"Wherever You take me, wherever I go, Your Spirit will guide me—I know.*
> *And whenever I need You, You'll always be there. I will trust in Your goodness that surrounds me and my heart will follow You."*

Taken from *"Where Are You Taking Me"* song by Roxanne Eilers

JUNE 28

"That's why I take pleasure in my weaknesses, and in the insults, hardships, persecutions, and troubles that I suffer for Christ. For when I am weak, then I am strong." (2 Corinthians 12:10 NLT).

GOD'S STRENGTH IN ME

WHEN WILL I see Christ's strength at work in me? What will it look like? I will see the strength of the Lord most visibly operating in my life when I am at my weakest point—-when my strength emotionally and physically is spent, but the work set before me must still be done, and another One's power undergirds me and carries me on. It will look like peace under pressure; quietness during turmoil, steadiness through the unknown, determination in the face of opposition, wisdom and guidance amid the confusion and perplexity, and unshakable faith lifted above the voices of doubt and discouragement. This is Christ's strength at work in me. I cannot produce it myself.

As I submit my body, mind and spirit to God and ask Him to empower me, He does just that. The more I depend on His power, the longer I can be about His business and work without feeling faint. But how often I forget and begin to rely upon myself and the human strength I feel I possess at the moment. Then, once again I am brought to that valuable point of being without strength—being absolutely weak and humbled, having to draw my resources once again from the Lord.

So as often as I see my infirmities and feel my inadequacies, I thank God, for then He can display before the world, the angels, and the demons His awesome works in and through my life—-thus bringing Himself the glory. Amen.

*"Sing praises to God, sing praises; sing praises to our
King, sing praises. For God is the King of all the earth;
sing to Him a psalm of praise" (Psalm 47:6-7).*

Sing the Blues or Sing God's Praises

When Paul the apostle was in prison, what a strong temptation it must have been to complain over his plight. Here he was working for God, doing what was right, and he was put in chains for it. It just doesn't seem fair. Paul could have sung the blues, but instead he sings the praises of God. His key word to the Philippian Church, to whom he wrote while in prison, was to be joyful and to rejoice! Paul says to *learn* to be content where you are, and that you can do this through Christ who strengthens you to choose and live in obedience to God. Paul's contagious spirit of joy and praise was known throughout the entire jail and Praetorian Guard where he was at. His life was a witness to God's goodness.

Now you may be thinking, it was easier for Paul because he wasn't sick like I am, or having to deal with the everyday pressures, issues and headaches that come from living in the world and struggling to be set apart for Christ. Paul was settled in one simple place—prison. He didn't have the demands I have to deal with. He didn't have to face the temptations I have to face. Listen, Paul was stuck in chains where no one would want to be. He was very limited in what he could do. He was not free, but in bonds, being chained to one of the guards at all times. He could have cultivated a complaining heart, but he didn't; he chose to cultivate and grow a thankful, grateful, joyful praising heart and therefore was a dynamic witness for the Kingdom. If we choose to have a grateful and thankful heart God will meet us and help us with our attitudes. We can start thanking Him for who He is in us wherever we may be.

JUNE 30

"So Abraham called that place The LORD Will Provide.
And to this day it is said, 'On the mountain of the
LORD it will be provided'" (Genesis 22:14).

RESOURCES AND PROVISIONS

*D*ON'T LOOK AT what you don't have—but focus on what you do have. Use up what you do have and God will give you more. You receive from God as you need it. God is never in a rush—we are. His timing is never off—ours is at times. Living one day at a time trusting God for your sustenance, resources and provision is living by faith.

This is God's way for us to learn faith.

The just shall live by their faith (Heb. 10:38).

July 1

[They had] "gone through Phrygia and the region of Galatia... they were forbidden by the Holy Spirit to preach the word in Asia. After they had come to Mysia they tried to go into Bithynia but the Spirit did not permit them"(Acts 16:6-7).

KEEP MOVING, GOD WILL LEAD YOU

*P*AUL HAD JUST gotten through receiving Timothy into the faith and together they evangelized the cities around Derbe and Lystra. When their work was up in these cities they passed by Mysia and came to Troas where God spoke to Paul in a vision. Paul saw a man pleading for them to come to Macedonia and help them. After Paul saw the vision, he felt a confirmation in his spirit that God had called them to go to Macedonia and preach the gospel there. So Paul obeyed the Lord, and sure enough they found those who were open to the gospel.

This was how the church at Philippi got started by Paul. Now, as we follow this passage, we can apply it to our own lives and how the Lord may lead us. Sometimes we have to start out somewhere, doing something, going somewhere to find out if it is an open or closed door. The Holy Spirit may forbid us to continue on that way through an inward prompting, a scripture verse, a word from a brother or sister in the Lord, a supernatural vision, circumstances, or however He chooses to speak to us. There may be no fruit in that place where we think there might be. God always knows better than we do because He has already been there and has the master blue print. Now sometimes we may try and try to push and go in a certain way to do something we feel is good and worthy for the Lord and the way is barred. Each time we try a door we see open, it closes or leads to a dead end. God knows how to confirm His leading, so keep seeking, keep asking, keep knocking and keep moving, being sensitive to the Holy Spirit. God will move you into the direction you need to be going in order for Him to bring you to your own Macedonia. Trust God's leading. The Holy Spirit was given to us

to guide us into all truth. When you have reached God's desired destination you will be productive. So keep moving.

JULY 2

"I waited patiently for the LORD; He turned to me and heard my cry. He lifted me out of the slimy pit, out of the mud and mire; He set my feet on a rock and gave me a firm place to stand. He put a new song in my mouth, a hymn of praise to our God. Many will see and fear the LORD and put their trust in Him" (Psalm 40:1-3).

WAIT IN HOPE

I WAITED AND WAITED for the Lord to answer and move on behalf of my request. I know He was listening when I cried out to Him. Then finally after I had waited and waited, He lifted me up out of the valley; He lifted my eyes away from my problems and concerns and secured my mind and emotions with peace. I feel like singing now and giving Him praise! I believe those who see me will see a difference in me and want to trust in God too.

(EILERS' PARAPHRASE)

JULY 3

*"You will seek Me and find Me when you seek Me
with all your heart"(Jeremiah 29:13).*

LOOK FOR ME

C AN YOU FIND God in all the goings on of life? Can you find God in your sorrows, in your joys, in your disappointments, in your successes? Can you find God in the little things of life and the big things? He is there to meet you at your point of need—He is there to rejoice with you and to encourage you. If you can't see God in the everyday goings on of life, keep looking and He will reveal Himself to you. In Him we live and move and have our being. God sees all, knows all and interacts with us daily.

JULY 4

"Preach the word; be prepared in season and out of season;
correct, rebuke and encourage—with great patience
and careful instruction" (2 Timothy 4:2).

PROPHETIC WORD

ANSWER HIS CALL
God has called you to teach His Word and bring it forth to the people. He has ordained you that you should bring forth much fruit and that your fruit should remain. Don't say I can't teach, I can't speak, for God Himself will put His words in your mouth. You may be small, but God is great and His gentleness will make you great. You have the anointing of God on your life to preach and teach the Word and to proclaim the truth to set the captives free.

Don't make excuses because My grace is sufficient. I have called you many times and now you must answer My call and go forward. I will not fail you, nor forsake you; I will make a way where there is no way, and I will place you before men and women where My Word will be light to them.

In the night seasons I have come to you to spend time with you and to lead you by a word of wisdom—allow Me to invade your life. Lose your life for My sake and in the end you will find it. O, the joy of finding My Word and eating it! Man shall not live by bread alone but by every word that proceeds out of the mouth of God. Take hold of My Word and learn to rightly divide it—line upon line, precept upon precept. Study to show yourself approved My workman that needs not be ashamed.

July 5

"Why do you say, O Jacob, and complain, O Israel, 'My way is hidden from the Lord; my cause is disregarded by my God'"(Isaiah 40:27)?

Has God Forgotten?

At times we may feel that God has completely forgotten our situation. The one we've been struggling with for months, perhaps years. We've prayed and cried and fasted, but things remain the same. Our hearts grow weary and we begin to despair, and ask God, *where are You?* Then the enemy comes in and uses our own fears and doubts against us. He whispers in our ears, *"Where is your God? Surely He would answer you by now. How good is He? How powerful is He? He's left you to struggle in this pit and you're sliding down fast aren't you?"* Get thee behind me, Satan, in the name of Jesus! I will believe my way is perfectly clear to Him, and His eyes are open to my cry. He will perfect the matter that concerns me. I will trust and not doubt, for my God will surely bring me out!

And He will because He never grows tired or weary. He is faithful. Speak God's Word, believe His Word, stand on it. Your way is not hidden from God.

JULY 6

"The LORD is my rock, my fortress and my deliverer; my God is my rock, in whom I take refuge, my shield and the horn of my salvation, my stronghold" (Psalm 18:2).

UPON THIS ROCK

*I*N MATT. 16:13-20 we read that when Jesus asked His disciples, *"Who do men say that I, the Son of Man, am?"* The disciples answered, *"Some say John the Baptist, others Jeremiah or one of the prophets."* Then Jesus said to them, *"But who do you say that I am?"* Simon Peter answered and said, *"You are the Christ, the Son of the Living God."* Jesus answered Peter and told him he was blessed, and that flesh and blood did not reveal this to him, but the Father in heaven.

The next verse is interesting to note. Jesus says, *"You are Peter (a stone) and on this rock I will build My church and the gates of Hades shall not prevail against it."* Many have asked the question *what did Jesus mean "on this Rock?"* What or who is the Rock? It is not Peter, because Peter or *Petros* means a stone, like a stone someone may throw. The word here in Matt. 16 is Rock, *Petra,* which is a giant mass of Rock, as a bulwark—a place of safety. The Rock is Christ. 1 Corinthians 10:4 calls Jesus the Rock. Matt. 7:24 says those who build upon the Rock will stand up during adversity and trial. The Rock is the Word of God; John 1:1 tells us the Word was God and the Word became flesh. The Rock was Christ.

Jesus is telling His disciples that upon the truth of Peter's confession, saying that Jesus was the Christ the Son of the Living God, He would build His church. He will build, not a church that belongs to man, but to God. It is His work and He will build it; He is the foundation and will build and shape and nurture His church with His truth. He will breathe life into it by His Spirit.

What God builds, the gates of hell will not prevail against.

What is God building in your life today? Remember it is His work,

and as you follow Him and obey His Word, nothing will be able to prevail against you. He will do it. No matter how loud the enemy roars to devour. It just won't happen to the one abiding in Christ. God has to put it together—we obey and abide—the gates of hell will not prevail.

JULY 7

"By faith Sarah herself received power to conceive, even when she was past the age, since she considered Him faithful who had promised" (Hebrews 11:11 ESV).

FAITH RELEASES POWER

*D*ID YOU KNOW that God uses our faith to bring power into a situation? He is just waiting and looking for the faith that pleases Him. This kind of faith is steadfast, unmovable, against hope believes in hope and acts in hope. In Hebrews 11:11 we read about Sarah, Abraham's wife, who grew over the years in her faith until finally she received power to conceive and bear a son, for she finally considered God faithful to do as He promised. She didn't always believe this way, because at one point she tried her own hand at bringing the promise to pass—the promise of a son. She gave her maidservant to her husband for a wife, and thought that perhaps it would be through this maidservant, Hagar, that God would build a family as the stars in the sky.

However, this was not God's plan and it did not turn out the way Sarah had hoped it would. She struggled and strove within herself and had to get back into faith in what God would do. She finally did believe without wavering, and the promise was rushed in and manifested through the power of God. When God sees Faith, He is moved to act.

We must allow our faith to grow strong, every day by feeding on God's Word, the Bible, praying and using our faith to believe God in every situation that calls for faith. We must begin to believe the possible in the impossible situation. This is God-faith. It will release the power to bring the promise into being.

JULY 8

"Strengthen the feeble hands, steady the knees that give way; say to those with fearful hearts, 'Be strong, do not fear; your God will come, He will come with vengeance; with divine retribution He will come to save you'" (Isaiah 35:3-4).

A WORD OF ENCOURAGEMENT

MAKE YOUR HANDS strong so you can serve the Lord and help others.

Walk with confidence and assurance knowing who you are in the Lord.

You are strong so don't be afraid of anything that comes against you, because your God will come and take care of it. Your God will lift you up out of the troubled waters and place you on firm ground.

Don't be afraid when all seems to be against you. God is for you and He is enough. Hide your heart in Him and trust Him with every fiber of your being. Let go of striving and worrying. Let yourself rest confidently, just like a little baby, against your Heavenly Father's breast. Rely on His goodness and care for you. Be strong in Him.

JULY 9

"...fixing our eyes on Jesus, the pioneer and perfecter of faith. For the joy set before Him He endured the cross, scorning its shame, and sat down at the right hand of the throne of God" (Hebrews 12:2).

...LOOKING UNTO JESUS....

I'VE GOT TO look to Jesus if I am to stay afloat in this battle of the spirit against the flesh. I will look at His face, into His eyes, at His gentle smile. I will admire His comely hair and beard, and see His light of glory. Oh, a lovely Savior indeed! I can smell the sweet fragrance of His robes and feel His strong arms around me. As I focus my gaze upon Christ, I certainly can't be focused on myself. Myself, or my failures, my fears, and my struggle with my old nature. The more time I spend on myself the more of a captive I become to myself. The more time I spend on Jesus, who He is, and what pleases Him, the freer I become to live life to the fullest and to overcome the flesh. It's a choice isn't it? Choosing to be Christ-centered instead of self-centered. In Him we live and move and have our being. As our eyes are upon Him, He begins to change us from glory to glory. It is a God thing.

JULY 10

"I eagerly expect and hope that I will in no way be ashamed, but will have sufficient courage so that now as always Christ will be exalted in my body, whether by life or by death. For to me, to live is Christ and to die is gain" (Philippians 1:20-21).

PERSECUTION FOR CHRIST

I HAD A DREAM the other night that I was with other Christian believers and we were being persecuted for our faith. We were calling on the name of Jesus and trusting in His deliverance. There came a time when I thought I would lose my life and clearly hung on to Jesus –I was even ready for Him to receive my spirit. Then I found myself delivered from my enemies.

This dream reminded me of the story of the three men in Daniel, chapter three. Meshach, Shadrach and Abednego would not bow to the great golden image King Nebuchadnezzar had set up. Whoever would not fall down and worship this image would be thrown into the fiery furnace. These three would rather die for Christ than to betray their faith in Him. They were indeed thrown into the fiery furnace; but God visited them and delivered them from getting even the smell of fire upon them. The result was that God's name was glorified.

So we, whether life or death, must pledge to be true to Christ in this life. He will always give us grace to endure whatever we must or He will deliver us out of it for His glory. Stay true—stay unmovable—stay faithful and you will receive a crown of Life. Do not ever compromise your faith for something temporal.

JULY 11

"Then God opened her eyes and she saw a well of water. So she went and filled the skin with water and gave the boy a drink" (Genesis 21:19).

FRESH WATER

*T*HIS STORY IS about Hagar and her son, who were banished from her mistress' presence, and left to wander in the desert of Beersheba. All their water was gone, and Hagar placed her son under one of the bushes and walked away so she would not see him die of thirst. The narrative goes on to say that God heard the boy crying and provided for his thirst. In a place where no water was, God opened Hagar's eyes to see a well of water that was ample to keep them alive.

Sometimes we find ourselves in a dry, barren, desert place and all our resources have been used up. We see no way through, and hopelessness and despair start to creep in. We feel like lying down and quitting—without strength and faint. We can't see where God is taking us. Then God opens our eyes.

> *Dear Father, right now I pray that You would open the eyes of those who need water to quench their parched throats. Show them where the well is at. Lead them where the waters are fresh. Bring them to Yourself, so spiritually they will thirst no more. Bring them to that door of hope so they can continue on in the journey. Amen.*

July 12

"He restores my soul; He leads me in the paths of righteousness For His name's sake" (Psalm 23:3).

RESTORED

*A*RE YOU WEARY? Suffering from emotional distraught? Anxious, agitated? Does your soul feel overwhelmed with care and concern? Do you need emotional healing from past wounds? Do you need quietness of soul and mind—need a peace that is ever present and comforting? God says that He is the restorer of the soul. He wants us to be emotionally healthy and growing, thriving in our souls and spirits.

When we encounter difficulties and challenges in our souls we cannot concentrate on growth, but rather we are seeking for relief. Bring it to Him. Ask God for relief. Ask Him to restore you. To restore means to *"relieve, to set again to its original condition that it was made for."* God made our minds and emotions to be stable and sound and to bring Him glory (2 Tim. 1:7). As believers in Christ we are to renew our minds and pull down strongholds that have embedded themselves in our emotions and not to give place for one minute, the lies Satan throws at us (Rom. 12:2, 2 Cor. 10:4).

So roll your care onto His able shoulders (1Pet.5:7) and by faith move on to spreading out your spiritual roots deep into the soil of His grace (2 Peter 3:18). Allow God to restore you emotionally and renew you for ministry. Let our prayer be, *"Lord, restore my soul."*

JULY 13

"For the vision is yet for the appointed time; It hastens toward the goal and it will not fail. Though it tarries, wait for it; For it will certainly come, it will not delay" (Habakkuk 2:3 NASB).

IN GOD'S TIME

GOD IS NOT in a hurry, nor in a rush. He does not move in haste. He is patient and longsuffering. He is not moved by man's impatience, panic or franticness. God moves gracefully as a waterfall and stronger than a mighty earthquake. His actions are done in wisdom, confidence and faithfulness. God has a very specific time when He chooses to work and move on our behalf.

We may not understand why He is taking so long when He sees and knows how serious the situation is. What is He doing? Why is He delaying the answer? Remember that God is God and He sees the past, present and future. He knows what things in our present will affect our future. Therefore, He waits until all is ready and the time is ripe—the season is finally at hand. Then He moves. Sometimes with majestic power and other times in gentle caresses of the Holy Spirit. Trust the timing of your God. If you are in the waiting room right now learn to wait with expectation and faith. God is building you spiritually and establishing your faith. He is preparing hearts, positioning people, events and circumstances; and as you trust Him everything will fall in line with His will for you.

July 14

"Arise, shine, for your light has come, and the glory of the LORD rises upon you. See, darkness covers the earth and thick darkness is over the peoples, but the LORD rises upon you and His glory appears over you" (Isaiah 60:1-2).

Light

*I*SAIAH 60—GET UP and let your light shine! Look what the Lord has done! He's given you light in the darkness. Even if the evil of darkness covers the earth and the deep darkness of depression the people, the Lord says He will be a rising light of hope and encouragement over you. His glory and favor shall rest on you, and many will see what He has done for you and how He shines through your life. And they will be drawn to Him. Get up and let your light shine! Look what the Lord has done!

"The Spirit gives life; the flesh counts for nothing. The words I have spoken to you—they are full of the Spirit and life" (John 6:63).

HOW TO SEE IT GOD'S WAY

IT IS ONLY the Holy Spirit that opens our spiritual eyes so we can understand spiritual truths, and have insight into what God wants to do in our lives and in the world around us. Only the Holy Spirit opens our hearts to hear from God. Our natural eyes and mind cannot comprehend the things of God, nor can we see the situations we encounter with God's perspective unless we walk in the Holy Spirit. Jesus told us that the words that He spoke were spirit and life. Jesus' words are alive and have power to change the conditions and events in our lives. That is why we speak what God says and not what our flesh tells us.

It may appear in the earthly realm that all heck is breaking out around you, and perhaps your circumstances are looking like they will swallow you up. You must go to God's Word and see what God is saying to you in the Bible. Take His words seriously. Speak what God says. Ask Him to reveal to you what is really happening around or in you, and what to do—to open your spiritual eyes to the matter. Use the power of God's words to battle your spiritual enemy. And then live above the situation and not under it.

How do we do this? The first step is to spend time getting closer to and fellowshipping intimately with the Father, the Son and the Holy Spirit. The rest will follow.

"And David was greatly distressed; for the people spake of stoning him, because the soul of all the people was grieved, every man for his sons and for his daughters: but David encouraged himself in the LORD his God" (1 Samuel 30:6 KJV).

More Encouragement

*D*AVID, IN THE Old Testament, was very distressed because his men were against him—they even wanted to stone him because their wives and children had been taken captive by their enemies. David felt overwhelmed at this time and it appeared all was against him. We may not have been in David's exact shoes, but we have felt very distressed over something in our lives at some time. Perhaps we have had great distress over family relationships, financial difficulties, health issues, just to name a few. What did David do when he was feeling very distressful? The Bible says that David *encouraged* himself and found strength in the Lord his God. So we, too, must turn to the Lord for our encouragement and strength in time of need. He will encourage us through the Scriptures and through His people; He will strengthen us with His Spirit in our inner man and give us grace to live in the present. Distress will eventually pass, but God's encouragement and Presence lasts forever.

JULY 17

"So do not throw away your confidence; it will be richly rewarded.
You need to persevere so that when you have done the will of God,
you will receive what He has promised. For, in just a little while, He
who is coming will come and will not delay" (Hebrews 10:35-37).

JUST A LITTLE WHILE

SOMETIMES I START out so excited with what I'm praying about! I have faith that God is answering and I know He is at work—it's just that my faith begins to wane a little when the answer takes time to come, and takes time to come, and more time to come. I start to get frustrated and doubt creeps in through some open door. This happened to me the other day. I was feeling so confident and full of faith until I had to wait for the answer.

The Bible says in Hebrews 10:35-38, that we are not to cast away our confidence which has great reward. But we have need of perseverance so that after we have done the will of God (waiting patiently in faith) we may receive the promise. For it is really just a "little while" as the Bible says and then God will come and answer! The just shall live by Faith!

So I took up the shield of Faith once more and the Sword of the Spirit, which is the Word of God, and I am walking back in confidence and joy!

JULY 18

*"For I will pour water upon him that is thirsty, and floods
upon the dry ground: I will pour My Spirit upon thy seed,
and My blessing upon thine offspring: And they shall spring
up as among the grass, as willows by the water courses.
One shall say, I am the LORD's; and another shall call himself by the
name of Jacob; and another shall subscribe with his hand unto the LORD,
and surname himself by the name of Israel"* (Isaiah 44:3-5 KJV).

A PRAYER OF BLESSING FOR YOUR CHILDREN

*D*EAR FATHER, PLEASE *pour out Your Spirit lavishly on my
children and on my children's children. And pour out Your
blessing on them so they will be spiritually healthy and grow
like strong trees by the flowing streams. Let them declare that they belong to
You and they are Yours. And may they lead many to You. Keep them from
the evil in the world and from falling into Satan's traps. Set Your hand
upon them and lead and guide them. May they walk in Your ways. Thank
You, Father, In Jesus Name, Amen.*

JULY 19

"He that dwelleth in the secret place of the most High shall abide
under the shadow of the Almighty. I will say of the LORD, He
is my refuge and my fortress: my God; in Him will I trust.
Surely He shall deliver thee from the snare of the fowler, and
from the noisome pestilence. He shall cover thee with His
feathers, and under His wings shalt thou trust: His truth
shall be thy shield and buckler" (Psalm 91:1-4 KJV).

PSALM 91

NYONE WHO ABIDES in the Lord's love and intimately fellow-
ships with Him will find a deep continual rest. Tell the Lord that
He is the only one you trust in, and that He is your wall of protection from all your enemies. For when the enemy comes around setting his
traps to catch your foot and trip you up, God will deliver you. And when there
is the outbreak of disease that could cut your life short, the Lord will be there
to heal and restore you. He wraps you in His blanket of security and watches
over you as a mother hen. The Lord takes care of all your needs so you do not
lack or want.

Again, the Lord will shield you from evil so you don't need to tremble
or become afraid of the wickedness that lurks around you throughout the
night, nor for the flaming arrows of destruction that are shot to disable you
spiritually. Again, the Lord stands as your righteous deliverer and healer
when sickness knocks at your door. People may be entrapped and fall flat on
their faces all around you, but you will be hedged in and stand firm against
tribulation and destruction of any kind. You will also see that God is just
and fair, so trust Him to handle all who do you wrong.

Remember to abide in the Lord's love and mercy and make Him your
safe place, then harm will pass over your door and away from your home.
Whenever you think you are failing, falling and about to crash spiritually, God's mighty angels will swoop you up in their hands and stand you
upright on your faith. They always stand guard over your life. The roaring

lion of darkness will try to devour you, but you can rejoice because in the Lord's name you will trample that lion down with all his cohorts.

The Lord says to you, *"Because you have shown that you love Me and are faithful to seek My face, I will personally rescue you in that area of distress and place where you need deliverance. You will find safety in My presence because you speak My name with reverence. Call upon Me at any time and My ear will bend down to hear you—My answer will be on its way. Don't worry about anything because I will never leave you or abandon you when trouble comes your way; I will send My angels to bring a great deliverance to you. I will lift you up for My own sake. Your days will be full and many on this earth and then you will see My face in glory!"*

JULY 20

"And we all, who with unveiled faces contemplate the Lord's glory, are being transformed into His image with ever-increasing glory, which comes from the Lord, who is the Spirit" (2 Corinthians 3:18).

BEHOLDING THE GLORY OF GOD

I LOVE SOAKING IN the presence of God and beholding His glory with my spiritual eyes. Today we will look at Moses' experience of beholding God's glory, and then the experience that we can have under the new Covenant in Jesus Christ. Please read

Exodus 33:7-11 and Exodus 33:18-23. "Glory" in the Hebrew—*Kabowd* means "brilliance, light, splendor, abundance, honor." Moses wanted to see God in all His greatness and splendor. God called His "glory" *"all of His goodness."* Thus the glory of the Lord is all that He is, His attributes and characteristics of beauty, power, purity, authority, holiness, wisdom, love, and mercy. It is as author, John Bevere, describes the glory as *"the immeasurable weight and magnitude of God."*

Moses wanted to see and take in all the splendor of God's person and presence. He was spiritually hungry and thirsty for God—to be filled and immersed in God. He wanted more of God and the more he got of God the more he desired.

God put Moses in the cleft of the Rock where he viewed the goodness and glory of God.

We also can view the glory and goodness of God through the Rock, Christ Jesus (Hebrews 1:3).

God covered Moses in the cleft, and we are covered by the blood of the Lamb, so we can enter into the holy place and look upon God in the face of Jesus Christ.

It says that Moses saw *"the back of God." Pulpit Commentary* says this means "God's works—the consequences of His activity." At this time God may have allowed Moses to view the past activities of when He created the

heavens and the earth. Moses could have been shown the recorded past of God's glory manifested by His works. Remember Moses wrote Genesis and described each day of creation as if he were there. That is a thought to think about.

In 2 Corinthians 3:18, God transfigures us so we can radiate His glory on earth. Let our light so shine that men may see our good works and glorify the Father in heaven. As we allow God to live His life in and through us, we radiate His glory. Moses veiled his face because the glory faded. But we can always glow with the light of God's glory because we have the Holy Spirit who resides in us and conforms our inward man to the beautiful image of Jesus. By soaking in God's presence, talking and fellowshipping with Him, we can experience and radiate the glory of God.

JULY 21

"...for He chose us in advance, and He makes everything work out according to His plan" (Ephesians 1:11).

PEOPLE IN OUR LIVES

IN GOD'S PLAN for us, certain people are placed in our lives to help us grow and mature in our Christian walk and to develop our character. God has placed someone in my everyday life who causes me great anxiety, worry, frustration and fear. I began to complain about it, and felt like I couldn't handle one more confrontation with this person. How long must I carry this load? How long must I be wearied and disturbed over her behavior and actions. When will I get some relief and peace?

God's voice spoke gently to me and said, *"One of the reasons I have placed this precious person in your life is not only for you to minister of My grace, love, mercy, hope and strength to this person, but also in order for you to grow in faith, patience, love and to become more like Me. Now rather than complain, rejoice and be exceeding glad for you will behold the fruit of your labors and great will your reward be in heaven."*

After hearing this I walked a little lighter, felt uplifted, encouraged, and my hope was renewed because I reminded myself that there is always a specific plan and purpose for why God carefully and wisely places an individual in our lives. We must get our eyes off of ourselves and back on the transforming ministry of Christ and His heart of healing and reconciliation.

"We walk by faith, not by sight"(2 Corinthians 5:7).

IT'S ALL ABOUT FAITH, NOT SIGHT

*a*S CHRISTIAN BELIEVERS, we march to a different drum beat than that of the world. It is a walk by faith. It is a complete dependence upon someone else—that is, God. It's like a child who depends solely upon the parent who loves him.

In all our doings of life, problems and perplexities of all kinds, we are to exercise our faith and belief that there is Someone so much bigger than everything we face and that He can be utterly trusted. When our faith has grown and matured we will know what it means to "rest in the Lord."

Our whole life rests on God's shoulders. The days we are allotted, the particular trials we are assigned, the people we are to reach in our lives and finally our departure to the Father—are all in His own loving, faithful hand. He will not, cannot, fail us.

We must not be moved by what we feel, see or think for these are subject to change.

In this particular chapter in 2 Corinthians, Paul is talking about when we put off this earthly tent of our bodies and affirms that we will be immediately present with our Lord and Christ. Then he says, *"Hey, Listen, even though we can't see where Jesus is—He's there. And even though we have never gone through this experience of dying—He is with us. He will carry us on safely over to the other side." (author's paraphrase)* Our son has gone on to heaven before us and now we cannot see this place where he has gone, but by faith, we can embrace and believe it is there because in reality it is, as God says it is. We just need to take one step at a time choosing to place our confidence in Him whether we see the thing promised or not. We do not "run" by faith—we *walk*. God teaches us how to do this. When we cannot see into the spiritual realm, we can depend on the Holy Spirit to guide us.

JULY 23

*"My sheep listen to My voice; I know them
and they follow Me" (John 10:27).*

LISTEN TO GOD

WHAT IS GOD saying to you today? Have you been listening to His voice—His call? His guidance? The Holy Spirit whispers to our hearts which way to go. When to say yes to something, and when to say no. In all our busyness we must quiet down enough to feel that nudge. God lives inside us and is always speaking to our hearts and minds.

What is God saying to you today? Whatever He says, do it. It takes practice to train our spiritual ears to be in tune with God's voice, and the Holy Spirit. Make it your aim today to be more aware and sensitive to what He may be saying to you.

JULY 24

"Therefore, since we have these promises, dear friends, let us purify ourselves from everything that contaminates body and spirit, perfecting holiness out of reverence for God" (2 Corinthians 7:1).

WALK IN HOLINESS

. . . Dear friends, let us turn away from everything wrong, whether of body or spirit, and purify ourselves, living in the wholesome fear of God, giving ourselves to Him alone. (2 Corinthians 7:1 TLB)

Oh, how God longs to have us walk in holiness! Every day we have a choice set before us to either "turn away" from evil temptations, or "turn towards them." We can't help thoughts from entering our minds, but we can keep them from nesting there. It is not a sin to be tempted, for even Jesus was tempted by the devil in the wilderness. We can resist temptations no matter how fierce they may come, or how persistent they are in trying to pull us away into sin. We have the divine power of the Holy Spirit living within us and we can say *"no"* to the lusts of the flesh. We can say *"no"* to ourselves and *"yes"* to God. Our aim is to please Him and not ourselves. We were made just for Him, and we belong to Him because He has bought us with a price, the death of His only Son, Jesus. Now His life pulsates through our entire being if we do not quench it. Oh, how I want to walk in holiness of heart and mind! Today, I make a fresh pledge of myself to the Lord—-to do what is right and good, holy and pure.

*"Great are the works of the LORD; they are pondered
by all who delight in them" (Psalm 111:2).*

THE WORKS OF THE LORD

HAT ARE THE works of the Lord in your life? What has God done for you in the past? What is He doing for you today? The works of God in your life are those answers to prayer. It is the move of His hand in a situation or circumstance; it's His miraculous touch or maneuver.

How often I have sat in awe shaking my head, astonished and stunned at the workings of the Lord. Psalm 111 says that God's works are: great, honorable, glorious, wonderful, powerful and just. Have you forgotten His works of the past because you feel overwhelmed with the trials of the present? The Lord says to remember His works of old and this doesn't just mean "the parting of the Red Sea" back in Biblical times; but it also means what He has personally done for you in the past.

I recall a time when Ike and I were pastoring a small church in the desert. I felt that it was time to try for a baby—I, being 39 years old at the time. We needed a home of our own with a certain number of rooms—a room for the baby, Ike and I and for an office. I watched God put a real estate deal together where it appeared it could not happen. We bought our first home and then I stood in awe as the first month we moved in I became pregnant. How God covered my every need. It was truly amazing! To this day when I am tempted to doubt I rehearse in my mind what God has done for me so many times, and my confidence in Him is renewed. Now, what are the works that the Lord has powerfully done in your life?

JULY 26

"No one will be able to stand against you all the days of your life. As I was with Moses, so I will be with you; I will never leave you nor forsake you" (Joshua 1:5).

AS GOD WAS WITH MOSES

*J*OSHUA, CHAPTER 1, tells us that after Moses died, Joshua was told by the Lord to lead the Israelites into the Promised Land. Joshua must've felt a little nervous and unsure at times of his leading abilities, and perhaps wondered if the Israelites would listen to him as they did to Moses. God knew Joshua's heart and knew he needed encouragement and confirmation for his call. The Lord said, *"No one will be able to stand against you all the days of your life. As I was with Moses, so I will be with you; I will never leave you nor forsake you. Be strong and courageous because you will lead these people..."* God confirmed to Joshua his call and enablement more than once—He repeats His encouraging words of faith and hope, *"Do not be afraid; do not be discouraged..."* Joshua needed this affirmation from the Lord, for in himself he saw all the inadequacies.

We, also, are called to fulfill what God has set before us. We may feel discouraged at times, or feel unsure of ourselves, afraid—the circumstance may appear too large for us to handle, too difficult, yet God cheers us on and tells each of us individually, *"As I was with Moses, so I will be with you."*

So Saint of God, stand upright and march on with your given assignment—lead those people God has given you to watch over, nurture, and teach.

"Strengthen the feeble hands, steady the knees that give way; say to those with fearful hearts, 'Be strong, do not fear; your God will come, He will come with vengeance; with divine retribution He will come to save you'" (Isaiah 35:3-4).

ISAIAH 35: 3-4

MAY STRENGTH FILL your hands so you can faithfully do the work of the Lord. May your steps be steady and sure beneath you, so you know where you are going. Encourage those who are feeling faint and spiritually frail. Tell them to be strong and not to tremble or be afraid in their situation because their God will come.

Yes. God will come when we need Him. He will show up at just the moment when you think the hour is too late—Your God will come.

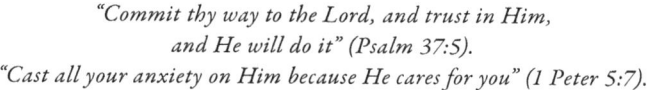

JULY 28

"Commit thy way to the Lord, and trust in Him,
and He will do it" (Psalm 37:5).
"Cast all your anxiety on Him because He cares for you" (1 Peter 5:7).

HAND IT ALL OVER TO GOD

"*THROW ALL YOUR concerns upon the Lord and He will hold you up emotionally and spiritually. He will give you all the strength you need to keep on trusting Him. If you cast all on Him, He will make sure you will remain steady in your faith" (Psalm 55:22 Eilers' paraphrase).*

These three verses are saying the same thing to us. Commit, cast, throw all your anxiety, cares (which in the Hebrew language is *deagah* which means carefulness, fear, heaviness, sorrow—it is that thing or those things which weigh you down and cause distress in your mind and unrest in your soul, those things that pull you apart) throw these all upon Him, the One who is able to carry and shoulder all things. Why should we cast it all on Him? Because it matters to Him about you and your situation. Your well-being matters to Him. And then if you continue to trust Him to take that which you rolled into His arms, He will do it—He will work while you rest.

July 29

"You open Your hand and satisfy the desires of every living thing" (Psalm 145:16).

HE BRINGS WHAT WE NEED

THERE HAVE BEEN countless incidents that I have witnessed God's hand of provision in my life. I would like to share one of those with you today. Whenever I recall it, my faith is always encouraged.

I was pregnant at the time, and we didn't have any insurance to cover the doctor checkups and hospital visits. My husband, the very sharp business man that he is, had already checked into all the possible insurances, but we couldn't afford any of them.

As I was filling out papers at the doctor's office, the nurse asked me what insurance I would be using. I explained our situation and she asked if I had heard of this one particular insurance company. I told her that my husband already looked into all of them. Still, she urged me to take the papers home to show him.

That night to our utter amazement, we found that this company would not only take me and pay for everything down to Lamaze classes and pre-natal vitamins, but also it would cover our baby two years after he was born. My husband scratched his head. He had never heard of that insurance company before.

Thank You, Father for Your hand that can bring out of nowhere, if need be, whatever we are in need of.

JULY 30

"Sometime later the brook dried up because there had been no rain in the land. Then the word of the Lord came to him: 'Go at once to Zarephath of Sidon and stay there. I have commanded a widow in that place to supply you with food'"(1 Kings 17:7-8).

GOD WILL PROVIDE

WHEREVER GOD PLACES us and whatever He asks us to do, He will always provide for our needs.

God told Elijah to go to the ravine of Kerith; there Elijah could drink from the brook and the ravens would bring him food at God's command. When the time came to pass, and the brook dried up, God sent Elijah to Zarephath where a widow would supply him with food and water, again at God's command.

How faithful God is to take care of His children. God is so creative in His wonderful provisions. He can use anyone or anything to accomplish His purposes for us.

Many times He allows us to use up the last little bit of what we have before He brings something else into our lives. Other times He lets us go without our need being immediately met, to see what is in our hearts, if we will keep on trusting in Him. Whatever way God decides how to provide for us, it is His responsibility and the matter is in His giving hand.

"The eyes of all look to You and You give them their food at the proper time." (Psalm 145:15)

JULY 31

*"Indeed, You have made my days as a handbreath, and
my age is as nothing before You... And now, Lord, what
do I wait for? My hope is in You"(Psalm 39:5-7).*

HOLD ON TO THOSE GOD-PROMISES

THE OLDER WE get the more we see how swiftly time goes by. We may find ourselves still hoping for unfulfilled dreams and wondering how they will ever come to pass. We look at our age and may feel anxious that the years have flown by and the promises the Lord has given us are still unfulfilled. We ask *"When?"* In the Bible, Abraham surely must have felt this way when he was waiting for a son to be born to him from his wife, Sarah. It appeared all hope was gone because Sarah was way passed her child bearing years (Genesis 15:1-6). But God knew what He was doing and waited until their faith was at a pleasing point, and then performed a miraculous conception and birth with bringing Isaac into their lives. Abraham's faith was steady and sure as he held on to God's promises with all that was in him (Rom.4:19-22).

I believe this story of Abraham and Sarah's faith is an example for us to follow and imitate. We are to hold on to God's promises no matter what it looks like, how long it takes, or how old we are. Never give up on what God has highlighted and illumined in His Word for you. Hold steady for He is faithful who promised (1Cor.1:9).

AUGUST 1

"I will steady him with My hand; with My powerful arm
I will make him strong" (Psalm 89:21 NLT).

GOD'S HAND

"*MY HAND WILL sustain him: surely My arm will sustain him.*"

I have seen God's hand at work all around me, in other people's lives, loved ones, and in my own life. What a joy to secretly pray to the Father who hears in secret, and to see His hand move invisibly to bring my prayers to visibility. I love His hand that has surely strengthened me in my times of need, and that continues to. I love His right hand, because that is where His Only Son resides. I love His healing hand that has reached down so many times to heal my broken heart, and shattered emotions. God's hand sustains me perfectly well when I feel weak and feeble at life's challenges. His hand holds my hand and together we walk through the valleys and up over the hills. I love the hand of the Lord because it is upon me, and protects me wherever I go.

"You hem me in, behind and before; You have laid Your hand upon me." (Psalm 139:5)

AUGUST 2

"The cords of death entangled me, the anguish of the grave
came over me; I was overcome by distress and sorrow. Then I
called on the name of the LORD: 'LORD, save me!'"
"...that I may walk before the LORD in the land of the living."
"I will sacrifice a thank offering to You and call on
the name of the LORD" (Psalm 116:3-9,17).

MY HOPE RESTORED

*P*RAYER: ALL THAT seems to come to me is trouble and sorrow. I do not ask for them—they barge their way into my life and bring turmoil, anxiety and distress to me. But I will not sit here helpless—I will call upon Your name, Oh, Lord. I will cry out earnestly to You that You would deliver and calm the trials of my soul. Because You are so gracious, Oh Lord, and righteous, I can be assured of Your help. I trust and depend upon Your mercy. Preserve my simple heart and mind. I am brought very low these days—I can barely see the light of hope. Save me!

Answer: The Lord has truly dealt bountifully with me! He brought great deliverance to my emotional and spiritual being. He has renewed my hope and faith. I will not die even though I am greatly afflicted. The Lord will wipe away my tears and steady my feet, so I do not fall into the enemy's pit of despair. I walk boldly before the Lord in the land of the living. The Lord has infused His life into my entire being and I am revived. Now, Lord, I will thank You for all my blessings, even in the midst of my troubles, and I will continue to call on Your name. I will hide myself in You until these troubles be passed.

AUGUST 3

"We do this by keeping our eyes on Jesus, the champion who initiates and perfects our faith. Because of the joy awaiting Him, He endured the cross, disregarding its shame. Now He is seated in the place of honor beside God's throne" (Hebrews 12:2 NLT).

BELOVED, LOOK AWAY FOR A WHILE

GOD ASKS US, as believers in the Lord Jesus, to be eternal minded—seeing with an eternal perspective. When we fix our eyes on the coming of Jesus, His presence and power and the glories of the new heaven and earth He will create, the temporary things of this age seem to fade and lose their first place priority in our hearts. Our eyes are lifted, even for a moment, away from our continual troubles and monotonous burdens and onto hope, a glorious future with God and one another, enjoying the pleasures of life eternal wearing our robes of righteousness.

It is vitally important that we lift our eyes away from our plight and situation and place them on the Lord rejoicing in Him, even if for a little while. Just this small detour away from the path of trial can give us a whole new understanding of our circumstance. Things will not seem to be so mysterious and impossible. We can see with God's eyes and hold that gaze into the possible.

Oh, God, help us to look away unto You, the Author and Finisher of our faith... and the things of earth will grow strangely dim in the light of Your glory and grace.

AUGUST 4

"The eternal God is your refuge, and underneath are the everlasting arms"(Deuteronomy 33:27).

THE EVERLASTING ARMS

WHERE ARE GOD'S arms? They are underneath us to hold us up and to strengthen us on our journey of life. Not only does He hold us up, but it is in His presence that we can find peace and security. Psalm 91:1 says that we can dwell in the shelter of the Most High, and when we choose to dwell in the place where God is, rest is the result.

In this busy age of hurry and worry God asks us to take time out to gaze upon His beauty and abide in His dwelling place, fall back into His everlasting arms and fellowship with Him. The result will be rest and peace of mind.

AUGUST 5

"He said, 'If you will listen carefully to the voice of the LORD your God and do what is right in His sight, obeying His commands and keeping all His decrees, then I will not make you suffer any of the diseases I sent on the Egyptians; for I am the LORD who heals you'" (Exodus 15:26 NLT).

FAITH AND HEALING

FAITH IS NOT cut and dried. It is a journey that we walk and grow up in. We exercise our faith—the faith that each of us is given by God. We feed it, water it, and work it. Faith is what pleases God. But faith is not just to get what we want from Him, it is a way of life—the way of reliance on His love for us. Just because we have faith doesn't mean that healing for our minds and bodies always manifests when we expect it to. I believe God honors unmovable faith that will continue to believe no matter what, but it is also His prerogative when and how we receive what we have been asking and believing for.

If we have been or are believing Him for healing in our bodies or minds, we must stay steady and rely on Him to guide us through and to this healing. He may do it supernaturally or He may use doctors or other natural means. He knows what He is doing. This, we can place our faith in for sure.

You may expect Him to supernaturally heal you instantly when He has designed for your healing to come about in a slow, methodical, learning pace—leading you to the places, people and things that will bring you your healing. Don't be discouraged—just do what He says to you in your heart. It is not the healing that is of utmost importance, but rather our heart's condition during our seeking of our healing. Don't be angry just because God has His way and His way is not agreeing with your way, or the way you have imagined. I do know that it is important to be honest with God. To continue to trust in His love, His way, His power, His wisdom. To take Him as your true Healer and to walk the path He has designed just for you. Always along the way He has other people we are assigned to touch and minister

to as we are healing. God wants us to be well and healthy and whole, but above that He desires us to be well, healthy and whole in our soul and heart towards Him, ourselves and others. If God does heal you instantly it is also for His glory. Go and heal others likewise. But if God has been taking you along the longer route, learn what He is teaching you, teach others, grow and fall more in love with the Healer, giving Him all the glory as you go from strength to strength.

"Now when the adversaries of Judah and Benjamin heard that the children of the captivity builded the temple unto the LORD God of Israel; Then they came to Zerubbabel, and to the chief of the fathers, and said unto them, 'Let us build with you: for we seek your God, as ye do; and we do sacrifice unto Him since the days of Esarhaddon king of Assur, which brought us up hither.' But Zerubbabel, and Jeshua, and the rest of the chief of the fathers of Israel, said unto them, 'Ye have nothing to do with us to build an house unto our God; but we ourselves together will build unto the LORD God of Israel, as king Cyrus the king of Persia hath commanded us.' Then the people of the land weakened the hands of the people of Judah, and troubled them in building, and hired counsellors against them, to frustrate their purpose, all the days of Cyrus king of Persia, even until the reign of Darius king of Persia"(Ezra 4:1-5 KJV).

OUR ENEMY'S PURPOSE

WHENEVER YOU ARE attempting to do something great for God expect opposition. I'm sure you have heard this before and many of you have experienced it. In the book of Ezra, chapters 4-6, we are told the account of when God's people were rebuilding the temple of the Lord. They were so excited! God's people all joined together and when they laid the foundation of the temple they sounded the trumpets and praised the Lord. The people gave a great shout of Praise to God. There were shouts of joy and weeping. At this time the enemies of Judah heard about the building of the temple foundation and because God's people would not allow them to participate in the building of the holy temple of the Lord, they set out to discourage the people and frustrate their plans. They tried to make the people afraid to go on building. The work was stopped for a period of time until King Darius issued a decree for God's people to continue.

From these passages, it is clear that when we step out to serve the Lord and obey Him in a matter, our enemies will first of all bring discouragement to us—doubts, worries, we can't get through a closed door, we are trapped in a situation—it seems no one is there to help us, we don't have enough funds.

Then the enemy will work on frustrating our plans and bringing them to nothing—appearing like things will never be accomplished. Finally, we are tempted to be fearful to move ahead with our work for the Lord. If we are aware that this is what our enemy is trying to do we can prepare for the battle with prayer, the armor of God, and the Word of our God. Remember no matter how hard it was for the people of God in Israel, the temple was completed for the Lord. The same for us—our ministry will be fulfilled and completed!

AUGUST 7

"Even before He made the world, God loved us and chose us in Christ to be holy and without fault in His eyes" (Ephesians 1:4 NLT).

CHOSEN

WHO ARE THE chosen people today? Ephesians 1:4 tells us that we (those who are believers in Jesus Christ) were chosen in Christ before the creation of the world. We are the chosen generation—the chosen people. How do you know if you are chosen? I like to explain it this way. God has a door and above the door is written "whosoever." If you go through that door there is a sign above the door on the inside written "chosen." That door is Jesus. You see God calls everyone to Himself and those who choose to walk through that door become one of the chosen. In the Old Testament, God's chosen people who were the Israelites, were circumcised in the flesh to show they belonged to God. Today God circumcises our heart, and we are sealed with the Holy Spirit as God's chosen people.

Are you one of God's chosen people? Jesus said, *"I am the way, the truth and the life; no man comes to the Father except through Me."* He said He was the door to the sheepfold. Enter in through this door and you will be one of God's chosen people. You will be part of a royal priesthood, a holy nation, a special people to bring glory to God and to do good works.

AUGUST 8

"But those who wait on the LORD shall renew their strength. They shall mount up with wings like eagles. They shall run and not be weary; they shall walk and not faint." (Isaiah 40:31 NKJV).

IN GOD'S WAITING ROOM AGAIN

WAITING IS ONE of the most difficult exercises to do. We can become so frustrated and filled with anxiety. What will the doctor's report say? When will I hear from my son or daughter? How long will I have to be in this situation? When will I get that phone call? When will the money come in? When will I know if I passed that test? When will my circumstance change? I could go on. It's as if by our own intense worrying we can make the phone ring, or get that answer, or solve that problem. But this is not so.

The Bible has much to say about waiting. God trains us through our periods of waiting. We learn perseverance and how to rest in God. Sometimes waiting seems to wear us out, but actually it is the fretting over the matter that exhausts us emotionally, physically, even spiritually. God tells us to wait in silence, quieting our heart before Him—not to be moved by what is going on. We are to wait and practice resting in the knowledge that God's hand is big enough to take care of whatever disturbs us. We are to keep our hope alive while we wait quietly. We can keep our hope alive though meditating on God's words of comfort and assurance. We are to keep to His ways as we wait, and do the things we know to do. Keep walking steadily with Jesus. God calls us to keep our gaze upon Him, His Word, His purposes and plans for us as we wait. He has already heard us and is working on our behalf. Again, we are to be of good courage as we wait, and we will find God pouring renewed strength into our heart. And what will we reap after all our waiting?

In Isaiah 40:31 we are told that when we wait on the Lord *four* things will take place in the spiritual realm.

1. Our strength will be renewed.

2. We will take off like we had wings; we will be flying victoriously and partaking of spiritual blessings.

3. We will go about our work and have strength to spare.

4. We will walk steadily in faith and hope and we will not fail nor faint.

We are reminded in Isaiah 64:4 that God will indeed act for the one who waits for Him. He will bring that answer He has been preparing you for. He will bring the good news you've been waiting for. God will work while you rest and wait on Him.

Scripture References used: Ps 62:1; Ps 37:1,34; Ps 27:14; Ps 69:3; Mic. 7:7; Lam. 3:26

AUGUST 9

"The temptations in your life are no different from what others experience. And God is faithful. He will not allow the temptation to be more than you can stand. When you are tempted, He will show you a way out so that you can endure" (1 Corinthians 10:13 NLT).

YOU CAN ENDURE

1 COR. 10:13 TELLS us that the struggles we go through are endurable and God gives us a way to deal with them wherewith we can stay above water and not drown. I believe some of these ways of escape so that we may be able to bear up under temptations and trials are: living in our present, entrusting everything to the hand of God, refusing to worry, keeping our eyes fixed on Jesus and His Word, knowing that things will pass and not last forever, being thankful and grateful, resisting Satan with the Word of God, and praying. These are just some. You see, God doesn't want us to fall or fail but to be strong and victorious. He never wants us to choose those things that will hurt our lives in order to cope. If you are feeling overwhelmed today try seeing your situation in another perspective—God's perspective. God is faithful to catch you and pick you up and stand you on your feet again. You can go through anything with God!

AUGUST 10

"I will instruct you and teach you in the way you should go; I will counsel you with My loving eye on you" (Psalm 32:8).

AN ENCOURAGING WORD FOR YOU

NO MATTER WHAT you are dealing with at this moment there is someone dealing with something much worse. I'm not belittling what you are experiencing right now; just know that God has given you all the grace you need to handle this difficult challenge before you. At these times it is crucial for you to be quiet before God and seek His direction on matters. Moment by moment. You are not left on your own—His eye is upon you and upon the whole thing to work on behalf of you. Allow yourself to completely surrender that thing, that situation, or that person to the Lord. Out of your hands and into His. Watch what He unfolds and worship at His feet for His awesome care and supernatural intervention.

AUGUST 11

"Lord, how they have increased who trouble me! Many are they who rise up against me. Many are they who say of me, 'There is no help for him in God.' But You, O Lord are a shield for me, My glory and the One who lifts up my head" (Psalm 3:1-3 NKJV).

AMIDST TRIALS

O LORD, THE ENEMY of my soul, Satan, has been shooting flaming arrows at me. They are countless. I'm going through emotional battles, physical struggles, and spiritual attacks.

He is casting doubts at my heart trying to get me to believe You will leave me in this horrible pit I'm in. He's saying these trials will never end.

Oh, but You—You my God, have thrown Your wall of protection around my mind, and my heart. Supernaturally, You are shielding me from the blows of the darkness. You are my God of great glory, and You keep my eyes looking up steadfastly on the prize and reward I have in You. My hope is ever in You.

August 12

"LORD, You have assigned me my portion and my cup; You have made my lot secure. The boundary lines have fallen for me in pleasant places; surely I have a delightful inheritance" (Psalm 16:5-6 NIV).

My Assigned Lot

Lord, You have assigned for me the things I must go through and experience in my life in order for You to achieve Your purposes in me. You have personally assigned certain circumstances, happenings, people and situations to me and my life in order to teach me lessons, mold me more like Christ, to purify my heart and also to mature my faith.

I have been assigned certain difficulties, trials, tests. They have been made especially for me in order to produce in me fruit and praise to You, O Lord. They are the very things I need in my life to help me to grow.

You, Lord, have made my position in life with You secure. I know who I am. I am Your child. I am secure in my identity with You. The calling You have placed on me is sure, and You will make certain it is accomplished and brought to full potential.

"Even though Jesus was God's Son, He learned obedience from the things He suffered" (Hebrews 5:8 NLT).

THE LESSON

WHAT DOES YOUR situation look like? Is it draining you of your hope and joy? No matter what is happening right now it will not last forever. Certainly it will pass, but the lessons you learn will remain. Learn the lesson the Lord is trying to teach you—learn eagerly and well. Don't just see the circumstance or situation for what it appears to be on the outside. Ask God for discernment to see and perceive what is really going on between the lines. With your spiritual eyes of faith God can show you the truth in the matter. Ask Him what He is teaching you—what does He want you to learn?

I know of one lesson God has gone over and over with me and that is to remember, that even if my lot in life appears to be negative, empty, lonely, fruitless, frustrating or messed up, God wants me to rejoice in who He is, and to find my joy in Him regardless of what is going on around me, in me, or with me.

I can surely say that if you cultivate the mindset that Habakkuk did when all looked bleak, doom and gloom, your hope and joy will return regardless of your plight. He said, *"Yet I will rejoice in the Lord. I will joy in the God of my salvation."* His confession of faith revealed his heart's belief and that was that the Lord was his strength! To Habakkuk, God would lift him up spiritually to a realm where evil would touch him not, but victory would fill his heart and life. Habakkuk chose to learn the lesson of rejoicing in his God even when everything seemed out of sorts and his efforts fruitless. When it looked like there would be no solution and things were dark, he hung on to hope. He hung on to God, and God raised him up to be victorious in his faith (Hab.3:16-19). Will you learn what the Lord is teaching you?

AUGUST 14

"...and His incomparably great power for us who believe.
That power is the same as the mighty strength He exerted when
He raised Christ from the dead and seated Him at His right
hand in the heavenly realms." (Ephesians 1:19-20).

THE *DUNAMIS* POWER OF GOD

OW THIS SAME power and might that dwells in God can dwell and operate in us by the Spirit of God who comes to take up residence in us when we put our faith and trust in Jesus Christ. Paul, the Apostle, wanted us to experience this *dunamis* (dynamite) power in our daily walk with the Lord. In Ephesians 1:17-23 Paul prays for the believer. He wants us to be enlightened and know the hope and the riches we have in Christ, and the power that we have access to through Him. This power is incredibly great. It is Christ's mighty power that works in us to do His good works and will. Even the weapons that we have been given to fight the good fight of faith with are mighty weapons (2 Cor.10:3-6).

So it is through this *unlimited divine power* of the Lord Almighty, the *El Shaddai*, that we are empowered to live the victorious Christian life—resisting sin and Satan, renewing our minds through God's Word, growing up in Christ, being a powerful witness for Him at home and then to the far corners of the earth.

AUGUST 15

"Let us hold fast the confession of our hope without wavering, for He who promised is faithful" (Hebrews 10:23 NASB).

CONFESSIONS OF FAITH

I DO BELONG TO Jesus. I am His child. I do declare my freedom in Jesus. I do declare my redemption through His blood. I declare before heaven that Jesus is my healer. Jesus is my healer. Jesus is my healer. It may seem like my head is swarming with confusion and my body feels weak and empty of strength. It may seem like I can't smile and all joy is gone, but, praise God forevermore; He is my strength; He is my hope and the lifter of my head and by His stripes I am healed. I do declare before heaven that Jesus is my deliverer. It may seem like I am caught up again in a net. It may seem like fears and doubts are the only thing I hear. It may seem like I am never going to rise above my afflictions and that I am beaten, but I want to say that Jesus is my deliverer! He will set my feet upon solid ground. He will put a new song in my mouth! He will raise me up and set His hand of blessing upon me. I am blessed. I am set free by the shed blood of the Lamb. I proclaim my victory in Him today. I declare that Jesus is my redeemer.

> *Father, it was Your Son who walked to Calvary and carried my cross of sin and shame for me. It was Your Son who was beaten mercilessly and nailed to the cross for my iniquities. It was Your only Son whose blood was poured out for me. For my life, for me. He bought me with that spotless blood and I am His.*

I will not listen to lies. I will not believe lies. I am covered with the protective blood of the Lamb. I believe the truth and the truth is in Jesus Christ. The truth is that He loves me beyond any human. The truth is that I am secure in His presence. The truth is that I have nothing to fear because

Jesus is always with me and in me. All my needs are taken care of. I declare that Jesus is my provider. All that I have asked for I receive because I abide in Him and do His will. He reaches down and satisfies my desires with good things. It may look like I am poor and without material goods. It may look like my house is going without. It may appear that I am in want at this moment, but the Bible tells me that the Lord is my Shepherd and I shall not want. The Bible tells me that Jesus is a rewarder of those who diligently seek Him. The Bible says that I am to call those things which are not as though they were. So I look to and fix my eyes on the invisible until it is made visible. I don't care how long or how short the time of actual manifestation lasts, He will and does provide. I will endure waiting of any kind and I will see the salvation of the Lord. I will see the Glory of the Lord revealed to me, in me and for me. Glory to God in the Highest!

AUGUST 16

"But Jesus immediately said to them: 'Take courage!
It is I. Don't be afraid'" (Matthew 14:27).

TAKE COURAGE!

*S*OMETIMES IT'S ALMOST impossible not to be overwhelmed by fear—fear of the unknown, fear of what could happen, or of what's not happening that should be. I remember a while back when I heard some news that was very disturbing; it brought great distress to my mind and heart. My mind was swirling with thoughts—-what to do? How to handle it? My focus on the Lord was waning—-neither comfort nor peace would come to me. I prayed, and then I was too exhausted to pray. I gave it to the Lord—-I took it back. Then I saw the words in Matthew 14:27. My friends, I can take courage, and you can take courage. Jesus is speaking here, and He says that we can take courage because He is here with us! Our hearts can be calm. He is here with us! We don't have to worry or fear.

He will guide us and direct our hearts to the answers we need. Before we are done praying the answer is on its way. He is here with us! Take courage, right now—Do not be afraid.

August 17

"Jesus answered, 'If I want him to remain alive until I return, what is that to you? You must follow Me'"(John 21:22).

Follow Him

*I*N THIS SECTION of Scripture, Jesus has just told Peter how he would die and glorify God. Peter sees John, one of the other disciples, and asks what will happen to him? Jesus answers with the above verse.

God has a personal plan for each of our lives. He sees us as unique individuals and has designed His purposes and plans according to who He made us to be with our particular temperaments, personalities, abilities and weaknesses.

When we busy ourselves with the time-wasting work of examining, envying, and worrying about other believers' lives and wondering what God is doing with them and has in store for them, this takes our focus off of God and what He wants to accomplish in us. The Lord is telling us here to just keep following Him and obeying what He asks of us to do. It really is none of our business what God intends to do in someone else's life unless He reveals it to us for His purpose.

So then, let us keep our eyes looking right on, one foot in front of another finding contentment in what God has disclosed to us for our lives.

AUGUST 18

*"Above all, you must understand that no prophecy of Scripture came about
by the prophet's own interpretation of things. For prophecy never had
its origin in the human will, but prophets, though human, spoke from
God as they were carried along by the Holy Spirit"(2 Peter 1:20-21).*

DIFFERENCE BETWEEN THE BIBLE AND OTHER BOOKS

WHY IS THE Bible different than any other book? 2 Peter 1:16-21 tells us why. Peter is writing and is serious in his declaration, that he and those with him did not follow deceptive cleverly imagined stories that were unfounded. They actually saw Him with their own eyes, the Lord Jesus Christ in His power and glory on the holy mount when His countenance was changed before them. They even heard God the Father speaking from heaven witnessing about His Son. But even though they had seen Christ, touched Him, heard Him and walked with Him and their witness was reliable, they had a more sure word of prophecy that we could believe in for ourselves—God's written prophetic Word, the Bible. Peter wanted us to know that the Scriptures did not come by some creative thoughts of a man who had his own opinions and agenda, nor did a man decide on his own to just sit down and write the prophetic Word. Men who were set apart specifically for God's purpose were made holy by God, and spoke and wrote down God's Word as they were fully anointed and controlled by the Spirit of God. They spoke what God told them to—He gave them His mind.

Again we see in 2 Timothy 3:16 that all Scripture is given by inspiration of God. That word "inspiration" is literally *"God breathed; breathed out by God"* (*Strong's Concordance, 2315*).

The Bible is no ordinary book; it is God's message to us. It is God revealing Himself to us and giving us a guide and standard for our lives here on earth. We are not on our own. The Holy Spirit is given to all who believe on Jesus Christ and He abides with us forever. It is also the Holy Spirit who helps us understand the Bible.

TREASURES FOR THE Heart

Remember: All other books come alive only through our imagination. The Bible is already living and powerful because it is God-breathed.

AUGUST 19

"...Look, there is an open door that I have placed right in
front of you; this door no one can shut..." (Rev. 3:8).

AN OPEN DOOR

ECAUSE IT IS God who will open a door for you, there is nothing or nobody who will be able to close it. Have you been praying about what you should do next? Is there a situation you need guidance and direction on? Do you need an open door clearly set before you? Ask the Lord to open a door just for you that He alone can open. Ask Him to reveal to you what and where that door is. Only go through this door when you have His green light (that is) a peace ruling in your heart and a witness of the Holy Spirit. Then walk confidently knowing that whatever lies on the other side of that door will be the best thing for you. God will provide everything you will need and equip you for whatever you will encounter there. Don't be afraid to meet a new challenge or situation for God has ordained your steps. Just trust His hand and move when He moves.

"This is love: not that we loved God, but that He loved us and sent His Son as an atoning sacrifice for our sins" (1 John 4:10).

FOR THE ONE WHOM GOD LOVES

HAVE YOU SUFFERED greatly throughout the years with a chronic illness, a struggle with finances, an addiction, broken relationships, and emotional pain? Are you worn and weary with the battle? Please don't give up on God, but make Him your fortress and refuge. Run to Him, not away from Him. Don't keep blaming Him or being angry with Him because of the continual pain of your circumstance. He still loves you deeply and knows what you are experiencing—He is moved with sympathy and exceeding compassion. I would ask you instead to begin afresh to ask and believe God to enter your condition and to bring you deliverance, healing, restoration and wholeness. Keep on trusting Him to do this, regardless of how things look or how long it takes. Let go of bitterness and self-pity and begin to look up and live in God. I am standing in faith with you because I count Him faithful who called you to Himself.

AUGUST 21

"Thy shoes shall be iron and brass; for as thy days are
so shall thy strength be"(Deuteronomy 33:25).

LIVE IN THE PRESENT

IT SAYS IN Matthew 6:34 that we are not to worry about tomorrow, for tomorrow will worry about itself. 2 Corinthians 12:9 tells us that God's strength is sufficient for all our needs. Philippians 4:13 says that I can do all things through Christ Jesus who gives me strength. This tells me that I can live in my present, and I will have enough strength to deal with it. A favorite Bible verse of mine is *Deuteronomy 33:25, "As your days so shall your strength be."* I live by this verse. This means to me that as my days are so will strength be given. How are our days? They are one at a time, one second at a time, one minute at a time, one hour at a time, one day at a time. I found that I could stand anything for a minute or an hour. I could endure anything for a period of time. So it happened that when I began to feel overwhelmed I would say to myself, *"I can stand this one moment at a time."* And I could. (*Taken from Seven Powerful Steps to Happiness*/Roxanne Eilers)

AUGUST 22

"The tongue has the power of life and death, and those who love it will eat its fruit" (Proverbs 18:21).

SPEAK LIFE! SPEAK LIGHT!

WHAT WE SAY to ourselves over time will eventually shape our lives. No wonder the Lord exhorts us over and over to watch what comes out of our mouths. God desires that we speak words that bring life and light into our lives and also into the lives of others. We can bring victory into our circumstances by what we say. Speaking God's Word brings victory and power. Instead of complaining and grumbling over hard times, God says to praise Him and be thankful. Choose to speak life and light into every situation and to every problem. Tell yourself the truth and refute lies. Anything that brings destruction, resist. Ask yourself, *"Does this bring me life or destruction in some way or form?"*

Now I speak life and light into your life today. I proclaim a blessing upon you and the wisdom of God to enter your heart afresh. I declare that you are able to stand up under that load or difficulty because God says you can and He is your strength. I proclaim the healing of God over your sickness—receive what He has already paid for. I speak refreshment to that person who is weary in heart. Faith be increased to all those who need it right now—keep listening to God's Word for this increases faith. I declare strength to that soul who is faltering and financial blessing to you who are in great need. Be blessed! Be increased! Give and it shall be given to you, pressed down, shaken together and running over shall men give unto your bosom. Now go in the Name of the Lord Jesus Christ, and speak words of encouragement to him who needs it at the appointed time.

> *Isaiah 50:4 "The Lord God has given me the tongue of the learned that I should know how to speak a word in season to him who is weary."*

August 23

"Know that the LORD has set apart His faithful servant for Himself; the LORD hears when I call to Him" (Psalm 4:3).

Prayer for Those Who Suffer

*D*EAR FATHER, EVERY day has been a battle for me—I fight to keep holding on in faith. I struggle to keep holding on to hope. This same painful thing keeps looking me in the eyes and threatens to steal away what peace I have managed to gather within myself. Please give me the strength to resist temptations that come to assault me—the temptation to always complain, or feel sorry for myself, or give in to defeating thoughts, or to lose faith in what You can do. Give me the grace I need for this moment and the next and the next—I am only human and frail and I need You so much to hold me up and pour Your healing power into me.

Please make me whole inside and out—ease my painful thinking and my suffering body. Restore me Lord, renew me, refresh me, so I can have a joyful heart. You said that nothing would come into my life that I would not be able to handle, but You would bring me through with a heart of praise. Lord, it is very hard to sing and be joyful when I am staggering in the depths of pain. Please help me to focus on You, who You are and what You have done for me. Help me to offer the *sacrifice* of praise. Lord, give me times of relief—give me Your assurance that even if things appear to go on and on and to be out of control and hopeless that You will hold me, support me, lead me, and work out every type of affliction I may be experiencing, somehow for my good, and to bring Your name glory. Thank You, Lord for hearing my prayer, Amen.

AUGUST 24

"...then hear from heaven, Your dwelling place. Forgive and act; deal with everyone according to all they do, since You know their hearts (for You alone know every human heart)" (1 Kings 8:39).

GOD SEES

THE LORD SEARCHES our hearts and knows all within us. The things seen and the things hidden. He understands our motives and why we do certain things—why we respond or act in a certain way. He knows the struggles we have with the flesh and with our thoughts. He understands the real meaning and reasons why we think the way we do. One thing we can count upon is the blood of Jesus that cleanses the deepest parts of our hearts that we think no one can see. *"Search me O God and know my heart try me and know my thoughts. See if there is any wicked way in me and lead me in the way everlasting" (Psalm 139).*

"O LORD God Almighty, who is like You? You are mighty, O LORD, and Your faithfulness surrounds You" (Psalm 89:8).

THE FAITHFUL ONE

HE BIBLE IS filled with scriptures that talk about God being faithful. Let us look at the word "faithful" and see what the Greek meaning is. The Greek word is *pistos* which means trustworthy, reliable and loyal. Let us look at some of the scriptures where God is said to be faithful.

Deuteronomy 32:4
"He is the Rock, His works are perfect, and all His ways are just. A faithful God who does no wrong, upright and just is He."

Psalm 36:5-6
"Your love, O LORD, reaches to the heavens, Your faithfulness to the skies. Your righteousness is like the mighty mountains, Your justice like the great deep. O LORD, You preserve both man and beast."

Psalm 40:10
"I do not hide Your righteousness in my heart; I speak of Your faithfulness and salvation. I do not conceal Your love and Your truth from the great assembly."

Psalm 71:21-23
"You will increase my honor and comfort me once again. I will praise You with the harp for Your faithfulness, O my God; I will sing praise to You with the lyre, O Holy One of Israel. My lips will shout for joy when I sing praise to You, I, whom You have redeemed."

Psalm 89:1
"I will sing of the LORD's great love forever; with my mouth I will make Your faithfulness known through all generations."

Psalm 89:2
"I will declare that Your love stands firm forever, that You established Your faithfulness in heaven itself."

Psalm 89:14
"Righteousness and justice are the foundation of Your throne; love and faithfulness go before You."

Psalm 91:4
"He will cover you with His feathers, and under His wings you will find refuge; His faithfulness will be your shield and rampart."

Psalm 92:1-3
"It is good to praise the LORD and make music to Your name, O Most High, to proclaim Your love in the morning and Your faithfulness at night, to the music of the ten-stringed lyre and the melody of the harp."

Psalm 100:4-5
"Enter His gates with thanksgiving and His courts with praise; give thanks to Him and praise His name. For the LORD is good and His love endures forever; His faithfulness continues through all generations."

Psalm 117:1-2
"Praise the LORD, all you nations; extol Him , all you peoples. For great is His love toward us, and the faithfulness of the LORD endures forever. Praise the LORD."

Lamentations 3:22-24
"Because of the LORD's great love we are not consumed, for His compassions never fail. They are new every morning; great is Your faithfulness. I say to myself, 'The LORD is my portion; therefore I will wait for Him.'"

1 Corinthians 10:13
"No temptation has seized you except what is common to man. And God is faithful; He will not let you be tempted beyond what you can bear. But when you are tempted, He will also provide a way out so that you can stand up under it."

1 Thessalonians 5:23-24
"May God Himself, the God of peace, sanctify you through and through. May your whole spirit, soul and body be kept blameless at the coming of our Lord Jesus Christ. The one who calls you is faithful and He will do it."

2 Thessalonians 3:3
"But the Lord is faithful, and He will strengthen and protect you from the evil one."

1 John 1:9
"If we confess our sins, He is faithful and just and will forgive us our sins and purify us from all unrighteousness."

Revelations 19:11
"Now I saw heaven opened, and behold, a white horse. And He who sat on him was called Faithful and True."

I think all these scriptures speak for themselves. Don't you? God *is* faithful.

AUGUST 26

"You who have shown me great and severe troubles shall revive me again. And bring me up again from the depths of the earth. You shall increase my greatness and comfort me on every side"(Psalm 71:20-21).

GOD'S PROMISE OF DELIVERANCE

ODAY YOU MAY be finding yourself in the midst of great and severe troubles—hard times—difficult days. You have God's solemn promise, if you put your trust in Him, He will make you strong, steady and renewed with life once again. He will bring you up out of the impossible pit you may be in. He will not forget you nor leave you there; He will not allow you to fall. He will lift you up again and bring your honor back to you. And the grief that you have endured will be completely comforted. He will cover you with His feathers and under His wings you will find refuge. Take hold of God and this promise today and make it your very own. God is faithful.

AUGUST 27

*"Therefore as you have received Christ Jesus the
Lord, so walk in Him" (Colossians 2:6).*

WALKING WITH JESUS

WHEN WE WALK with Jesus we are walking with a *friend*—someone who knows and cares about us. He loves to share our life with us, celebrate our joys and sympathize with us in our sorrows. When we walk with Jesus we are walking with a *King*. He is someone who is of royalty and of great honor. He is pleased to have us join Him at His banqueting table and to fellowship with Him.

When we walk with Jesus we walk with a *Savior*—someone who forgives us and rescues us from the slippery pit of darkness. His power delivers and saves us from ourselves, the enemy and the world system that bombards us.

Again, when we walk with Jesus we walk with our *God*, our *Creator*—the one who searches us and knows all about us, and who holds a place in His heart for us. It is God who calls us His very own. When we walk with Jesus we walk with the *Father*. He calls us His sons and His daughters and pours out His Holy Spirit on us. We are accepted into the family of God, and we can crawl up into His lap—He's our Daddy.

When we walk with Jesus we are walking with *someone very special*. May we walk with reverence, awe, wonder, joy, peace, love, wisdom and all those good things.

AUGUST 28

"When you pass through the waters, I will be with you; and when you pass through the rivers, they will not sweep over you. When you walk through the fire, you will not be burned; the flames will not set you ablaze" (Isaiah 43:2).

HOPE IN THE STORM

THE LORD CREATED you and formed you; therefore, He knows how you are wired. He knows what makes you tick. He said He will not allow you to go under when passing through the deep waters of trial. If you listen, you can hear Him calling your name. He is telling you it's going to be all right because you belong to Him. And when you are in the fires of affliction He says that you will not get burned up. He knows how much you can handle, and if you take the way He has provided for safe escape, that is by running to Him and holding to His hand in trust and doing what He shows you, you will be able to stand in the day when everything seems to be falling down around you.

There is a place in the wild tempest and storm where there is a quiet rest in God. Let Him lead you there. Don't listen to all the shouting and confusing voices that would overwhelm you. God is holding your hand, and He is telling you how precious you are to Him and so dearly loved. You just watch—He will bring you the people you need to help you out and support you. Again, if you will listen, He is saying, *"Fear not; for I am with you."*

AUGUST 29

"So do not fear, for I am with you; do not be dismayed, for I am your God. I will strengthen you and help you; I will uphold you with My righteous right hand" (Isaiah 41:10).

I WILL HELP YOU

IN ISAIAH 41:10, God says to you this day, *"Don't be afraid of anyone or anything because I am here with you. Don't be overwhelmed with the mountains of difficulty and the uncertainty of things in your life. Don't look around you at everything that is happening—keep your eyes on Me; I am your God and I will give you the strength you need to make it through whatever you are facing. I hold your future in My hand, so trust Me with your life. I will help you to know what to do in your circumstances and you will not faint under the heaviness of your burdens because I will hold you up with My own righteous right hand."* (Eilers' paraphrase)

August 30

"Yet You, LORD, are our Father. We are the clay, You are the Potter; we are all the work of Your hand" (Isaiah 64:8).

Clay in the Potter's Hand

THE BIBLE TELLS us that we are clay in the Potter's hand, the Potter being God. We may want to form ourselves a certain way—we may want to become someone important, influential, popular, recognized, or someone behind the scenes, quiet as a mouse, staying in our safe little box. We plan our way, but God directs our steps. He already knows what He is making us into. He already knows what kind of vessel we will be most effective as. We may want to be a lovely rose vase chiseled with delicate markings, or a strong and sure solid mug, but God may want you to be an ordinary water glass who will bring water to the spiritually thirsty. Don't fight what God is doing in you right now. Don't question every time things don't go the way you want. Place yourself once again in the Potter's hands and let Him work.

Sometimes God has to take what we have made of ourselves and remake us into another vessel as seems good to Him. God is actively at work molding and shaping your life with God precision. Every time you submit to His will a little more, you are becoming a vessel of honor meet for the Master's use. Every time you say *"yes"* to the Lord and obey Him you are being molded into something absolutely beautiful and highly useful (Is.64:8, Is. 45:9; Jer. 18:6).

AUGUST 31

"Paul, a servant of God and an apostle of Jesus Christ to further the faith of God's elect and their knowledge of the truth that leads to godliness- in the hope of eternal life, which God, who does not lie, promised before the beginning of time, and which now at His appointed season He has brought to light through the preaching entrusted to me by the command of God our Savior" (Titus 1:1-3).

HOPE OF ETERNAL LIFE

*D*ID YOU KNOW that God promised us the hope of eternal life before the beginning of time? He planned for mankind's future with Him—to live forever with God in righteousness, joy and peace. God even set eternity in every man's heart. We don't want to die, but we want to live on and on with health and vitality. We know deep down there is something more after we leave this body of flesh. Because there is life after death, how then ought we to live this life in preparation for the next. This life is not all there is—God said so. But there are countless people who have not heard the good news of eternal life in Christ. But just at the exact time on God's calendar He made His Word known and heard through preaching, which preaching has been committed to you and me as believers in the Lord Jesus Christ. The message is *that the wages of sin is death, but the gift of God is eternal life through Jesus Christ.* It is a gift that was promised long before you were ever born, but it can now be appropriated today by receiving Jesus Christ as Savior and Lord—believing in Him and then demonstrating this faith by following and living for Him. Eternal life—God, who cannot lie promised this gift to all who will believe.

*"The LORD is good to all; He has compassion
on all He has made" (Psalm 145:9).*

GOD, MY GOOD FATHER

WHAT A GOOD Father You are! You shelter me from the problems that swirl around me. You hold me up high on the tallest mountain so that none of my enemies can touch me. You whisper gentle words to my weary heart. What a good, good Father You are. You cheer me on even when my feet are dragging; You quickly take hold of my hand when I am about to fall into a sneaky trap of the enemy and You detour my way. You scoop me up into Your arms. Then You lift me up out of the pit that I find myself in so many times aimlessly trying to find my way out.

You have set a crown on my head and kissed my brow. You are my good Father. You gather me up into Your heart of love, and it is there that all my fears are soothed. My good, good Father.

SEPTEMBER 2

"The rod and reproof give wisdom: but a child left to himself bringeth his mother to shame" (Proverbs 29:15 KJV).

THE ROD OF REPROOF

*I*N PSALM 119:67-68 the psalmist admits that he had gone astray and didn't give heed to the words of God. Therefore he was afflicted or disciplined by the Lord. Hebrews 12:5-11 tells us that we are to be encouraged in our faith whenever we are disciplined because it is a good Father who lovingly disciplines His child. God says we are not to lose heart when we are chastened, because we are truly loved and cared for. There is a certain comfort in knowing that God cares enough about us to teach us what we need to know and to keep us from falling into the pit. *"Your rod and Your staff they comfort me" (Psalm 23).* Discipline is hard and something that we need to endure. We are being trained by it to walk in the ways of righteousness. And it is only for a short time according to God's time table. He reminds us that all discipline is for our good so we can walk in His holiness. Yes, the rod of reproof is not desirable; it is painful, but the Bible says that *"later on, it produces a harvest of righteousness and peace for those who have been trained by it."*

If we go back to Psalm 119 to the psalmist, he says that yes, he went astray, but after he was chastened he turned and obeyed God's Word. Then he tells the Lord that He is good and what He does is good—even when it comes time for discipline. Continuing down in that psalm the writer's heart is finally in the right place for God to teach and reveal spiritual truth to. He says *"teach me Your word; I keep Your precepts with all my heart. I delight in Your word."* His final conclusion is in verse 71. *"It was good for me to be afflicted so that I might learn Your decrees."*

When you find yourself in a time of affliction search your heart and ask God to show you the purpose. If it is for instructing you to walk in His way

and to turn from your own way of doing things, repent and obey His word. You will say with the psalmist that it was to your overall advantage to be disciplined for now you are more aware of what God desires for you.

SEPTEMBER 3

"A psalm. For giving grateful praise. Shout for joy to the LORD, all the earth. Worship the LORD with gladness; come before Him with joyful songs. Know that the LORD is God. It is He who made us, and we are His; we are His people, the sheep of His pasture. Enter His gates with thanksgiving and His courts with praise; give thanks to Him and praise His name" (Psalm 100:1-4).

JOYFUL SHOUT!

EVERYBODY STAND UP and shout for the Lord has done marvelous deeds right before our eyes! How happy I am to serve Him. I will sing a new song and glorify the Lord with my voice when I come into His presence. I will bow down and declare that the Lord is God! He is my God. He created me wonderfully with skillful hands. I could not bring my own self into being. I was created to be His own child, the little sheep of His great pasture. I am so excited about God that when I come into His gates I will jump up and down with grateful thanksgiving! I will come into His courts with praises on my lips! Thank You, Lord, for You are so good! Thank You, for Your mercy that goes on and on and on. I will declare Your Word forever to all peoples in my life-time, and my voice will continue to be heard even when I am gone from this earth.

SEPTEMBER 4

"Do not call to mind the former things, or ponder things
of the past. Behold, I will do something new. Now it will
spring forth; will you not be aware of it" (43:18-19)?

A NEW THING SPRINGS FORTH

TODAY IS A new day! Be happy! All your sins are forgiven—past, present and future. Jesus' sacrifice on the cross was enough to take care of all your sin for all time. Step lighter today because you have been set free from the bondage of the darkness of guilt and shame! Don't keep looking behind you and hanging back in the past—those days are gone and only memories remain. God is doing a new thing in your life now. Look ahead and expect victory to greet you. Say yes to God's invitation to walk with Him today. He is here for you and is the only one who will satisfy your deepest desires. Embrace life today! Use your weaknesses as stepping stones to spiritual growth. Believe in the impossible. God is doing a new thing in you—a fresh new thing. Anticipate new dreams and visions of His call on your life. Step up higher with Him! Today is your day to move forward and put the past behind you.

SEPTEMBER 5

"God is our refuge and strength, an ever-present help in trouble. Therefore we will not fear, though the earth give way and the mountains fall into the heart of the sea, though its waters roar and foam and the mountains quake with their surging. There is a river whose streams make glad the city of God, the holy place where the Most High dwells. God is within her, she will not fall; God will help her at break of day" (Psalm 46:1-5).

GOD WATCHES OVER ME

IN GOD I find my place of rest and safety. He daily strengthens me for the day's tasks. And when I find myself in any trouble, I can count on God to be there for me, to help me know what to do and how to handle my difficulty. Because He is always with me to deliver me, I won't let myself be afraid of anything. Yes, even if a major earthquake comes upon me, and it shakes the earth so hard that the mountains crumble into the sea; and though a tsunami threatens to overtake me, I still will not fear. I know that God's river of life continually flows into and through me, and that if I were to die I would live forever in the city of God—heaven. But as long as I have breath and live on this earth, I know that God's dwelling place is in my spirit, and because He is within me I will be unmoved by troublesome circumstances—I can go through anything, for God will help me at my time of need.

(EILERS' PARAPHRASE)

"'If you can'? said Jesus. 'Everything is possible
for one who believes'" (Mark 9:23).

FAITH THAT RECEIVES FROM GOD

GOD IS ALWAYS searching our hearts to find the kind of faith that will please Him. What kind of faith is that? It is the faith that believes and doesn't doubt. It is a faith that calls those things that are not as though they were. It calls the impossible to become the possible. Again, it is a faith that simply receives when everything seems to be against us and opposite of all we have been believing for. This faith that pleases God continues to stand fast. It grows stronger and stronger and becomes completely unmovable, having absolute confidence in God's ability to act.

What are you believing God for today? Is it the salvation for a loved one? Finances? Healing? Direction and guidance? What is that thing you are praying and hoping for? Believe God—leave no room to be shaken in faith, but grow stronger and stronger in your faith, confessing that you do have what you are praying about. Believe you have received it. Then be patient and wait, thanking and praising God as He works and brings your request into manifestation. Be convinced, persuaded that God hears and acts on your behalf. When God sees your faith pleasing Him the impossible becomes possible.

"For God so loved the world that He gave..."(John 3:16).

GOD'S LOVE IN ACTION

THE OTHER NIGHT I was praying and God impressed upon my heart something I wanted to share. I could hear Him saying, *"Tell them I love them so much—so very much."* I believe He was saying He loves everyone so deeply and fully and desires intimate fellowship with them. The Bible says that *"God so loved the world"*...that He did something about it. *"He gave His one and only Son that whoever believes in Him would not perish but have everlasting life."* Love always shows itself through action. God loves, so He gave. God loves, so He delivers. God loves, so He saves. God loves, so He strengthens. God loves, so He heals. God loves, so He provides. Love is always shown through actions.

"I am crucified with Christ: nevertheless I live; yet not I, but Christ liveth in me: and the life which I now live in the flesh I live by the faith of the Son of God, who loved me, and gave Himself for me" (Galatians 2:20 KJV).

JESUS' FAITH

*J*ESUS WAS THE greatest person of faith that ever walked this earth. He believed that what He prayed for would happen. He always did the will of the Father and pleased God with His faith. He spoke to sickness and when He rebuked it, it fled; He spoke to the sea—it calmed; He spoke to the demons—they were cast out. He believed God would work miracles through His hands. Now Jesus is the Author and Perfecter of *our* faith, and He is always teaching us faith and how to believe for greater things. As we study the faith of Jesus, I believe we will grow in our faith until it too pleases God. We live not just by our own faith, but we also have a portion of Jesus' faith because He lives in us. We live by the faith *of* the Son of God. We have access to greater faith when we plug into Jesus. The more we come to realize the revelation of Christ living in us, the more we can operate and walk in faith.

September 9

"Pray without ceasing. In everything give thanks: for this is the will of God in Christ Jesus concerning you. Quench not the Spirit. Despise not Prophesying. Prove all things; hold fast that which is good" (1 Thessalonians 5:17-20 KJV).

The Prophetic Word

THERE IS A difference between foretelling and forth-telling in prophesy. Foretelling is telling what will be in the future; forth-telling is speaking forth the word of God. This prophetic word for today is forth-telling.

Prophesy, O Daughter of Israel: washed in the blood of the Lamb, I prophesy. The Lord, the Lord of Hosts is His name. He has called us in righteousness. He has called us to walk before Him in the land of the living. Walk before Me with your lamps full of oil. Watch for Me at the gates—watch for My hand to perform all the good that I've promised. Yes, the years that the locust have eaten will be paid back—every day, every second that was stolen will be returned with years of fruitfulness. O weary child, lift up your head. I have not forsaken you. I am with you in your groaning; I will wipe away your tears, and I will comfort you again. Listen when I call—listen when I speak; move when I move.

September 10

"Unless the Lord builds the house, its builders labor in vain" (Psalm 127:1).

To Those Who Build

*A*RE YOU PLANNING something new? Are you venturing out into unfamiliar territory? Are you building a family, a business, retirement, a ministry? Are you starting over in life entering through doors that will lead you to new episodes in your life? Are you deciding to go back to school? Have a baby? Go to a new church? Begin a new chapter in your life? My advice is that you would do well to listen carefully to what your Heavenly Father has to say about it.

Psalm 127:1 tells us *"Unless the Lord builds the house, its builders labor in vain."* Can we personalize this and replace "house" with what we are dreaming and desiring to build? We can put all our efforts and hard work towards building something great, but unless God is the chief builder and supervisor we are building on shaky ground.

One of my life's verses is Zechariah 4:6 which says, *"Not by might, not by power, but by My Spirit says the Lord of Hosts."* God is not saying to do nothing for "all hard work brings a profit" but ultimately we are to build our foundations through daily prayer before God.

September 11

*"Very truly I tell you, unless a kernel of wheat falls to
the ground and dies, it remains only a single seed. But
if it dies, it produces many seeds" (John 12:24).*

A Seed in the Ground

JESUS WAS SPEAKING about His own death, burial and resurrection in this passage. Jesus was broken and thrown in the deepest darkness carrying our sin and shame. He was judged for us and took our sentence which was death. But while He was in the grave, God was preparing Him for the day of the resurrection! Jesus would not be held and buried forever, but just like the kernel of wheat in the soil has to die, when it resurrects it brings forth much fruit. Jesus knew the outcome of His death and burial, and even though it was excruciating for Him—He kept His eyes on the prize of the resurrection and the many "new kernels" the "plentiful harvest of new lives" His life would bring forth. He was securing our redemption and salvation and tasting death for everyone. He took the sting out of death for those who believe in Him.

We become a seed in the ground when we lay down our lives for Jesus. We are buried with Him through baptism and raised again in newness of life through the Holy Spirit. Thus many other seeds are planted through our life in Christ. We also, may have to bury things in our own lives that we hold dear, in order for them to be raised up again ready to be used to reach many. We die to the things of the world in order that we may live unto God.

September 12

"He was foreknown before the foundation of the world but was made manifest in the last times for the sake of you" (1 Peter 1:20 English Standard Version).

God Knows Our Future

REVELATION 13:8 TELLS us that the Lamb of God (Jesus) was slain before the creation of the world. To me this clearly means that before the world was even created, and man fell into sin, before there was a you and a me, God had already seen the future of His Son, Jesus, that He would be slain for the redemption of the world. God knows the future and He sees us forgiven, justified and glorified already seated with Him in heaven. God said to Jeremiah that before he was formed in the womb He knew him and had set him apart to be a minister for Him. God knows you and what the whole blue print of your life is all about. He knew you before you were even born. He set you apart for His glory and appointed you to be a minister of the gospel. He knows the mountains and the valleys that you will go through and have already gone through. He sees the end and the finished work in your life, and He will give you just what you need to live for Him and grow up in Him.

Can you trust God today with your future? It may look hazy, unclear and sometimes scary. But God sees it all and will equip you for what the future holds. Do you believe this? Your ultimate future is sitting and ruling, glorified with Him, rewarded for all the fruit you bore on earth. Trust the One who already planned the solution for our sin before the world was even created.

"For we are God's handiwork, created in Christ Jesus to do good works, which God prepared in advance for us to do" (Ephesians 2:10).

PURPOSE

WE ALL WANT purpose in our lives and for our lives. We want our life to count for something important. When we leave this world we want others to know we were here. We want to leave a legacy. We want our words and thoughts and loving actions to be remembered. I remember when I was seventeen years old and I felt I had no purpose in life. Why I was here—I had no clue. I thought that this was all there was and then you're gone. I walked as if in a dream that I couldn't wake up from—no meaning to life, no meaning to my life, what's the use of it all? Then I remember the day that Jesus reached His hand down to me from heaven. He used a beautiful loving lady to speak with me. She told me the good news that there was hope in life, and there was purpose and a reason for living. She introduced me to the Living Jesus. That was the day I met Him and gave to Him my life. I told Him I would follow Him forever. He began to take me on my life journey. I began to see that my purpose was to love and serve Him, to love others, and to share Him with others to give them hope. I was called to use my gifts and abilities to the max and to become all that God had planned for me to be.

I was alive, reborn spiritually, and stepped out into a world of obstacles, but God had given me a special gift that He gives to all who come to Him, and that is FAITH. It is the gift of God!

Today, I am still on my wonderful and exciting and sometimes difficult journey, walking hand in hand with Jesus. I am getting to know Him more and more as the real living person He is, not was. He is not just found in history books of the past. He is found on earth and in heaven. Do you need purpose, help, direction, healing, hope, then come to Jesus and ask Him to show you the way. He will. God is always in the business of restoring and making useful again—not just in a regular way, but extravagantly!

SEPTEMBER 14

"For, who has known the mind of the Lord so as to instruct Him?
But we have the mind of Christ" (1 Corinthians 2:16).

THE MIND OF CHRIST

WHAT DOES IT mean to have the mind of Christ? In this passage of scripture we are told that the Spirit of God knows the mind and heart of God. God's Spirit is within us, as believers in Jesus. The Holy Spirit in us knows the mind of Jesus and transforms our mind daily to think more like Jesus. He reveals God's heart and thoughts to us using the Word of God. As we allow this Word to penetrate our soul, our mind is renewed and changed to think how Jesus thinks. What does God think about? Some of God's thoughts include: love, peace, compassion, victory, forgiveness, reconciliation, joy, power and so much more. The Bible says we have the mind of Christ, therefore, as we pray that the Holy Spirit within us reveals the heart of God to us, and as we pull down evil strongholds in our minds, bringing every thought captive to Christ and God-thinking, this mind of Christ is practiced in us.

"Put on therefore the Lord Jesus and make no provision to ful-
fill the lusts of the flesh" (Romans 13:14).

SEPTEMBER 15

"I will obey Your decrees; do not utterly forsake me" (Psalm 119:8).

CHOOSE OBEDIENCE

OBEDIENCE IS SOMETHING we must choose to do as followers of Jesus. The Word of God instructs us and teaches us God's ways. It teaches us to walk in the truth (Ps. 86:11), to walk in the light (Is. 2:5), to walk as children of the light (Eph. 7:14), to walk in love (2 John 6), to walk in humility (Mic. 6:8). If we are His children, His words resonate in our hearts and we choose to obey them.

We will walk in the truth. We will tell ourselves the truth and resist the lies the enemy brings.

We will walk in the light. We will walk in the light of the knowledge that God has shown us for our lives.

We will walk as children of the light, leading others to His light.

We will walk in love. We will forgive those who have wounded us; we will be kind to those who act unlovely; we will give without resentment.

We will walk in humility. We will lift up our brother or sister who seems to go unnoticed. We will have the proper perspective of ourselves and not think of ourselves more highly than we ought. We will be ready to wash someone's feet.

Obedience is something we must choose. How shall we then walk before God?

September 16

*"I remain confident of this: I will see the goodness of the
LORD in the land of the living" (Psalm 27:13).*

Grief Gives Way to Joy

*(I wrote this October 23, 2012. Little did I know I would
need to be encouraged by these same words years later after
losing my 22 year old son, Joseph in an accident in 2016.)*
It is hard to believe that when we are in a season of grief, that it will end
when it hurts so much. It seems like an eternity. We grieve the losses that
we experience in our lives. It can be loss of a loved one, a friend, a pet, a job,
a dream, reputation, health just to name a few. Losses hurt so much and we
may feel overcome by the emotions that come with them. I found that if we
can keep in mind that our grieving is just for a season and it will end—this
can give us hope. God says that He will once again give us the *"oil of joy
instead of mourning and a garment of praise instead of a spirit of despair"
(Isaiah 61:3).* John 16:20 tells us that we will grieve at times, for this is part
of life, but our grief will be turned to joy as we seek the heart of God even
in our sadness. God gives us His Holy Spirit to comfort us in our time of
sorrow, and it is the Holy Spirit who will lead us through our season and
bring us out to the other side of sorrow, which is joy and thanksgiving. And
why does God bring us through our sad moments? Because He loves us and
He wants to display His goodness and mercy in and through our lives. He
desires to beautify our spirits even in our darkest moments.

God never wants us to stay stuck in our grief, but rather to acknowledge it,
feel it, work through it, accept it and then in time, move on to joy. God can
restore our heart of sorrow with a heart of praise and gladness if we let Him.

SEPTEMBER 17

"Stop doubting and believe" (John 20:27).

BELIEVING AGAIN

BELIEVING WHAT YOU can't see, but somehow seeing it—this is Faith.

There is a lesson for us in everything written in the Bible. In Mark, chapter five, we read about a ruler of the synagogue whose daughter was so sick she was dying. He came to Jesus and asked Him to lay His hands on her so she could be healed. Jesus went with him. However, there was a delay. A woman who had an illness ran up behind Him and touched the hem of His garment. She was instantly healed. Jesus stopped walking and called her out. He wanted to honor her faith and confirm her healing to her. All this took time. Finally to the despair of the ruler of the synagogue someone came and told him his daughter had died. Jesus heard this and knew that the ruler needed to stay in faith, keep his faith activated. So here is what Jesus said. *"Do not be afraid, only believe."* In other words, don't let your situation paralyze your faith with fear of what is, what isn't or the unknown. Keep the level of your faith up. Tell God you do believe Him. You will continue to believe Him.

This ruler of the synagogue chose to continue to believe even against reason—against what reality told him. He kept his eye on Jesus as Jesus kept walking to the house. He may have told himself over and over, *"I do believe. I will believe. Jesus will take care of it. I don't know how but I know He will."* And, my friends, Jesus did just that. He raised the little girl from the dead.

He will do just that for you too. You may not know how, but He will. He always honors faith. You will know you have faith that is active when you find yourself resting more in God's peace, and less of being in a state of turmoil. It is a process sometimes, and we need to learn this lesson desperately. Do not be afraid of what has happened or is happening now, or will happen. Only believe.

SEPTEMBER 18

*"And as the bridegroom rejoices over the bride, so shall
your God rejoice over you" (Isaiah 62:5b NKJ).*

OUR HEAVENLY BRIDEGROOM

I REMEMBER THE DAY I got married. I will never forget what I saw when I looked into my bridegroom's eyes. What did I see? I saw such tenderness and love; my heart felt secure with him. I saw the promise of complete commitment forever to cherish me, and a longing to shelter and care for me. I felt his protecting spirit for me.

That was over forty years ago. The Lord takes me back to those days at times when I need to make a fresh pledge of my heart to my husband and to remember just how much he loves me; and how both of us being so imperfect, are striving to grow in the love of God and love for each other.

Our Heavenly Bridegroom's love for us is perfect and unblemished. He finds great delight and joy in us, and in who we are in Him. He is the ultimate tender lover, the cherisher of cherishers, the great protector and His commitment to us is for eternity.

What do we see when we look into His eyes? Do we need to renew our pledge of love to Him—to love Him only and to trust Him when times are sunny and times are dark?

Prepare yourselves and rejoice; be exceedingly glad for your Bridegroom comes quickly!

SEPTEMBER 19

"But He giveth more grace. Wherefore He saith, 'God resisteth the proud, but giveth grace unto the humble'" (James 4:6 KJV).

GRACE THAT IS ENOUGH

I ASKED GOD HOW I would be able to handle the challenges that lie before me, and He answered, *"My grace is enough for you."* I asked Him how I would pay my bills when I am so short on finances, and He answered, *"My grace is enough for you."* Then I asked Him how can I hold on to peace of mind in the middle of conflict, and He answered, *"My grace is enough for you."* Again I asked Him how I would be able to endure my particular trial, and He gently and patiently answered again, *"My grace is enough for you."*

"You see" He said, *"My grace is always sufficient because it becomes whatever you need. It is your strength, your provision, your healing, your hope and encouragement. If your need increases My grace is increased for and in you. My grace is enlarged to accommodate your specific need. There is nothing you cannot face or do because My grace is enough for you. In your greatest weakness you will find My greatest grace and strength. You can do all that I ask of you, for My grace is always available to you.*

September 20

"But our citizenship is in heaven. And we eagerly await a Savior from there, the LORD Jesus Christ" (Philippians 3:20).

Heaven More Alive Than Earth

SINCE THE LOSS of my beloved son, Joseph, who was killed when he was hit by a car, my focus has ever shifted more towards heaven being my home. Heaven is a real planet, a real country, a real city, immeasurable and vast where we, as believers in Jesus Christ, truly have our citizenship. The Bible tells us in Philippians 3:20 that our citizenship is in heaven. What is a citizen of a country? It means we "legally belong to that country and have the rights and privileges and protection from that country." We owe our true allegiance to the ruler of that country—the ruler of heaven being the Lord King Jesus. We are already spiritually seated with Him in the heavenly realm. We are given the authority to push back darkness and overcome all the power of our enemy, Satan. We have the right to live a life of abundance, victory and joy. We can experience answered prayer, spiritual power, protection, wisdom and righteousness. We are citizens of another world—heaven. Again, the Bible tells us to set our affections on things above and not to get caught up with things on this earth. People, this world and its substance and matter is not all there is. Heaven is much more alive and real than earth, for heaven was created first, with earth merely a shadow and pattern after heaven. So heaven is not just a place to float around in and do nothing but sing. Rather it is a place teeming with life, bustling with love and activity. Saints are busy visiting each other, inviting Jesus over for dinner, using their gifts, creating new things, experiencing God's perfect love and presence. There are trees, mountains, beauty, flowers, rivers, and much more.

I believe that at times God may permit the saints in heaven to see their loved ones on earth in order to cheer us on in the heavenly race. They have become part of that great cloud of witnesses who are very much alive.

There are mansions in heaven. Jesus said we would have a mansion that

He so lovingly is preparing. We, as saints of God, through the blood of Christ that covers our sins, have a connection to heaven. We are plugged in to the circuits of heaven. Heaven is our home, so don't get stuck in this life on earth. Live for God and love as He loves. Bring His Kingdom spiritually to this world, pushing back the darkness of this age, bringing light and life to all who need.

"...who was declared the Son of God with power by the resurrection from the dead, according to the Spirit of holiness, Jesus Christ our Lord" (Romans 1:4).

RAISED BY THE SPIRIT OF HOLINESS

*J*ESUS CHRIST HAD the power to raise Himself up from the dead, and because of His Spirit of holiness, death could not hold Him. If He had had one little tiny bit of sin, death would have grabbed hold of Him and He would not have been able to rise from the dead by His own power.

Sin holds the body in the ground. It is a consequence of sin. But, my dear friend, Jesus was sinless, spotless and holy, and therefore had the right to raise Himself up from the bowels of the grave. Remember Jesus said in John 2:19, *"Destroy this temple, and I will raise it again in three days."* He was speaking about His physical body. And that is exactly what He did, Praise God! The Spirit of Holiness rose up within the body of Jesus and *Zoe Life* (the very life and breath of God) took hold of the body and raised it from the dead! Now the way is opened for us to come before the throne of God and enter into a sure relationship with Him. We have the promise that one day God's Spirit of holiness will rise up within our dead bones and raise us up again! How marvelous and awesome!

*"Blessed are those whose strength is in You, whose
hearts are set on pilgrimage" (Psalm 84:5).
"...they were foreigners and strangers on earth. People who say such things
show that they are looking for a country of their own" (Hebrews 11:13-14).*

LISTEN, PILGRIM

WE ARE PILGRIMS on this earth, foreigners and strangers because this is not our country (spiritually speaking) that we are from. We are born of God now and our citizenship is in heaven with Him. The Bible tells us that God has prepared for us a city and that He will be our God in that city. Heaven is that city where life is busily going on. We know where we are headed, that is why we must not get bogged down with the weights of this life. Always keep the eternal perspective in your heart and before your eyes because that is where you are being drawn. We are to be about our Father's business here on earth, for we are His ambassadors set forth to represent Him and His heavenly Kingdom and city—bringing as many people as will go with us. So don't hold on too tightly to this world's possessions because we cannot bring them with us to our destination. We are on a "sacred quest" that is, to our heavenly home. Jesus said that in His house were many mansions, and that He is preparing a place for us there. Set your heart on where you are going, where Christ is. If we look heavenward, sometimes we can see our home in the distance with our spiritual eyes and it is not far from us. Keep on course with a steady heart and mind until you pass over where you will finally be home!

SEPTEMBER 23

"But when the right time came, God sent His Son, born of a woman, subject to the law" (Galatians 4:4 NLT).

GOD'S TIMING

GOD IS NOT an anxious God. He is never wringing His hands in a heavy sweat. He never worries. He is always at peace. He is Peace. God is fully aware of our life's situations. He knows everything that makes us fall into the arms of worry, and He knows every solution that will bring us the peace we so long for. God is not in a hurry. So many scriptures remind and exhort us to wait for, and wait on the Lord. Therefore, let us slow our lives down and live each day to its fullest, pleasing God with our faith and confidence in His continual care over us. Remember, that when God sent His only Son into the world, it was at His exact and precise timing. Timing is very important to God. He was waiting for certain things to happen and come to pass; He was waiting for the "right time" to introduce His Beloved Son to the world. And it will again be in the fullness or right time when Christ will return to earth. God always has a purpose for long waiting periods and delays in our life. Trust His timing—it's always right.

September 24

"So we fix our eyes not on what is seen, but on what is unseen, since what is seen is temporary, but what is unseen is eternal" (2 Corinthians 4:18).

Spiritual Sight

YOU'VE BEEN PRAYING and standing in faith yet it appears not much is happening. Is God still at work on your request? You begin to wonder because you are looking at the impossible through human eyes. You must use your spiritual eyes when you look at the impossible, and gradually you will grow confident that all things are possible with God. Don't concentrate on the trouble or the waves of the circumstance, but rather keep your focus on Jesus and where He is taking you. View the situation with eyes of victory, for Satan is a defeated foe and can only go so far for so long. Don't let your imagination run away with you in imagining the worst happening, the negative, the mountains that appear gigantic. No, my friend, let your mind dwell on following and tracing the loving hand of God in your life, for then you are stepping from the temporary into the eternal perspective which always pleases God, and lifts you above your circumstance.

SEPTEMBER 25

"Brothers and sisters, I do not consider myself yet to have taken hold of it. But one thing I do: Forgetting what is behind and straining toward what is ahead, I press on toward the goal to win the prize for which God has called me heavenward in Christ Jesus" (Philippians 3:13).

FORGETTING THE PAST

WHAT IS PAUL saying here in this passage? I believe Paul is telling us that if we are lingering in our past or over our past, it is difficult to move forward and to have a clear vision of our goal. The word *"forgetting"* means to completely forget and to continue to forget. Anything that would get in the way of running the race and pressing onward, must be forgotten and left alone. Now, sometimes God asks us to go back and to make some things right, and to forgive, or to be healed in an area that keeps bringing pain into our lives. But He will direct us and show us what things these are—and we are not to live there, only visit until what needs to be accomplished is accomplished. I believe that Paul was getting bogged down with his past memories of when he persecuted and killed the Christians. Perhaps it was hard to forgive himself. But there comes a time when God tells us, as He told Paul, to get up and go forward, forgive who you need to forgive and move on—don't hold grudges; they just weigh you down. By an act of our will and choice, we must not allow the past, with our failures and shortcomings, to hinder us from doing God's work and will. Heaven must be kept in the view of the believer.

SEPTEMBER 26

"That night all the members of the community raised their voices and wept aloud. All the Israelites grumbled against Moses and Aaron, and the whole assembly said to them, 'If only we had died in Egypt! Or in this wilderness! Why is the LORD bringing us to this land only to let us fall by the sword? Our wives and children will be taken as plunder. Wouldn't it be better for us to go back to Egypt?' And they said to each other, 'We should choose a leader and go back to Egypt'" (Numbers 14:1-4).

MURMURING

THE ISRAELITES WERE traveling through the desert and they grew impatient with what God was doing with them. They spoke against God and Moses; they spoke in unbelief. They accused the Lord of bringing them out of Egypt's bondage just to let them die out in the wilderness. They would not believe in the Lord's provision, love or guidance. They complained and said, *"We have no bread, no water—"* and then they hated the bread that God did give them from heaven. They were sick of it. God was not happy with them. Many were greatly disciplined unto death.

Today, we are under the grace of God and we are rarely disciplined unto death, but the lesson here is the same and one we should take heed to. Are you growing impatient with where God has brought you in your life so far? Are you angry with how things are going? Do you accuse the Lord of bringing you to your present position in life just to let you fail, faint, be without, lose all you've worked hard for, or to have you perish? God wants good things for His children, but there are times when our hearts are tried and tested to see what is in them. Will we still believe in the Lord's provision, love and guidance? Or will we complain, *"We don't have this; we don't have that—we deserve better; we are not where we want to be?"* Are we even sick and tired of God allowing us to struggle and grow in our faith? If we are thinking in this way, we must discipline ourselves, and set our hearts right before the One who does all things well. He honors faith.

September 27

"Sing the glory of His name; make His praise glorious. Say to God, 'How awesome are Your deeds! So great is Your power that Your enemies cringe before You. All the earth bows down to You; they sing praise to You, they sing the praises of Your name'" (Psalm 66:2-4).

Incredible God!

GOD HAS RESOURCES for you that you never even thought of. He has people for your life that you haven't even met yet. I am in awe of how God works! When I think of what God has done in my own life and in the lives of those around me, I fall on my face in wonder and awe. When I see glimpses of His plan unfolding before me, I shake my head and am humbled—I am stunned by His ways! This God who calls Himself our Father, whose love is profound and deep—this God who promised to complete the work He began in our lives—this God who carefully knit our spirit to our body inside our mother's womb and called us to Himself even before we were born—this God is more than amazing. He truly does hold every detail of our lives in His hand. He does fulfill the desires of those who love and reverence Him. When He reveals His glory, His beauty, His power, His presence, His love and care over us—what can we do? We are what is called "blown away" "undone" "speechless" "forever in love" by and with this God—this wondrous God—this relationship seeking God—this fully committed God. This God who we can pledge our entire hearts to. This God who is the only one worthy of all our worship, adoration, honor, and praise! Awesome…so, so incredibly beautiful and wondrous.

SEPTEMBER 28

"To everything there is a season, a time for every purpose under heaven: A time to be born, and a time to die; a time to plant, and a time to pluck what is planted; a time to kill, and a time to heal; a time to break down, and a time to build up; a time to weep, and a time to laugh; a time to mourn, and a time to dance; a time to cast away stones, and a time to gather stones; a time to embrace, and a time to refrain from embracing; a time to gain, and a time to lose; a time to keep, and a time to throw away; a time to tear, and a time to sew; a time to keep silence, and a time to speak; a time to love, and a time to hate; a time of war, and a time of peace" (Ecclesiastes 3: 1-8).

EVERYTHING HAS ITS TIME

GOD DESIRES THAT we encourage our heart to be content in every season that comes into our life. There is an appointed time for everything under heaven. God has fashioned the world and time to operate in seasons. Think of what season you are in right now. Has God called you to do something new—go in a new direction? Is it your time to heal in areas where you have been broken down? Has God asked you to step outside of your box and to launch out into uncharted waters? Are you going through a season of loss? Whatever is causing you grief, God is ready to comfort and console. Is it time to throw away things that just clutter your life? Let them go. Is it your time to rejoice and dance before God for all He has done? Then dance and sing unto Him with all your might! It may be your time to keep quiet about a matter and just take it to the Lord in prayer.

God says it is always in season to love one another—so let us love with a pure heart. Sometimes you will find yourself in a season of battling in spiritual warfare; this too will pass and you will experience a time of peace. Whatever season you find yourself in, know that it will change—for one thing you can be sure of is things will change. Take advantage of where you are at today and serve God with all your heart. I am in a season of gaining

experience, wisdom, confidence and perseverance. It is also my time to grieve a loss, and stand in God's strength.

Thank God, He has a purpose for every season we encounter. Remember the main purpose is to form us into the image of His Son. Hard days, easy days, live them all for the glory of God, and always be alert to where God is asking you to respond as Christ would.

September 29

"Yes, my soul, find rest in God; my hope comes from Him. Truly He is my rock and my salvation; He is my fortress, I will not be shaken. My salvation and my honor depend on God; He is my mighty rock, my refuge. Trust in Him at all times, you people; pour out your hearts to Him, for God is our refuge" (Psalm 62:5-8).

My Rock

I MUST TELL MY soul to wait quietly for the only One who can help me through this storm. Because He is all powerful and can do anything, I can expect His help and His strength when I feel overwhelmed. He is my security. My sure foundation when the earth is falling apart beneath my feet. He is an immovable Rock! He will save me. He will pour strength into my being. He will hold me up and not let my foot slip back into the pit. He understands my lot and takes my side—He defends me and validates my feelings. God is the only one who will make me whole again—He will restore my fragmented heart. Again, I climb up into Him—my Rock, and He keeps me safe. I hide in Him and lean into His love. I have made up my mind that I will put my trust in Him all the time no matter what I have to face or am facing at this moment. I will cry out to Him and tell Him all that is on my heart. I am confident that He will move on my behalf.

PSALM 62:5-8 (EILERS' PARAPHRASE)

September 30

"Jesus looked at them and said, 'With man this is impossible, but with God all things are possible'" (Matthew 19:26).

His Promise/Your Faith

GOD WANTS YOUR faith to be strengthened. He wants you to become *fully convinced* that what He has promised you, He is also able to perform. He asks you to believe even when everything appears contrary to hope. He desires you to judge Him to be absolutely good in His nature, and faithful to all His promises. God wants your faith to come to the conclusion that He is always able, and delights, to do the impossible in your life.

What are you believing God for today? Find your promise in His Word and hold fast to it regardless of any obstacles that may come. Remember: His Promise + My Faith = together activates that which is impossible to become possible!

OCTOBER 1

"He who tills his land will have plenty of
bread...."(Proverbs 28:19 NKJV).

HARD WORK WILL PAY OFF

WHEN A FARMER works his land what does he do? He clears it of rocks, stones, branches and other large obstacles. He turns the soil, hoes it, the soil is turned upside down over and over. Nutrients, mulch, and fertilizer are added and mixed into the soil. The farmer waters it and softens it, making the final preparations for the seeds to be planted. But it won't stop there.

Weeds must be pulled up so they won't choke the crops, continual irrigation, and the fight to keep bugs and pests from devouring the plants. Finally, yet more work to do, the harvesting and separating the edible from the chaff. Then after the grain is ground into bread and baked, the farmer sits and eats a slice of the nutritious and delicious warm wheat bread with fresh butter. Yum!

Now, if you have a dream, vision or goal that you desire to bear fruit with, you must *work* it. You must develop it, prepare for it, remove obstacles or work around them. Don't let the weeds of failures choke it out. Resist negative messages that come to take away your hope, faith, and vision. Learn from mistakes, take instruction, then add more learning and wisdom, prayer and perseverance. Then wait when it's waiting time. Finally, you will reap if you faint not. You will reap abundantly!

OCTOBER 2

"Now therefore arise, go over this Jordan, you and all this people to the land which I am giving to them—the children of Israel. Every place that the sole of your foot will tread upon I have given you, as I said to Moses" (Joshua 1:2-3).

POSSESSING THE LAND

WHENEVER GOD ASKS us to go forth and possess the land, which includes His promises, there will always be a struggle in the spiritual realm. To possess, live in, live out, walk in, His precious promises, we must fight to possess what is ours. When God told the children of Israel to go in and possess the Promised Land, they had to move the other people out of that land. This took war and fighting. Each time, however, that God brought them to the next piece of the land they were to possess, He told them how to do it. God had different strategies each time because He knew the people of the land, and what needed to be accomplished before the land could be conquered. Thus, we, as God's children today, must seek His face on the things that concern us. If we have a certain promise we are standing for, God wants us to move in and possess it and bring it to reality in our lives. He wants us to seek His face to show us what we must do in order to overcome obstacles and opposition that threaten to keep us from receiving all that God has for us. Move in and possess the promises of God in His timing, in His way and for His glory!

OCTOBER 3

"... or because of these surpassingly great revelations. Therefore, in order to keep me from becoming conceited, I was given a thorn in my flesh, a messenger of Satan, to torment me" (2 Corinthians 12:7).

A THORN IN THE FLESH

WHAT IS THE thorn in the flesh? The thorn in the flesh is something or someone who causes you great distress and suffering. Paul struggled with a thorn in the flesh, which the Bible says, was a messenger of Satan who came to torment him. This could have been a person who caused Paul a great amount of stress, or it could have been a physical ailment, or perhaps a circumstance that rose up in his life over and over that was an irritation. Whatever it was Paul asked the Lord three times to take it away from him. God's answer was always the same, *"My grace is sufficient for you."*

Whenever we are experiencing the thorn in the flesh, and we've prayed and prayed for God to deliver us and He doesn't, we tend to grumble and moan. God knows how much we can bear. He has allowed us to experience this particular thorn for His purposes. Can we trust Him each time we are pricked by this thorn? I believe we can ask Him why we have this thorn. Perhaps it's to keep us humble, develop our perseverance, stretch our faith, or keep us from sinning. We do know that whatever it is God's grace is able to keep us from falling.

October 4

"I tell you the truth, if anyone says to this mountain, 'Go, throw yourself into the sea,' and does not doubt in his heart but believes that what he says will happen, it will be done for him" (Mark 11:23).

GOD CAN DO THE IMPOSSIBLE

*I*F WE HAVE faith and doubt not, can we really tell a mountain to throw itself into the sea? God thinks so. In fact He tells us that nothing shall be impossible for us if we believe. I believe that He is speaking figuratively and literally here in this verse.

If there is a situation that we find ourselves in, which appears to have tremendous obstacles blocking the way for us, we can pray in faith and ask God to make the mountain of circumstance, threat, oppression, or depression move, and it will move so we can pass on through to the other side.

And if there is an actual mountain or physical thing that stands in our path threatening to thwart God's work or His plans for us, I believe that we can pray in faith believing, and God is able and will remove, crumble, cast away, or whatever need be, that which is a wall to us. Always keep in mind, however, God's sovereignty and timing, but never give up praying and believing. Remember, the Children of Israel passed through the Red Sea as God parted the waters that stood in the way of their escape from the Egyptian army.

OCTOBER 5

"Therefore I tell you, whatever you ask for in prayer, believe that you have received it, and it will be yours"(Mark 11:24).

PRAY WITH CONFIDENCE

WHATEVER WE ASK for we shall have it, if we believe we have it. *What* does this mean? Haven't we all at times prayed for something and believed with all of our hearts that God would give it to us, but then, we were disappointed that we didn't receive what we thought we would. Is there a contradiction in God's Word? Absolutely not! We must take the sum total of all the Scriptures on that subject and compare them. Compare scripture with scripture and we will have a better understanding of what God is trying to say to us. Compare these scriptures together: John 15:7-8; John 16:23-24; Psalm 37:4; and 1 John 5:14.

If we compare just these four scriptures with today's verse, we can clearly see that: If we abide in Jesus and His words abide in our hearts, God will hear us and answer, and bring Himself glory.

And if we delight ourselves in God, He will place in our hearts His desires and we will pray according to His will: therefore we will pray with confidence knowing that God will answer our prayers. But again, remember that God is completely sovereign and does whatever He knows will benefit us. We are to leave all the results entirely up to Him and His perfect wisdom.

OCTOBER 6

"On the last and greatest day of the Feast, Jesus stood and said in a loud voice, 'If a man is thirsty, let him come to Me and drink. Whoever believes in Me, as the Scripture has said, streams of living water will flow from within him.' By this He meant the Spirit, whom those who believed in Him were later to receive. Up to that time the Spirit had not been given, since Jesus had not yet been glorified" (John 7:37-39).

THE WORK OF THE HOLY SPIRIT

JUST AS OUR bodies need to drink water in order to be kept alive and healthy, so our spirits need to drink the living water in order to be sustained and strengthened. That water is the Holy Spirit. *"And if the Spirit of Him who raised Jesus from the dead is living in you, He who raised Christ from the dead will also give life to your mortal bodies through His Spirit who lives in you." (Romans 8:11)*

The Holy Spirit of God is the life of God in us. He will not only give strength and life to our bodies right now, but He will also resurrect our mortal bodies at the resurrection of the dead. The Holy Spirit of God empowers us to live for Him, displays the fruit of righteousness in our lives, gives us love, guides, comforts, and teaches us, and will never leave us. We were sealed by Him at our conversion to Christ, and the Holy Spirit is our down payment guaranteeing our glorious inheritance to come.

OCTOBER 7

"...pray continually..."(1 Thessalonians 5:17).

PRAYER CONNECTS US TO GOD

PRAYER IS TO our spirits as breathing is to our bodies. It is an absolute necessity for us in the spiritual realm. Prayer is our connection to God who is our source of power and life. God desires us to be in a constant attitude of prayer. Not of a pious pretense of mumbling repetitive words or chants, but always being ready to communicate with Him at all times. Prayer is not just a duty we perform in the morning when we rise, and then before we go to bed at night. It is a vital living experience between God and us. Our hearts intimately entwined with His. We draw close to Him through prayer.

We see in the last chapter of the book of Ephesians, that prayer is part of the armor of God we are told to put on and use. We are to use faith when we pray and approach our Heavenly Father. We are told to pray and intercede for others, confess our sins to the Lord, and to bring all of our requests and petitions to Him. The habit of praying is to replace the destructive habit of worrying.

Prayer brings us into God's realm, and because Jesus Christ has washed us in His blood, and we are dressed in His righteousness, our prayers are powerful and effective. This means we can pray with confidence and our prayers will help bring about miraculous changes into our situations, in people, places, and in ourselves.

"Sh-h-h, be quiet. Put all the noises that clamor at your thoughts at rest—for just this moment in time. Breathe in My presence and know that I am right here with you. Know that I am so big that I can, and will take care of everything that is weighing you down. I will be exalted among all the people of different nations; I will be exalted throughout the entire earth. And I will be exalted in you, My child" (Psalm 46:10 Eilers' paraphrase).

BE STILL—GOD IS HERE

THERE IS SO much busyness and hurry these days. We need to slow down and let the heaviness roll off of our shoulders and on to the Lord who made us, and who has the answer to every single thing. Sometimes God wants us to just sit in His comforting, nurturing presence of peace and to be quiet. Can we trust this minute to Him? How about the next? And the next? It takes practice, but the more we pull ourselves back into the present, enjoy who God is, and cast all our cares upon Him, the less difficult it becomes.

"Be still, and know that I am God; I will be exalted among the nations, I will be exalted in the earth."

(PSALM 46:10)

OCTOBER 9

"Let us fix our eyes on Jesus, the author and perfecter of our faith, who for the joy set before Him endured the cross, scorning its shame, and sat down at the right hand of the throne of God. Consider Him who endured such opposition from sinful men, so that you will not grow weary and lose heart" (Hebrews 12:2-3).

ENDURE FOR THE GREATER GAIN

WHEN THE JOURNEY looks like it's taking forever, and the mind, spirit and body grow weary—don't give up. We must let our hearts fix their sights on Jesus only, His strength, His purposes, His plans, His deliverance. Remember that Jesus endured His cross, for the joy that was set before Him.

He determined to keep His eyes on the higher gain, which was the redemption of you and me and our fellowship with Him for eternity. He endured. He put up with the painful sufferings and accepted the Father's will—death on a cross.

Likewise, my dear fellow servant in Christ, do not faint nor grow weary in your work for righteousness. Endure the discomfort for the greater gain and good—to bring fruit and glory to God. You will reap if you don't give up.

OCTOBER 10

"He shall not be afraid of evil tidings: His heart is fixed, trusting in Jehovah. His heart is established, he shall not be afraid…"(Psalm 112:7-8a ASV 1901).

NO FEAR OF BAD NEWS

ONE OF THE most alarming news we can hear is "War!"—-Especially in our day and age when nuclear weapons are so advanced and can cause untold destruction for the human race. Where can a person find security? Where can we find safety when evil surrounds us and terror seems to loom out of nowhere?

When I feel the icy fingers of fear begin to take a grip upon my heart, I shall do as the Psalmist wrote in Psalm 112:7-8. I will dig my heels deeper into the soil of my Lord Jesus Christ. I will speak to my heart and remind it to trust and not be afraid because God is in control. He is the Sovereign One and does as He chooses. He gives and takes away. He wounds and He heals. He kills and makes alive, and no one can ask Him, *"What are You doing?"* If our God is in control, then nothing will touch us unless it is permitted by the love of God for our best. He is our protecting Father and we can hold firm to His promises of protection. We can tell our hearts to be at rest because He is in control of all—-of life, of death, even of war.

Bad news will come to us all throughout our journey on earth, but we can train our hearts to stay unmovable and steadfast, trusting in the Almighty God. We can choose to trust or to fear. God is there to assist us when we choose to trust, and there to strengthen us when we are waning with fear.

OCTOBER 11

"But to each one of us grace has been given as Christ apportioned it. This is why it says: 'When He ascended on high, He led captives in His train and gave gifts to men'"(Ephesians 4:7-8).

GIFTS GIVEN TO USE

WHEN WE ARE given unique gifts from above, we have a responsibility to develop them and to use them to bring Glory to God. Some are given one particular gifting, others have several, or multiple giftings. The Bible tells us that we have been given grace for developing and using our gifts. There are different kinds of abilities. Some we are born with, such as teaching, singing, writing or encouraging others. Then there are those gifts that operate in our lives as the Holy Spirit works through us in a supernatural way. These include the gifts of healing, prophesy, miracles….When we recognize that we have been given a gift that can be used to bless others and encourage the Body of Christ, which is the Church, we are expected to ask the Lord what He wants us to do with it, and how He wants us to develop and use it. It takes perseverance, practice, and hard work sometimes to develop gifts in the rough, that we have been given. Then, it takes patience and practice being sensitive to when the Holy Spirit is moving upon us to use our gifts. When we are aware of His nudging, we can yield to Him.

To whom much is given, much is required; let us therefore, not hide our talents, but invest in them for the Lord.

OCTOBER 12

"Call to Me, and I will answer you, and show you great and mighty things, which you do not know" (Jeremiah 33:3).

I WILL SHOW YOU

HE OTHER DAY when I was feeling overwhelmed with the trials I was struggling through, I could hear the enemy's voice saying, *"I'll show you; I'll show you. You want to do God's work and write Bible studies and teach them—-you want to seek God's face diligently, then I'll show you real troubles and trials. I will make it so hard for you...."* I thought for a moment, yes, the trials have increased for me, and I can feel the enemy's fists beating against me. Then God showed up and spoke to my heart loud and clear. *"Call unto Me...and I will show you. I will show you great and mighty things that are happening around and within you that you don't even know about. I will show you My Power when you are weak, My joy when you are in grief, My answers when you call, and My delivering and providing right hand!"*

OCTOBER 13

"There is no fear in love. But perfect love drives out fear" (1 John 4:18).

WHEN FEAR STRIKES

HOW EASY IT is to allow our hearts to become fearful. The enemy knows how to get us to fear—he knows where we are weak and what will trouble our hearts. What do we do when we are afraid, and our hearts are gripped with the torment of fear? Go to God. Always go to Him. Tell Him all about your fear and terrors. Ask Him for His peace in the matter that is so disturbing you. Then with your *will* choose to believe He has heard you and that He is doing just what you asked. Choose to believe there is nothing to fear when you put your trust in God. Believe He will always take care of you and be there for you whatever your need be. Believe and practice the Scriptures that tell us not to be afraid. It might be difficult at first to experience victory over your fear. But as you keep choosing to rely and trust yourself to God's love, you will find the fears begin to diminish. Faith will take hold of your heart and peace will enter once again. You will feel stability of mind and able to handle whatever you need to.

OCTOBER 14

"My prayer is not that You take them out of the world
but that You protect them from the evil one.
My prayer is not for them alone. I pray also for those who will believe
in Me through their message, that all of them may be one, Father, just
as You are in Me and I am in You. May they also be in us so that the
world may believe that You have sent Me" (John 17:15 & 20, 21).

TWO PRAYERS THAT WILL BE ANSWERED

TWO PRAYERS WERE prayed by Jesus when He was with His disciples, before He was crucified. He was praying not only for the disciples, but for you and me who would believe on Him through the Word of God. When Jesus prays, His prayers are always prayed in perfect faith, and in accordance with the Father's will.

According to the above Scripture passages, what prayers of Jesus will be answered then? First, God, the Father, will not take us out of the world, but He will put His hedge of protection around us, and keep us from being devoured by the evil one. Then, the whole God-Head, Father, Son and Holy Spirit, will live inside of us, bringing unity to our lives, unity with Him, and with other believers. We will be effective witnesses for Jesus.

OCTOBER 15

"The Lord said to Satan, 'Where have you come from?' Satan answered the Lord, 'From roaming through the earth and going back and forth in it.' Then the Lord said to Satan, 'Have you considered My servant Job? There is no one on earth like him; he is blameless and upright, a man who fears God and shuns evil.' 'Does Job fear God for nothing?' Satan replied. 'Have You not put a hedge around him and his household and everything he has? You have blessed the work of his hands, so that his flocks and herds are spread throughout the land. But stretch out Your hand and strike everything he has, and he will surely curse You to your face'" (Job 1:7-11).

CONSIDER MY SERVANT

ODAY I WENT to minister before some of God's people. When I got up to sing, I felt very timid and unsure of myself. My confidence was very small. I felt tiny in the room full of ladies. As I finished my song and sat down, I felt so discouraged. I knew how to sing—I had sung before many, many audiences, and today it was as if it were my first time. The discouragement grew into anger, and I began to tell the Lord that if He wanted me to minister in song, then I had to have the confidence needed to bring it forth with His power and anointing. After thinking about it for a while, feeling more and more inadequate, I began to question whether God had even called me to sing. Perhaps I should just concentrate on another part of ministry. At the end of the day, I asked the Lord why He had allowed for me to feel so humiliated. The story of Job came into my mind. I could just hear the Lord saying to Satan, *"Have you considered My servant, Roxanne? She will trust Me about her ministry and where I am taking her, because she believes in My call on her life."* Then I could hear Satan reply, *"Just let me put some kinks in her voice and delivery and she will doubt her call."* God allowed him to do just that, today. And I reacted just like Satan said I would. I doubted my call in this area of ministry. But as soon as I recognized it was the work of the enemy, I asked the Lord to forgive me for blaming Him falsely of not being there for me. Then I asked Him to forgive me for doubting my call.

Dear One, is God bringing up your name before Satan, exclaiming how proud He is of your devotion to Him and His Word, and how faithful you've been with what He has entrusted you with? And is Satan replying, *"Oh, but just let me take this away from her, or allow me to put stumbling blocks in her path so she ceases from being so successful in that area!"*

Let us be that faithful and trusting servant—-trusting the hand of God in our lives, knowing He never makes a mistake with even the tiniest incidents in our lives.

OCTOBER 16

"Do you not know that those who run in a race all run, but one receives the prize? Run in such a way that you may obtain it. And everyone who competes for the prize is temperate in all things. Now they do it to obtain a perishable crown, but we for an imperishable crown" (1 Corinthians 9:24-25 NKJV).

THE GREAT RACE

THE APOSTLE PAUL is talking here about being in a race and running in such a way to obtain the prize. We are running in God's spiritual race and one of our prizes is an imperishable crown of reward, which crown, God's Word tells us, we will cast down at the feet of Jesus. Dear friends, our focus here on earth is to be continually set on the One who has called us into this great race. We are to run that we may gain Christ, the greatest Prize ever, and be found in Him, and that we may know Him, experience Him and His resurrection power in our daily lives, sharing in His sufferings. Then, we are to die moment by moment to our own selfish, self- seeking ways.

As we run, we are instructed to discipline our bodies, minds and spirits, bringing them under the Lordship of Jesus Christ and His Word, while reaching, stretching, and pressing forward towards the prize of the upward call of God in Christ Jesus.

So with these thoughts in mind, let us run this holy race with everything that's in us. We can endure and break through whatever suffering is thrown in our path by fastening our eyes on Jesus, who gave us our faith and who finished His own race from the Father, who completed His own call on earth and has sat down at the right hand of God's throne cheering us on with the saints that have gone on before us.

OCTOBER 17

"And the Lord said, 'Shall I hide from Abraham what
I am doing....'" (Genesis 18:17 NKJV)?

GOD, WHAT ARE YOU GOING TO DO NEXT?

GOD VISITED ABRAHAM while he was sitting in front of his tent. Abraham was told that Sarah, his wife, would indeed have a son at the appointed time. Then as Abraham raised his eyes toward Sodom, where his nephew, Lot lived, God knew that he was deeply concerned with Lot, being in that wicked place, and what was to become of him and his family. God showed Abraham that Sodom and Gomorrah, the two sinful cities, would be destroyed.

Abraham begins to plead and intercede for his nephew, Lot, and his family to be spared and kept safe. God hears Abraham and gives him the assurance he needs in his heart. Lot and his family are taken out of the city by two angels and then Sodom and Gomorrah are destroyed.

There are things that God wants to reveal to us, things in our lives, or in the lives of our loved ones, events and circumstances that will happen in the future. Why does God want us to know something ahead of time? I believe, it may be for us to prepare ourselves, adjust our plans, or intercede earnestly in prayer for someone or something.

The Lord desires us to ask of Him about our situations, what direction we are to take in our lives, in our jobs, with loved ones.... By faith we are to cry out to Him and ask Him to make our path clear, and open our eyes to His purpose and plan. And as the Lord makes our steps known to us, unfolding before us which way to take, or maybe just to wait and be still, we can be comforted and at peace because we know that God will always do what is best, and He will listen to our cries.

He sees, He knows, He reveals, He acts, we obey, and then we grow in our faith.

OCTOBER 18

"But I will sing of Your power; Yes, I will sing aloud of Your mercy in the morning; For You have been my defense and refuge in the day of my trouble. To You, O my Strength, I will sing praises; For God is my defense, My God of mercy" (Psalm 59:16-17 NKJV).

A PRAYER

O HOW STRONG IS our God—He is to be adored! In the morning I will run to Him. What do You have for me today? What is Your wise plan for me today? O Knower of all men's hearts! Reveal Your truth and guide me. I know You love me and call me Your own.

I am hiding today in the place where You have beckoned me. The days have been oppressive and evil lurks about me. I am sitting with You, Dear Holy Spirit, in Your divine fortified place. These are times of trouble and the schemes of mortal man would make me afraid, would intimidate me. So I am fleeing under Your wing for safety.

O my Strength, all glory to You, O Deliverer of Men! O God, I am amazed and comforted at Your power and guardianship over me. Because You love me, You will act on my behalf. Thank You, Savior. Amen.

OCTOBER 19

"For we wrestle not against flesh and blood, but against principalities, against powers, against the rulers of the darkness of this world, against spiritual wickedness in high places....Above all, taking the shield of faith, wherewith ye shall be able to quench all the fiery darts of the wicked" (Ephesians 6:12, 16).

THE FIGHT

OUR WRESTLING IS against the works and temptations of the devil. The Bible calls it "a wrestling." When two are wrestling, they are opposing each other, and their chief aim is to bring the other down so he can't get up again. We must master our enemy in our Christian warfare. We should never allow the enemy to master us and to hold us down. God has given us everything we need to be a conqueror in battle. However, we must learn to use the weapons He has given us. We must know our weaknesses and vulnerable areas and guard ourselves. We are not ignorant of Satan's devices and tactics. It is always to take down his opponent using fear, doubt or discouragement. Be alert then, and stand your ground, keeping that shield of Faith up for then you will wrestle to win.

October 20

"...to know the love of Christ which passes knowledge...."(Ephesians 3:19 NKJV).

The Love of God

IN THIS CHAPTER of the book of Ephesians, a few verses above 19, we are told some vital information to follow. We are told to be strengthened with the might of God's Spirit so that our faith in Christ will be solid. When our faith in Christ is strong and unwavering, we can begin to grow in the love of God. First, we are to have knowledge about His love, then we are to grow and be grounded in it. It is the will of God that we not only know His love cognitively, but also experimentally and continually. This will give us a sense of the security we have in Him, and we will begin to grasp that His love will never allow us to go through anything that has not been customized and carefully planned just for our good and spiritual growth. Faith works by Love. The two work hand and hand. The more we step out in faith and take God at His Word, the more we can believe it and receive it. Thus, our love in Him is matured.

OCTOBER 21

"Moses answered the people, 'Do not be afraid. Stand firm and you will see the deliverance the LORD will bring you today. The Egyptians you see today you will never see again'" (Exodus 14:13).

INCLUDE GOD AND WATCH HIM WORK

THERE ARE TIMES when what we see with our eyes or hear with our ears brings us to believe a faulty conclusion in the matter. The Israelites were trapped in the wilderness and the Red Sea was before them. They looked up and saw the Egyptian armies and their chariots charging towards them. Surely, they concluded that they would die, so great fear came upon them. You see they didn't have all the facts. They didn't bring God into the equation. Moses had to calm their hearts and he says, "Stand still and see the salvation of the Lord, which He will accomplish for you today!" God intervened and did the impossible—He parted the Red Sea, something the children of Israel would have never imagined could happen. God brought them away from the Egyptians who drowned that day. In your situation, God can still do the impossible. Bring Him into the equation when you are trying to figure out what to do. Inquire of Him. Believe Him to do something that may not seem possible to you. Trust Him to do a wonder. Stand still and watch Him work!

OCTOBER 22

"In this the love of God was manifested toward us, that God has sent His only begotten Son into the world, that we might live through Him. In this is love, not that we loved God, but that He loved us and sent His Son to be the propitiation for our sins" (1 John 4:9-10 NKJV).

THE WONDER OF GOD'S LOVE

THE WONDER OF God's love is shown to us in His action of sending us His beloved Son, Jesus, so we could have our sins forgiven through the blood that He shed on the cross. We then will be able to live life to its fullest, and no longer be a slave to our sinful nature. What freedom if we really apply this truth to our hearts!

When we didn't even have God on our minds, when we didn't even care about Him, He had us on His mind, in His heart and cared deeply about us. With His love He pursued us. All we have to do is to receive this love and walk in it by faith.

God is always romancing our hearts closer to Himself. He whispers, He cries out, *"I love you. I love you. I love you for always."*

OCTOBER 23

"And there is no one who calls on Your name, who stirs himself up to take hold of You . . ."(Isaiah 64:7 NKJ).

HOLD ON

GOD IS SPEAKING to the soul who will call on His name in faith. To the one who will get himself excited and fired up for God and the things of God. The Lord is seeking for that one, whoever will, take hold of Him and not let go.

Will you take hold of God and determine to keep holding on to Him no matter what you have to face? Watch Him bring you through your fiery trials! Stir up the anointing within you by praying in the Holy Spirit. Earnestly fan into flames your fervor for God and the things of God. Let your fiery trials just cause you to call on the Name of the Lord for mercy and keep holding tenaciously on to God even stronger.

OCTOBER 24

"Now think it over and see what you can do" (1 Samuel 25:17).

WHAT CAN YOU DO?

*T*HIS STORY IN 1 Samuel is about the time when David was fleeing from King Saul who sought to destroy his life. David comes into a certain area and asks for favorable treatment from the master of the place, Nabal at Carmel. He asks for food, water, shelter, whatever Nabal can give him. Nabal disregards David's men who have come to make the request. David in turn, becomes very angry and is bent on putting to death all the males belonging to Nabal. Nabal's wife hears of the incident and her servant tells her to *"think it over and see what she can do."* How can she prevent bloodshed and pursue peace? She is a wise woman and packs food and wine on donkeys and sends them to David. She then follows them and stands in the gap before David. David receives her gifts and provisions and grants peace.

This story could have ended in bloodshed and violence if Nabal's wife had chosen to seek vengeance with David. But they both left vengeance up to the Lord. When the situation comes into your own life for you to figure out what to do when anger and vengeance are pressing in, what will you do to make for peace? See what you can do to choose peace and pursue it. Pursue peace with all people. Hebrews (12:14) Blessed are the peacemakers. (Matthew 5:9) Obey God's Word and you will be blessed. (Psalm 34:14)

OCTOBER 25

*"True humility and fear of the Lord lead to riches,
honor, and long life" (Proverbs 22:4 NLT).*

THE WAY TO SUCCESS

*I*N THIS VERSE we are told one of God's secrets to being successful. So often we find ourselves striving to be somebody, trying to please everybody. We want to be noticed for our achievements, and desire to be complimented on our talents and abilities. I know, I have worked so hard to develop my talents of writing, singing and artwork. I've prayed for God to use everything I've got and to make me successful in life, to have the finances to live comfortably, to be honored for all my hard work and to live a full rich life.

God has said that we must have "true humility" that is, to have a humble, submissive, and meek heart. If God gives us success can we give Him all the glory, and remain humble in heart?

Then God says that we must have a deep reverence and understand who He is and what He's done for us. Remember, God resists the proud, but gives strength and mercy to the humble in heart. The reverence of the Lord is the beginning of wisdom. And having wisdom means we will apply God's Word, the Bible, to our daily lives. The Bible tells us how to be successful, respected, and live a long fruitful life.

October 26

"Study this Book of Instruction continually. Meditate on it day and night so you will be sure to obey everything written in it. Only then will you prosper and succeed in all you do"(Joshua 1:8).

How to Prosper and Be Successful

WHAT ELSE DOES God say about prospering and being successful? According to the book of Joshua 1:8, we are to study God's Word. Study means to really *learn* it. An example, is when we are studying for a test we write down key words, we rehearse it, and think about it. So also included in "study" is the daily meditation, the pondering upon what God's Word is saying to us. How we can apply it to our daily lives, and then how we can obey it.

We are to apply and work at obeying all of what we know in the Bible, then, we can expect two things—to prosper and to be successful in our everyday lives. What is prosperity? It is the multiplying of the good things we want to do or receive. What is success? It is the division and distribution of all the good we have done or are doing or have received.

Dear Lord, please help me to study and apply Your words to my life. Then I will get to know Your heart better and what You desire. Amen.

OCTOBER 27

*"Trust in the Lord and do good. Then you will live safely
in the land and prosper" (Psalm 37:3 NLT).*

PROSPERITY

WHAT DOES THE Lord say to do in order for us to be kept safe and to prosper? We are to put our trust in Him alone. Trusting means to rely solely on Jesus. It means not worrying. Next, we are to live a good life—a holy life. What is the good life? It is thinking upon, applying and obeying God's Word in our everyday words, thoughts and actions towards ourselves and others.

I want to feel safe wherever I go, so when I'm trusting the Lord and doing what's right, I can experience a greater confidence and peace.

Thank You, Lord, for Your protective hand You place upon me and for blessing me. Now I can be a blessing to others, thus being obedient to You. Amen.

OCTOBER 28

"Those who listen to instruction will prosper" (Proverbs 16:20 NLT).

LISTEN AND PROSPER

WE HAVE BEEN looking at how we can prosper and succeed in life. Here we have yet another exhortation on what we are to do so that we may prosper. We are to listen to instruction; we are not just to *hear* when others instruct us, we are to really *listen*.

Listening includes: thinking about it, understanding it, finding how it applies to you. When others give us instruction, we can listen to it and then evaluate whether or not we want to use it or discard it. We have that choice, and also God will give us wisdom about the matter. If what we are told is of value, then great is that value. It can only help us bear good fruit. This, my friend, is prosperity. It is when we become unteachable and stiff necked, that we are in danger of falling and taking the wrong path.

Pray for a teachable and humble heart today, so you can learn and benefit, not only yourself, but for others also.

October 29

"Then the Lord answered Job from the whirlwind" (Job 38:1).

God Answers

IT IS SO marvelous that God answers our prayers and requests. Sometimes we may feel the heavens are brass and God has forgotten us, but the truth of the matter is that His eye is always on us, and He carefully watches over us. God answered Job.

When God answered Job out of the storm, He was showing a side of Himself that Job needed to see in order to be encouraged in his faith. God showed Job His power, omnipotence, and absolute greatness, and these attributes of His could be seen in nature.

God also answered Elijah the prophet, but this time it wasn't in the great and powerful wind, or the earthquake, nor fire. God revealed Himself to Elijah in a gentle whisper. When Elijah heard the whisper of God, he went out of the cave he was in, to talk with God.

How does God speak to you? Sometimes perhaps in a loud voice where you stand at attention, listen and obey. Or perhaps at times, in a gentle whisper, where you are comforted and encouraged. However way God may speak to you, when you really listen to what He is saying, you will be richly rewarded. So keep on praying and God will keep on answering.

OCTOBER 30

"He will delight in obeying the Lord. He will not judge by appearance nor make a decision based on hearsay"(Isaiah 11:3-4).

TRUST THE RIGHTEOUS JUDGE

WE TALK ABOUT God being the Righteous Judge. Do we really believe it?

One night, at 3:00 in the morning, I rose up to get a drink of water. My eyes were drawn to the blinking light on our phone machine. Pressing the button for play, I listened to the message. It was not a good report and my heart started to beat faster. It was one of our friends who left the message that their father had shot their mother, and then took his own life. She was instantly an orphan. What a shock to us all.

As the day neared for the funeral, I began to wonder if Bob had gone to hell for what he did. Instantly I felt the presence of God surround me and words spoken to my mind. Instantly I knew that I could trust God with the eternity of my friend's parents. The message I heard in my heart said to me, *"You can't even imagine how deep and wide and great My compassions and mercies are. They are way beyond your understanding. Her parents are safe and I am taking care of them. I am the very Just and Righteous Judge."*

My heart and mind were at once flooded with peace. I knew that God would take into consideration the depression and illness in her father's life. God knew his motives and the insanity of the moment.

Do you believe God is the Righteous Judge? I do. I cannot judge another one's life on what I see and hear. Only God will have the final say. Some ask, what about those who've never heard about Jesus and have died? Will they be ushered into the flames of hell? The Bible tells us that God is the Righteous Judge, and He will judge those people upon what they do know about Him and how they lived their lives. The Bible says in Revelation 20:12-13, that the dead were judged according to what they had done. And

then again in Romans 1:19-20, God tells us that *"... What may be known about God is plain to them ...."*

Rest assured in your Righteous and Merciful Judge.

OCTOBER 31

"But the fruit of the Spirit is love, joy, peace, longsuffering, kindness, goodness, faithfulness"(Galatians 5:22 NKJV).

DYING TO THE FLESH

ONCE, I FOUND myself in a very trying situation. It was a situation where every fiber of my inner most being and temperament were being tried. My mother in-law had come to live with us. I found that every work of the flesh I had considered to be dead to, were very much alive. That of being irritable, judgmental, prideful, just to name a few, showed their ugly heads. How could I allow the holy fruits of the Spirit to take pre-eminence? It was a work only God could do. It was a daily dying to the flesh that wanted to be grouchy and irritable because it seemed provoked. It was choosing the fruit of the Spirit of gentleness and kindness to rule my heart. It was a true dependence on the work of the Holy Spirit in me. So my prayer back then is the same for me today. I want to die daily in the old sinful nature, and to rise up and live in the newness of Christ.

O God, help me crucify the old nature. I die to being disagreeable. Help me to be honest with my feelings, but to also walk in the supernatural realm of the spirit of love.

November 1

"I will bless the Lord at all times; His praise shall
continually be in my mouth" (Psalm 34:1 NKJV).

Praise at All Times

THIS PSALM WAS written by David around the time when he fled from King Saul and ran to Abimelech to find safety. Unfortunately, he was recognized by one of the servants of the Philistines and was confronted by King Abimelech. David was so afraid that Abimelech would kill him or Saul would find out he was there, so he pretended to be insane. However, even though David was terrified, he blessed and praised the Lord. How can one who is so afraid still bless the Lord and speak of His praises? When I am afraid, sometimes my first response is to draw back into myself and avoid the situation. When I address the Lord, it is for His help and deliverance from fear. Perhaps David already knew, through the eyes of faith, that God would deliver him because later in verse 4, he speaks of being delivered from *all* his fears. And David was delivered out of his dangerous situation. Of course he sought the Lord and prayed, but it was his faith in what God would do and already had done, that caused him to praise at all times. We can learn from David, that although we may be in a time of trial, fearfulness, or tribulation, we do need to pray for God's deliverance, but *always* in faith to praise Him for the answers, and then to keep on praising Him because He is good.

"Then the Spirit entered me and set me on my feet" (Ezekiel 3:24 NKJV).

Possessed Of God

WHEN GOD WAS commissioning Ezekiel, one of the things He did when Ezekiel had fallen on his face before Him, is found in this verse. When God's Spirit entered Ezekiel, He set him upon his feet. Later on down in the chapter, Ezekiel is made dumb, but when God chooses to use him to speak, He opens his mouth to speak to the House of Israel.

We, as believers in the Lord God, have His Holy Spirit residing and abiding on the inside of us at all times, but are we so yielded as to allow Him to do with us as He pleases? Do we allow Him to move through us supernaturally if He chooses to? Will we allow Him to speak through us and keep silent when He says to? Oh Dear One, to be so possessed of the Spirit of God that we are completely pliable in His hand. Then He can really use us to do great things—all reserves unstopped. What glory then!

NOVEMBER 3

"Oh taste and see that the Lord is good; Blessed is the
man that trusts in Him"(Psalm 34:8 NKJV)!

A GOOD GOD

LATER ON IN David's Psalm 34, he talks of his intimate knowledge of his loving God. He tells everyone that God is good. So because God is good, we can rejoice when we decide to place our trust in Him because He will work everything out for our good. A good God does good things for us. We can exult in joy over knowing a God like this. We can also continually engage in daily tasting for ourselves this goodness. And at the times when nothing makes sense, we can lean on this extravagant goodness of God to show us the way. He will bring good out of what was meant for evil against us.

NOVEMBER 4

*"I will turn the desert into pools of water and the
parched ground into springs" (Isaiah 41:18).*

A PRAYER FOR RENEWAL

*H*AVE YOU BEEN feeling dry these days? Do you lack a zeal to
witness? Is your desire to travail in prayer wavering? Have you
no energy to worship? Your soul needs to be watered, your
spirit renewed. Let us pray this prayer together.

*Dear Father, please let Your Holy Spirit sweep down on me
and pour out Your springs upon me. Let them overflow within
me. I am dry and thirsty, worn and weary. Refresh my prayer
life, rekindle my heart of praise, hold me up and let Your power
surge through me. Bring me back into Your oceans of grace and
mercy, peace and everlasting love. Amen.*

NOVEMBER 5

"Do not be like a senseless horse or mule that needs a bit and bridle to keep it under control" (Psalm 32:9 NLT).

DON'T BE STUBBORN

WHEN THE LORD shows us the way to go and what to do, He expects us to obey Him. God will tell us to do something more than once, just like a mother does her child. But if we keep resisting His will, He will have to allow circumstances and situations to come into our lives that get us back on track and willing to obey quickly. We cannot afford to be stubborn in God's Kingdom. We lose blessing and God has to put pressure on us to conform to His ways. Oh, how peaceable it is when we hear His lovely voice and we say, *"Yes, Lord."*

I have been in both places and I do not like the bit and the bridle put in my mouth. I like to just follow the Master's hand with the apple in it. His will is a sweet will. Ours, one that is selfish, unless given over into His hands. Will you go easily or have you needed a bit and bridle these days? Pray with me.

Dear Lord, please make me willing to do Your will at all costs. To go where You bid and to answer Your call. Give me grace to follow You and not to wander off on my own. Bring me under the complete control of the Dear Holy Spirit and be glorified in me. Amen.

"But seek first His Kingdom and His righteousness, and all these things will be given to you as well" (Matthew 6:33).

SEEK FIRST THE KINGDOM OF GOD

*I*N MATTHEW 6:33, we are told to seek first the Kingdom of God and His righteousness. What does this mean?

I believe it means to be wrapped up in God and His business. It is diligently pursuing after God's reign in our lives. Is He Lord over every area—or just a few? It is striving to do what's right and what will bring God the glory. It is making God, His Word, His will, and His reign, the most important aim in our lives. He comes first on our agenda—not second.

The opposite of seeking His Kingdom first, is to run after the things of the world instead—to make possessions and money our aim. It is being anxious about our needs, acting like an orphaned child. Jesus outright says don't do this. You are acting just like someone who doesn't know God—someone who feels he has to rely only on himself to survive.

Jesus concludes with the promise that if we do seek His Kingdom first all these other things will be thrown in as well.

November 7

"Because the Sovereign LORD helps me, I will not be disgraced. Therefore have I set my face like flint, and I know I will not be put to shame" (Isaiah 50:7).

Set Your Face like a Flint

NEVER LOSE SIGHT of your calling that God has anointed you to. Things may be falling down all around you—circumstances of trial and turmoil, struggles of loved ones and friends, daily challenges, loss, personal problems—but don't lose sight of your calling. Keep marching on, one foot in front of another to accomplish what God has set before you to do. Chip away, little by little, doing the little things God shows you to do. Stay focused and don't let the vision die. Don't get sidetracked. You were called for such a time as this. There will always be some kind of tribulation, some kind of problem that will come up because this is life. However, set your face like a flint and be unmoved in your calling.

NOVEMBER 8

"I will make rivers flow on barren heights, and springs
within the valleys. I will turn the desert into pools of water,
and the parched ground into springs" (Isaiah 41:18).

HOLY SPIRIT REVIVAL

ISAIAH 41:18 SAYS, "I will make spiritual rivers flow all over your barren heart. I will create bubbling joy in the Holy Spirit in your deepest valleys. I will turn your dry and desert seasons into soaking seasons in the Holy Spirit. Then I will change the weary and tired ground of your soul into watered springs of living water. (Eilers' paraphrase)

It is just like Jesus said in John 7:37-38, *"Let anyone who is spiritually thirsty come to Me and drink his fill. Whoever believes in Me as Scripture has said, 'rivers of living water will flow from within them.'"* This sounds like the rain of revival to me. When the Holy Spirit shows up—life and joy spring up and overflow inside the heart. Hallelujah! The Holy Spirit says at this time that He will do that thing that you have been inquiring of Him. He will make things new and revive your tired and empty soul. *Get under the pouring and rain of My Spirit and I will revive you! I will rebuild the broken places in your heart as you soak in My presence and Spirit.*

If this is you today raise your hands and receive from the Holy Spirit what you need spiritually in order to thrive and bear fruit. Pray with me.

> *Come, Holy Spirit and saturate my life. I raise my hands up*
> *to You and receive power, as You fall upon me and fill me up.*
> *Soak me from head to toe with Your Spirit and anointing! Let*
> *me walk under Your anointing, sleep under Your anointing,*
> *wake under Your anointing! Hallelujah! All praise and glory*
> *and honor to the Lamb who sits on the throne. Bring Your fire*
> *and burn away my dross; purify my mind and heart—ignite*
> *revival in my heart and bring Yourself glory. Amen and Amen*

NOVEMBER 9

"I lift up my eyes to the mountains—where does my help come from? My help comes from the Lord, the Maker of heaven and earth. He will not let your foot slip—He who watches over you will not slumber; indeed, He who watches over Israel will neither slumber nor sleep. The Lord watches over you—the Lord is your shade at your right hand; the sun will not harm you by day, nor the moon by night. The Lord will keep you from all harm—He will watch over your life; the Lord will watch over your coming and going both now and forevermore"(Psalm 121:1-8).

GOD'S WATCHFUL CARE

GOD PROMISES HIS watchful care over us, and to send His presence to be with us. In Psalm 121, we are told that our help comes from the Lord and He will watch over and keep (preserve) us. He will not slumber nor sleep. He is always available for us and ready to take care of our needs. In verse 5 it says *"The Lord is your keeper..."* This word "keeper" in the Hebrew language is *Shamar* which means "to hedge about, guard, protect, attend to, keep, preserve and watch" (Strong's 8104). God places a supernatural hedge about us; even Satan knows God has set this hedge around His people in Job 1:9-10. God shelters us with His hedge. It protects us from evil. I believe there are three components that make up this hedge.

Psalm 34:7 tells us it is the angel of the Lord who encamps around us to deliver us. Then in Psalm 139:4-5, the Lord hems us in all around by the Holy Spirit. I also believe our faith and obedience to God keep that hedge up around us. So the hedge is God's mighty angels, His own embracing Holy Spirit, His protecting and preserving hand, and our faith and obedience. The only way something can touch us is if He lifts His hand and allows it to pass through to us for His own purpose and glory, and for our good and growth. In Exodus 33:14, God says He will send His presence with us to help us face whatever comes into our lives, and He will give us rest. Our God will never leave us nor forsake us. He is our true helper.

November 10

"He lifted me out of the slimy pit, out of the mud and mire; He set my feet on a rock and gave me a firm place to stand. He put a new song in my mouth, a hymn of praise to our God. Many will see and fear the LORD and put their trust in Him" (Psalm 40:2-3).

Why Does God Deliver Us?

WHY DOES GOD rescue us and deliver us? I believe one of the main reasons why He helps us and preserves us is so that we would tell others of His goodness and love. Also, that we would bring the lost into the fold, to set the oppressed free, and to bring light and hope to those whose lives are in a perpetual darkness.

Yes, our God will take care of us and watch over us. He will meet our needs. He will have mercy on us and faithfully guide us and lead us to where the wells of refreshment are for our souls. And even the hardest and most trying circumstances that threaten to take us under will be used to bring us closer to Him. God will help us to see that there are paths even in the mountains, and He will lead us safely through and bring us to our desired haven. Why?

Because He loves us so much and wants us to have mercy on others, take care of the needy, lead and guide those wandering lambs to green pasture and safety, to bring the living water of Christ to the parched souls of men. Sometimes God will use us to help escort some weary soul through their own mountainous way. God is our teacher and our perfect example. What He does for us, in the measure we can, we are to do unto others.

November 11

"Therefore, since we have these promises, dear friends, let us purify ourselves from everything that contaminates body and spirit, perfecting holiness out of reverence for God" (2 Corinthians 7:1).

CLEAN UP FOR REVIVAL!

I WAS READING IN 2 Chronicles 29 that the temple of the Lord had been terribly neglected, the furniture was broken and the holy utensils were badly tarnished. King Hezekiah had the Israelites clean out the temple; everything needed to be cleaned up and the trash and unclean things thrown out. The furnishings needed repair, the utensils cleaned and polished; fresh oil was to fill the lampstand and sweet incense was to be brought back in to ascend up to God. Then when the temple was purified, cleansed and ready, they stood before the Lord and worshiped and praised Him with great song and shouts and instruments. There was a shout through the streets for the people of Israel to return to the Lord and repent and serve Him. The priests and the Levites devoted themselves to the Law of the Lord and people gave offerings.

What does this have to do with us today? In 2 Corinthians 6-7, we are told to clean up our temple which is the temple of the Lord; it is our body where Christ lives in us. The Lord is adamant about us separating ourselves from all impurity of spirit and flesh. He says to touch no unclean thing, and I will receive you…I will use you and make My life shine through you to the world. God will live and walk in us because He lives in us. So Paul, the apostle, admonishes us to clean up our lives, our hearts and our minds— everything that contaminates body and spirit. Clean up and revival will happen in us and pour out to others. Is the Lord telling you not to watch a certain show, clean up your mouth, purge out hidden secret sinful thoughts? It's time to Clean up for Revival! We will burst forth in song and be filled with the powerful oil of the Holy Spirit's power! Hallelujah!

NOVEMBER 12

"Try to please them all the time, not just when they are watching you. As slaves of Christ, do the will of God with all your heart. Work with enthusiasm, as though you were working for the Lord rather than for people" (Ephesians 6:6-7 NLT).

A SERVING HEART

HOW OFTEN DO we murmur and complain under our breath when we have to do things that we don't necessarily enjoy doing? I am guilty of having a complaining heart when my husband asks me for something, and I am preoccupied with the things I like to do at the moment. God has been dealing with my own heart over this one because He is always concerned about our heart attitude, not just our actions. If I get up and get a cup of coffee for my husband, but in my heart I am grumbling, this is not pleasing to God who tries the hearts. Rather, may I develop the mind-set that I am serving my Lord Jesus and so determine to have a grateful and gracious heart in the matter—to serve another with a giving heart. This takes practice and prayer, but thank God, we can change our attitudes through the power of the Holy Spirit who works in us to do good works.

"I know, LORD, that our lives are not our own. We are not able to plan our own course" (Jeremiah 10:23 NLT).

Direct My Steps, Lord

*J*EREMIAH 10:23 SAYS *"Lord, I know that people's lives are not their own; it is not for them to direct their steps."*

Prov. 3:6 *"In all your ways acknowledge Him and He will direct your steps."*

Our lives are not our own; we have been bought with a price—the precious blood of the Lamb. Therefore, we are to live for Him in all ways and in all things. We must allow God to direct our lives and the steps we are to take on our journey. Our steps, as believers, are ordered by God and He delights in our way. How does God order our steps? I believe we are led and directed by the Word of God and the Holy Spirit, circumstances, and an inner witness. The Word of God is a lamp, a light unto our feet so we can see where we are walking. It is a beautiful thing to watch the Lord lead and direct where He has planned for us to go. His Word will speak to us personally in confirming or directing. The Holy Spirit will make the way clear through His leading. Circumstances will work out so that you can move ahead. He will make your paths straight for you and remove the obstacles when it is time. Then you will experience a peace inside your heart—an inward witness. Allow God to guide you through His Word. It is a joy and a blessing!

NOVEMBER 14

*"My beloved spoke and said to me, 'Arise, My darling, My
beautiful one, come with Me'" (Solomon 2:10).*

PREPARE FOR YOUR GROOM

OH, HOW I long for you to prepare yourself for Me, your groom. Deck yourself with garments of righteousness and holiness! Sew the pearls of goodness and humility upon your veil of purity, then, let it flow down from your head to your shoulders to the ground. Bring to Me a heart of passion and love—I pursue after you with all My heart—you are My beloved and the wedding is at hand. There will be dancing and singing, feasting and great joy for all who attend our wedding. Spend time with Me while these are the days of preparation…get to know Me; you will find yourself becoming more and more beautiful as you gaze upon My face. Do not wear your veil over your face for you are Mine, and I want your face to shine with the sweet oil of the Holy Spirit. The big day is drawing near—don't forget to prepare yourself for Me. Shall we meet tonight? I am always ready to be with you—I am passionate about you. My darling, My dove—come away with Me.

NOVEMBER 15

"Saying, 'The Lord is risen indeed, and hath appeared to Simon'" (Luke 24:34 KJV).

A GLIMPSE OF GLORY

I WAS THINKING ABOUT the resurrection of Jesus this week, and the Lord gave me a tiny glimpse of what it was like that morning. The light was so bright it was blinding, the exertion of power from the Holy Spirit that brought Jesus out of the tomb was like an atomic bomb. Jesus' face was filled with super victory and joy as He opened His eyes! Tremendous excitement was radiating from Jesus as He stepped forward out of the grave clothes, because He had just conquered death in the face! The demons screamed in complete defeat. He made the way for you and me—to live forever with Him and to be resurrected from the dead at that day! Jesus' victory and triumph was remarkably outstanding and He knew it! Today we greatly rejoice!

There is a saying that goes back to the time of the early church that when a believer was marching off to be martyred, with his hands tied he was led to the stake, and the soldier would ask him if he had any last words. He would shout out loud for all to hear, *"He is Risen!"* Little did the guards know that in the nearby hills the Christians were watching the whole time and they would echo back, *"He is Risen indeed!"* So they say that was how the Christians would greet each other. He is Risen! He is Risen indeed!

November 16

"Finally, be strong in the Lord and in His mighty power" (Ephesians 6:10).

Keep Strong

I WOKE UP THIS morning and thought about the Father's goodness to us. He is so good all the time. I believe that He always does what is right and just—He brings good out of what was meant to be against us, meant to shake us, and move us out of faith and into the darkness of doubt and fear. Jesus is building an army of believers that will shake the darkness and the world in His Name! We need to go through difficulties in order to become unmovable in the Lord. Keep strong in the strength of the Lord and keep your eyes on His ability to preserve you to the end. Walk in His power and love, and praise Him for what He is doing in you. He is always worthy of our praise and adoration. *"Surely goodness and mercy will follow you all the days of your life and you will dwell in the house of the Lord forever!"*

NOVEMBER 17

"But I trust in You, Lord, I say, 'You are my God'" (Psalm 31:14).

WHAT TO DO IN TROUBLED TIMES

I KNOW WHAT I will do when tough times come against me, I will choose to rely, trust in, place all my confidence in God who is my strength. He is my God. Personally and intimately, I know Him. And I know He is faithful in all His ways. He will never let me down. He sees everything I am going through—the difficult times and the good times. This, I know, is that He will deliver me from those people who seek my hurt and from situations that cause my heart to fear.

O God, when I turn my gaze to Your face and I take my focus off of circumstances and people, I behold Your glory, and I feel secure in Your merciful love. I know You will never ever leave me alone to battle my trials by myself. You are with me. You will put to silence the enemy of my soul who spews out lies and destruction.

Ah, Your goodness is so precious. It will never run out. Because I trust in You without wavering, You prize me with Your blessings, and You hold me safe in our secret meeting place within Your presence.

Taken from Psalm 31:14-20 (Eilers' paraphrase)

November 18

"And Miriam sang this song: 'Sing to the LORD, for He has triumphed gloriously; He has hurled both horse and rider into the sea'"(Exodus 15:21).

He has Triumphed!

WHEN THE ISRAELITES left Egypt, where they were slaves under Egyptian rule, the Egyptian armies pursued after them with horses and chariots. The Israelites were sore afraid as they saw the riders coming in the distance. God, however, had a plan and caused the Red Sea to open in two for the Israelites to pass through to the other side. When they were almost to the other side, the Egyptian armies were following close behind them, also going through the dry ground of the parted sea. God's people were frightened, but God had a plan for their complete deliverance. He caused the waters to come back together again, and closed in on all the Egyptians with their horses and chariots while the Israelites were safely on the other side. The horse and rider he has cast into the sea! Miriam, Moses sister, led the people in exuberant praise to God dancing and singing! How happy they were when God showed up. And how happy are we when we find relief from a heavy burden we've been carrying, or after fighting and resisting the powers of darkness, or after we have been assailed with much fear and trembling over matters, and our deliverance has finally come. Our God shows up! And just one touch from His little finger upon our distresses and calamity, and we are changed from despair to hope and joy! We get our perspective back and we praise and adore our God who moved on our behalf.

NOVEMBER 19

"Submit yourselves, then, to God. Resist the devil,
and he will flee from you" (James 4:7).

DO NOT BE MOVED

THE ENEMY IS tricky. He will use all his ability to work against us. He will try to pry open a door that was once open to him, to see if he can gain a foothold again. That is why resisting him is so crucial.

He doesn't want to lose his ground. He fights all the harder when he sees he's losing. That is when we lift up the shield of faith, which will ward off his flaming darts. We must stand without flinching. We must stand determined not to give in to the least of his tactics. I believe when we stand our ground, and we are determined to take back any ground we have lost, there will be a huge battle that will go on inside of us. The battle is in our mind. God is greater, and the great Lion of Judah roars over His people and fights for them and their sure victory!

Do not be moved by the schemes and devices of Satan. He uses fear, doubt, guilt, and deception as his main tools. If they have worked in your life in the past, he will expect them to still work, so he will test you on every side, until he knows he has no access in those areas of your life. Stand therefore, for your victory will be manifested in due time.

NOVEMBER 20

"Even to your old age and gray hairs I am He, I am He who will sustain you. I have made you and I will carry you; I will sustain you and I will rescue you" (Isaiah 46:4).

TRUST ME TO CARRY YOU

DO YOU TRUST Me child? Let Me carry you. Don't worry about anything but talk to Me about it. Let thankfulness surround your soul. Rest in Me as we walk this way together. My love for you is so great—you can rely wholly on it to never change. It is steadfast and true. In this valley I will carry you, and you will find Me faithful. Set your face like a flint to trust Me to bring you up out of this valley. Depend on My love for you. I will protect you and deliver you from the evil one. I am more than just a close friend, I am your God—I am your Maker, your understanding Father. What I am doing in your heart may not make sense to you at this time, but I know that each step of trust is making you more like Me. Trust Me to complete the good work I first began in you when you first believed in Me. This is a season of learning to lean yet more into My Love for you. It is a season in which I am teaching you total dependence on Me.

Rest now. Let Me carry you.

November 21

> *"I waited patiently for the LORD; He turned to me and heard my cry. He lifted me out of the slimy pit, out of the mud and mire; He set my feet on a rock and gave me a firm place to stand. He put a new song in my mouth, a hymn of praise to our God. Many will see and fear and put their trust in the LORD"* (Psalm 40:1).

Psalm of Victory

THE DARKNESS WAS thick around me and evil engulfed my soul. Fears and doubts clamored loudly in unison. My flesh was weak. I felt sick from my relentless tormentors. I felt like I was slipping, and called out to the Lord. I reminded Him of His promise to deliver me and establish my footsteps. I had no appetite. I was stripped of all joy. The enemy lingered in hopes to take me down to the dust. I called out again to my God. I told Him I trusted Him, and asked Him to lift me out of the miry pit—my enemies were too strong for me.

Then God said, *"Enough!"* I felt my feet being lifted up and set upon a rock. My steps were steadied. He brought me out of the pit and hid me in His tabernacle under His wing. The light broke through and the evil fled at His rebuke.

God has His reasons for heavy trials that afflict us.

We must trust His hand that He knows just when to lift us out. He is building us and teaching us lessons we can only learn through the fires of great trial.

"The weapons we fight with are not the weapons of the world. On the contrary, they have divine power to demolish strongholds. We demolish arguments and every pretension that sets itself up against the knowledge of God, and we take captive every thought to make it obedient to Christ" (2 Corinthians 10:4-5).

MIGHTY BEFORE GOD

WHAT DOES IT mean that the weapons of our warfare are mighty before God? The battle is in the mind of the believer, and thus we must learn to pull down strongholds and bring every thought captive to the obedience of Christ. If God says for us to do this, then we can be sure that it is possible.

One of the chief weapons of our warfare is the Word of God. The Bible says our warfare is *"mighty."* Let's look at this for a minute. *Mighty* means strong, powerful, able. What does our warfare have the power to do? The Word of God has the power to demolish, pull down, destroy, take down, take apart, any strongholds that the enemy has trapped us in. What is a *stronghold*? It is like a military stronghold, demons stand guard over. No matter how strong walled a fortress they think they have in or over our thoughts, it can be demolished by the Word of God.

So we are to pull down every thought that argues against the Word of God. The devil will throw thoughts into your mind to make you doubt and fear. He wants you to believe his lies and falter in your faith. Whatever the enemy has used in the past to bring you down, he will try again, to see if you really have fortified your mind against his wiles.

Then, we take captive every thought of ours, and bring it under subjection to the Word of God—to conform to what God says—truth instead of lies.

NOVEMBER 23

*"...until we all reach unity in the faith and in the knowledge
of the Son of God and become mature, attaining to the whole
measure of the fullness of Christ" (Ephesians 4:13).*

GROW UP IN HIM

WE CANNOT LIVE this Christian life with a lackadaisical attitude. We must be alert and ready to fight against the wiles of the devil. Watch that you enter not into temptation. Getting by on mediocre living for God will not do anymore. In these days there must be a focus and a zeal—a determination and a passion, that will carry us through safely in every battle of the soul.

We must cultivate our love of God, until we grow strong and unflinching in it. It is His love that casts out all fear. When we know and are assured of being loved and cared for by God, we can have a confidence and a peace that keeps us in and through the fiery furnaces of life's trials. God is calling all Christians everywhere to rise up, and grow up in the knowledge of God and in His love, and to be a mature child of God ready to do all the Master's bidding.

"Now to Him who is able to do immeasurably more
than all we ask or imagine, according to His power
that is at work within us" (Ephesians 3:20).

I BELIEVE

NEVER GIVE UP in the fight for good. Hold fast to your faith in times of great hardship. God's got a plan. God's got a purpose. Hold fast to Him and confess your faith to Him. Tell Him, *"I do believe. I do believe You love me. I do believe You are breaking all the chains from off my life. I do believe I am victorious in You. I do believe the anointing of the Holy Spirit breaks the yoke of any bondage off of me. I do believe I will come through and that victoriously!"* God is with me, in me, for me. He fights for me and with me against my foes. He always wins! I am holding fast to what God said in His Word. I am casting down every argument and lie that is contrary to the Word of God. I stand fast, unmovable, unshakable. I belong to the Holy Spirit. My mind belongs to Him, and I will not tolerate doubts or fears of any kind. I live, speak, eat, breathe, the Living Word of God empowered by the Holy Spirit!

November 25

*"being confident of this, that He who began a good work in you will carry
it on to completion until the day of Christ Jesus" (Philippians 1:6).*

Wonderfully Preserved

HAVE YOU EVER doubted that God would keep you and bring you safely into His Kingdom? The devil throws countless lies at the believer, and tries to get us to live in fear of losing the salvation God gave us through faith in Jesus Christ. Or he tries to bring doubt that God will finish the work He began in us. Many great saints have wrestled and fought against such doubts and fears. The good news is that no matter how we feel, or what thoughts the enemy throws our way, the truth of the matter is, that our salvation in Christ is perfectly secure and God, Himself, will make sure that we arrive safely into His Kingdom. Not only that, but we can rely on God to keep working in us until the day He calls us home. We are His and He is ours. God began the work in us, and He will complete it no matter how rough the waters get. We will be wonderfully preserved blameless unto His Kingdom.

NOVEMBER 26

"The temptations in your life are no different from what others experience. And God is faithful. He will not allow the temptation to be more than you can stand. When you are tempted, He will show you a way out so that you can endure" (1 Corinthians 10:13 NLT).

IT'S NOTHING NEW

OMETIMES WE MAKE the big mistake of thinking that the particular temptation or testing we are experiencing is, or has been, experienced only by us alone. No one else has gone through this like I am. I had once thought this myself, having to continually struggle with a particular testing of the spirit and soul. One day, however, as I was searching the internet for some more understanding on my problem, I was drawn to a site that God knew I needed to read. I had found that there were others who had and did indeed battle what I was battling with—although it was not a large percent of people. So there were other believers who God had allowed to pass through these very same fires that I was going through, and God had brought them through to stronger faith, even though the condition remained.

Thus, when you are tempted to conclude that you are all alone in your suffering, know that someone has gone, or is, going through, the same trial in various ways and degrees. But God is faithful to give you a way to be able to bear up under it. One sure way is always choosing to believe God's Word instead of thoughts, feelings or whatever would cause you to doubt. Know that He is faithful to sustain you.

NOVEMBER 27

"But Moses told the people, 'Don't be afraid. Just stand still and watch the LORD rescue you today. The Egyptians you see today will never be seen again'" (Exodus 14:13 NLT).

FIGHT OR REST

THERE IS A time to fight and a time to rest in our Christian walk. A time to stand fast in the war waged against our soul. A time to stop striving and to begin relaxing in the arms of Almighty God. There are different seasons for all these things. If you are going through a difficult time of trial ask the Lord which season you are in.

I remember the other day I was engaged in spiritual warfare and I fought so hard bringing every thought captive, resisting the devil's lies. I thought I had the victory, but found myself so stressed again that I cried out to the Lord. Then God showed me that it was a time to stand fast, and also to rest in His ability to take care of me and all my concerns. I was not to battle anymore, but to stand still, and see His salvation. So I did and victory gradually became mine. How does God want you to handle your particular trials you are facing right now? Ask Him.

*"Therefore, there is now no condemnation for those
who are in Christ Jesus" (Romans 8:1).*

No Condemnation

O YOU EVER feel a continual guilt nagging at you? Do you ever feel that you aren't forgiven of all your sins? How about condemnation and other like negative thoughts and feelings? You are not alone. Countless believers in the Lord go through these types of temptations. And they are temptations. The enemy of our soul wants us to feel that we are unforgiveable and unloved by God. He throws lies out to our weakest area in order to trip and trick us into believing God is somehow not pleased with us, and that we are such a sinner that God has turned away from us.

These are all lies from the pit of the devil. The Word of God tells us that if we confess our sins, God is faithful and just to forgive us our sins and to cleanse us from ALL unrighteousness. That means ALL. Past, present, and future sins have been paid for by the blood of Jesus Christ. We are clean! We need never to go around with a guilt complex. God never changes His love for us—never. Jesus' sacrifice on Calvary took care of the sin of all humanity. We just need to believe it and receive it. To be a Christian strong in faith, it is important to note that we must resist all the lies of the enemy, and hold fast to the truth of the Word of God.

NOVEMBER 29

*"Truly my soul waiteth upon God: from Him cometh my
salvation. He only is my rock and my salvation; He is my
defence; I shall not be greatly moved" (Psalm 62:1-2 KJV).
"We are hard pressed on every side, but not crushed; perplexed,
but not in despair; persecuted, but not abandoned; struck
down, but not destroyed" (2 Corinthians 4: 8-9).*

WAITING IN THE STORM

I THINK ONE OF the most difficult things we can go through is having to wait for our deliverance when we are in great pain, discomfort, depression and discouragement that seems to last for days and days. Our heart can begin to feel very weary, and we may start getting thoughts of hopelessness about our struggles. I wrestle with clinical depression and anxiety disorder, and when my medication is not working, all havoc can break loose. The enemy preys on my weakness of a chemical imbalance in my brain. The "feel good" chemicals are very low therefore I find myself feeling depleted and down. I am susceptible to unreasonable fears, doubts, torments, anxiety and emotional vulnerability.

One day I was experiencing all of this chaos, and I told the Lord I was really hurting, and that I was tired of this particular infliction. His words were clear to me from Psalm 40 and 62 that I was to wait (even in my misery) patiently for Him to bring me out and for my medicine to take effect.

When we feel like we can't go on a minute more because we are sorely pressed, know this, that God never makes a mistake in what He allows into our lives. He will indeed come to our deliverance, but we must train our hearts and minds to wait as best we can on His timing. God knows your personal struggle. He said He wouldn't fail us and He never does. Trust Him today.

"The LORD brings the counsel of the nations to nothing; He makes the plans of the peoples of no effect. The counsel of the LORD stands forever, the plans of His heart to all generations. Blessed is the nation whose God is the LORD, the people He has chosen as His own inheritance" (Psalm 33:10-12 NKJV).

PRAYER FOR AMERICA

Based on Psalm 33:10-12

DEAR FATHER, THANK You for this great country of ours. We pray that the counsel and plans of those who plot evil against our country be brought to nothing. That they would have no lasting influence over our people. We ask You to make the plans and schemes of those individuals who intend to stir up violence and unrest, evil of every kind toward our nation, of no lasting effect. Let those who plot ungodliness against our nation get snared in their own devices. Let Your blessed and powerful, perfect counsel and Your plans for America stand forever and be accomplished. Oh, Lord, do all that is in Your heart to all our generations. Help us to work along with You. Make our nation a blessed nation once again, a happy people who trust in You. Take away our disgrace and trouble as we turn our hearts and souls to pursue exceedingly after You. You have chosen this great nation for Yourself to be a witness and a beacon of light to the nations. We bow our knee to Your Lordship, and ask You to forgive us our transgressions, proudness of heart, running after idols, perverting Your truth. Cover this land with the blood of the Lamb, Jesus Christ, Your only Son, and turn the tables in favor for good. Let Your praises be heard loud and clear throughout this nation. We ask in Jesus' name, Amen.

DECEMBER 1

"Have not I commanded thee? Be strong and courageous; be not terrified nor affrighted, for with thee is Jehovah thy God in every place whither thou goest" (Joshua 1:9 Young's Literal Translation).

FOR THIS DAY AND TIME

LORD, GUIDE MY anxious heart. Help me, and teach me how to navigate through these uncertain and somewhat scary times in our world. Show me what is true and what is not. You said that Your people were not to be full of anxiety, but peace. Is this really possible, Lord, in this day? How can we do this? I can hear Your voice and feel Your hand turning me around to look at You. Speak to me, Lord, I am listening.

"Have I not reassured you that whatever I allow to touch your life will always be something that someone has gone or is going through in various manners. The test is always to strengthen you. It will always be something that you will be able to handle and that will not take you down. You will always be able to walk through it. I have also promised to be with you and give you My peace.

There are two keys I have given you on how to maneuver through the forest of trials and make it through. The first one is, you must keep your eyes on Me. Not on the problem, not on how bad things appear, not on the darkness and confusion, but on Me and My power over situations. My love, My plan, My purpose and Will. Second, You are to guard your mind from fearful and unsettling thoughts. Do not allow them to linger and control you. You must choose to think on what is good, right and just. Know this, that at the appointed time I will always answer you. Do not be alarmed. I've got you in My hand. Remember your times

(your life and all that concerns you) are in My hand. Allow your faith to grow strong during these days. I will keep you. I will only allow you to be in the furnace of fire for a short time. Remember again, the Refiner knows exactly when to take the silver out of the furnace, and not a second too late or too soon. Trust My plan. Trust My purpose. They come from My heart of Love. I've got this one, too."

DECEMBER 2

"And without faith it is impossible to please God, because anyone who comes to Him must believe that He exists and that He rewards those who earnestly seek Him" (Hebrews 11:6).

GROWING FAITH

WE CANNOT BE passive in our faith in God. It must be active and constantly in motion. Believing and trusting the very hand of God for all things. We must trust Him for deliverance, healing, provisions, peace, guidance, hope, for our very life, and all that concerns us. We must exercise our faith every opportunity that comes our way. A faith not worked is a weak faith and will not hold up under the floods of adversities. But even in the floods we can develop more faith, as we choose moment by moment to cling to our Savior and His Word. Faith grows, and as it grows it receives answers to prayer and a more intimate life with God. He is the author and finisher of our faith, and if He sees us not growing in our faith, trials will come our way so we can learn to live a little more by faith and not by feelings or sight. Faith pleases God, and He can work with even a small amount of faith if we let Him. However, He truly desires it to grow so greater things can be accomplished for His Kingdom and mountains can be removed, so we can receive what we are believing for.

DECEMBER 3

*"But I trust in You, LORD; I say, 'You are my God. My
times are in Your hands; deliver me from the hands of my
enemies, from those who pursue me'" (Psalm 31:14-15).*

MY TIMES

*I*T IS OF great comfort to me that my God and Savior has my
entire life in His hands. He has designated all the events that
would or have come into my life. Because I belong to Him, I
can thoroughly put my confidence in His plans for me. Nothing comes to me
unless it is allowed by my Gracious Father's hand. The day I die is ordered and
in His hand. Nothing can take my life until my appointed time. Every hardship I encounter is designed for me personally.

I recall the day I heard that my only child, my 22 year old son, was hit by
a car and did not survive. God knew beforehand that I would have this horrible tragedy barge into my life. Because He knew beforehand, He lovingly
prepared my heart in various ways so that when the worst happened, I could
say with all my heart, *"The Lord gave and the Lord takes away; Blessed be
the name of the Lord!"* I raised my eyes and my arms up to heaven and wor-
shipped the God who loves me.

Can we take what God allows to come into our lives with a heart that is
willing to praise, thank and adore Him? Because all that we are, all that we
have, all that we will ever be, are in the strong hands of the One who knows
us better than we know ourselves. Can we have peace even in the worst of
times?

DECEMBER 4

"Remember Your word to Your servant, for You have given me hope. My comfort in my suffering is this: Your promise preserves my life" (Psalm 119:49-50).

GOD'S PROMISES

I BELIEVE THAT WHEN we search the Scriptures, God will illumine certain sections, verses, even individual words to our hearts. These words speak to us and build hope within us. Many of them are promises made to all those who put their trust in the Lord. When we are experiencing a difficult season, I believe God wants us to bring His promises, His Word, which He has given us, before Him. Recite it before His ears and in His presence. God's promises cause us to have hope, and hope brings us comfort in our affliction. Rehearse those great and precious promises God has shown you in your time with Him in the Word. Say them out loud. Cling to the truth of them. Believe them. Hold steadfast to the hope that they bring, and your soul will experience great peace and contentment.

DECEMBER 5

"My eyes stay open through the watches of the night, that I may meditate on Your promises" (Psalm 119:148).

A HOLY MEDITATION

*I*T IS DURING the night hours that I long to read and meditate on God's Word. In the Greek, to *meditate,* means to "study, ponder, exercise myself in, practice" (Strong's 3191). In the Oxford Dictionary "to ponder" means to "think about (something) carefully." I think that God wants His people to take His Word and slowly chew upon it, considering what is being said and why. We are to allow our minds, our thinking, to get a hold of God's living words, and eat and digest them as a meal for our soul and spirit.

There are different times of the day and at night when we can meditate and ponder the Scriptures. When we take the time to do this, we are fortifying our heart and mind against the enemy's schemes. We are also instructed in Psalm 119:18, to ask God to open up the eyes of our heart so that we may not only understand what's been said, but that we would search and find the treasures of truth that may appear hidden to us. If we just read the Scriptures quickly, or glance over them without thinking about them, we miss out on a blessing. Take a verse to memorize and break it apart word for word, and you will be illumined by the Holy Spirit who will teach you the truths that lie within.

DECEMBER 6

"Before I was afflicted I went astray, but now
I obey Your word" (Psalm 119:67).
"I know, O LORD, that Your regulations are fair; You
disciplined me because I needed it"(Psalm 119:75 NLT).

GET BACK ON TRACK

HERE ARE TIMES when we get off track from where God wants us to go or what He wants us to do. We begin to follow our own heart and our own devices instead of seeking to know the Father's heart and where He is leading. This can happen innocently by being too busy doing what we think is the Lord's work. We have no time with Him. Or we can choose to take a certain path out of disobedience because we want what we think will bring us satisfaction. Sometimes our eyes become blinded by the things of the world, and we lose that clearness of vision God is calling us to. So when this happens, we can count on it, that our good Father will bring us gently back in line and in tune with Him. Many times this happens in the form of some kind of affliction or trial we encounter that draws us back to the heart of God, trusting in Him for all our needs. It is best, therefore, to always strive to stay close to Him so you need not be chastened.

"God paid a high price for you, so don't be enslaved
by the world" (1 Corinthians 7:23 NLT).
"Furthermore, because we are united with Christ, we have received
an inheritance from God, for He chose us in advance, and He makes
everything work out according to His plan" (Ephesians 1:11).

A HIGH PRICE

THERE WAS A price to pay for God to make us acceptable in His sight. It cost God everything to ransom us back to Himself. It cost Him the very death of His own beloved Son, God Himself. God gave Jesus as the payment to bring us back into fellowship with Him. It cost Jesus everything. It cost the shedding of His precious blood on the cross, forever paying the penalty for all sin, for all time. Since our debt was paid for, we have become free from the bondage of sin and alive unto God. We have passed from death into life eternal through placing our trust in Jesus Christ. We are no longer slaves to sin, to obey it and the lusts thereof. We, instead, belong fully and wholly to God, who has made us His very own beloved child. We have been born into the great inheritance that each child of God has received. We have His seal upon our hearts—the Holy Spirit. The Holy Spirit is the down payment on our inheritance. He is the deposit in God's heavenly Kingdom, guaranteeing our rights as a child of God, until we acquire full possession of it, that is, the redemption of our physical body and our position of ruling and reigning with Christ. The Holy Spirit is God's pledge to us that what we have believed is real and true, and the One in whom we are trusting will do all that He has promised. Since God gave us His all, dear Saints, let us give our all to Him and glorify His holy name.

DECEMBER 8

"My soul, wait silently for God alone, For my expectation is from Him" (Psalm 62:5 NKJV).

ANTICIPATION

GOD WANTS US to always be in expectation for what He will do for and in us. We've prayed. We've been waiting. We don't see the answer. We pray again. No sign of change—things appear to remain untouched. The tempter tells us God is not coming through this time. He will not answer your prayer, but will keep you dangling. Doubts and fear will set in, discouragement, and then our faith level goes down. Wait! God says, as you are waiting for Him to move on your behalf, to wait expectantly. This means to be continually expecting the answer to come. This means to keep anticipating His workings. Do not be moved in the least by what you hear or what you see, just keep your faith level high in expectation. Keep your eyes open for the moving of His hand.

DECEMBER 9

"To Him who loves us and has freed us from our
sins by His blood" (Revelation 1:5).

THE BLOOD OF JESUS

WHEN JESUS DIED on the cross and rose again, redemption was completed for us. Jesus had to shed His blood. He had to be a living sacrifice in order to bring us back to God. His blood is so powerful to cleanse and deliver the vilest sinner. That old song, "There is Power in the Blood" is so true. The blood of Jesus delivers, heals, forgives, washes, saves, protects and preserves us. When we stand under the precious flow of Jesus' blood, we are in perfect harmony with God the Father. This is our position in Heaven. We are seated in heavenly places in Christ because of the blood of the Lamb. If you are ever afraid, cry out to the blood of Jesus and He will deliver you. If you have a need, cry out to the blood of Jesus and He will hear you. It is because of the blood of the Lamb that we can bring all our requests before God and find help in our time of need. *"Cry out, the blood, the blood, the blood of the Lamb washes whiter than snow!"*

December 10

"Therefore He is able to save completely those who come to God through Him, because He always lives to intercede for them" (Hebrews 7:25). "In the same way, the Spirit helps us in our weakness. We do not know what we ought to pray for, but the Spirit Himself intercedes for us through wordless groans" (Romans 8:26).

INTERCESSION

*I*N THESE TWO verses we see that both, Jesus and the Holy Spirit, are making intercession in heaven for us while we are upon earth. We have need that they lift us up in fervent prayer continually. God has not left us on our own to live the Christian life. He is with us and is constantly holding us up in prayer. Jesus continues to shepherd us, His flock.

In John, chapter 17, we get a glimpse into what some of the requests may be that Jesus intercedes for us before the Father. He prays that God would keep us, protect us from the evil one—that would be the schemes, snares and works of Satan. God allows him to go just so far in tempting us. Then Jesus prays that God would use His Word to set us apart from the world. The truth of God's Word activates faith in our hearts to live for Him. Next, Jesus asks that God would make us perfect in union with Him, that God would mature us in our spiritual growth. Jesus finally concludes with sharing His great desire, that we would be with Him forever in heaven to behold His glory, and that we would be filled with the knowledge of the Father's love.

Aren't you thankful that we have such wonderful, faithful intercessors to cry out on our behalf!

DECEMBER 11

*"...give thanks in all circumstances; for this is God's will
for you in Christ Jesus" (1 Thessalonians 5:18).*

A THANKFUL HEART

C AN WE BE thankful when we are not feeling well, or struggling financially, or worried about a wayward child, or a broken marriage? I could go on. The point is that God asks us to have a heart of thanksgiving even when we go through disappointments, trials, suffering of all kinds. You may be thinking how can I thank Him that I have a terminal disease, or I just lost a child by a drunken driver? God wants us to thank Him for the good that will come out of these situations. He promises to work all things for our good. We can thank Him for His wisdom, and that He knows all things and has a plan and purpose. We can thank Him for His unchanging love that He has for us in the midst of all our suffering. We can be grateful and thankful that we are being made more and more like Jesus. We also can be thankful for all our needs that He has taken care of, and for giving us eternal life. A thankful heart is pleasing to God.

DECEMBER 12

*"He came and preached peace to you who were far away
and peace to those who were near" (Ephesians 2:17).*

PEACE

*D*ID YOU KNOW that the gospel of Jesus Christ is one of proclaiming peace and goodwill? Mankind does not have to be
at odds with his Creator, God. Jesus came for this very pur-
pose, to reconcile us to the Father. Even at Jesus' birth the angels in the heavenly realm proclaimed to the shepherds that night, *"Peace and goodwill to all
men."* Jesus was sent into our world to ransom us back to the Father. He came
to break down the wall that separated and kept us from fellowshipping with
God. We no longer have to be regarded as an enemy of God, because Jesus
made the way for us to become God's own child and friend. God's gospel is
the gospel of peace and good news. When mixed with faith, this gospel of
Jesus Christ works in us to bring us to wholeness in spirit, soul and body. God
is thinking peace and good will thoughts towards you today. He wants what
will bless you. He said, *"Peace I leave with you; My peace I give to you. Let
not your heart be troubled; neither let it be afraid"(John 14:27).* So we have
peace *with* God (no more enmity or separation between us). We also have the
peace *of* God (tranquility and security of heart).

DECEMBER 13

"And who knows whether you have not come to the kingdom for such a time as this" (Esther 4:14 English Standard Version)?

FOR SUCH A TIME AS THIS

REMEMBER, IF GOD didn't think you could make it through these chaotic times, He would not have allowed you to be here. You've got what it takes to touch your world where you are. You've got what it takes to stand up for what you believe. You've got what it takes to do all the things God has for you to do. This year, this era, this day, this time, this moment is given to you. God's got you, and all you have to do is keep your eyes on Him and follow Him wherever He leads. Don't borrow from or trouble your mind about tomorrow. If you wake up with your heart still beating and your breathing, there is something you still have to do in this life. Times can get really rough, I know, but if you couldn't do it, God would not have you here. Really.

DECEMBER 14

"The Spirit you received does not make you slaves, so that you live in
fear again; rather, the Spirit you received brought about your adoption
to sonship. And by Him we cry, 'Abba, Father'" (Romans 8:15).

ABBA

As a child of the Living God, we have the privilege and right to call God our Abba, Father. The word *Abba* is "Father" in the Aramaic language. It shows the intimate affection and trust between a child and his father. It is a warm, closely knit relationship. We, as children of such a loving Father, can have complete confidence in Him and in His care for us. It is likened to when a little child looks up at his father with tenderness and trust, and calls him "Daddy" or "Papa." When the two words are added together such as "Abba, Father" this signifies how great the Fatherhood of God is towards us. Our Heavenly Father adopted us unto Himself through faith in His Son, Jesus, and has given us this intimate sonship to enjoy. So being a child of the best and most perfect Father, we can always approach Him with boldness, and not be afraid or timid that He will turn us away. We can run into His arms and feel safe and loved. Always. (gotquestions.org)

DECEMBER 15

"Into Your hands I commit my spirit; deliver me,
LORD, my faithful God" (Psalm 31:5).

GIVE HIM YOUR ALL

*T*HE LONGER I live this life, the more I am convinced that God's Word is absolutely true, and that we can entrust our total being upon it. We can trust God with our daily life and for our eternal destiny. We can entrust our very spirit, soul, and body over to His care and keeping. He brought us forth from our mother's womb and gave us life. He has sustained us thus far, and will continue, until the day we take our last breath and cross over behind the veil. Even then, He will carry us over, for He will never leave us to flounder on our own. We haven't ever passed that way before, that is dying, but He has experienced it and knows what we need in order to make it through our journey safely and peacefully. The longer I live, the more I trust Him, and the more I love Him. I believe we grieve His heart when we doubt Him or allow fear to control our thinking. Remember, it is faith that pleases God. He delights in blessing the soul who, without any reservations, gives himself, and all that concerns him, over to His care and keeping.

DECEMBER 16

"He is not afraid of bad news. His heart remains secure, full of confidence in the LORD. His heart is steady, and he is not afraid. In the end he will look triumphantly at his enemies" (Psalm 112:7-8 GOD'S WORD Translation).

SECURITY

THERE IS A great peace that comes when we know we are secure and safe. God tells us that when we trust in Him He will keep us safe, and take care of us as a Father His child. When circumstances come to cause our hearts to fear, we can be at peace knowing, that whatever the situation, whatever the concern, God will handle it and show us exactly what to do. He will guide our very steps and thoughts as we abide in His Word and in His love. We can remain steadfast and immoveable in our faith, for our confidence is in someone who will never disappoint us, let us down, or leave us on our own. He knows the way and will take us through. The world may crouch and huddle in fear of what's happening around them. However, we know what to do and who to go to. We can keep our hearts from terror and fright. It is important for us, as believers, to grasp this truth and not to allow our thoughts to run away with fear or dread. Don't let anything disturb your peace of heart and mind you have in God.

DECEMBER 17

"When I am afraid, I put my trust in You" (Psalm 56:3).

FEARFULNESS

*T*ODAY, I WANT to look at the Christian's struggle with fear. Countless scriptures tell us not to fear, but the emotions of fear are so strong and intense that many times we succumb to them. God is certainly not the author of fear in any way. We are not given a spirit of fear, but a spirit of power, love and a sound reasonable mind. Fear exaggerates situations, and when we listen to it, it can paralyze us from doing the right things that can bring us stability and peace. I have been assaulted with fears of all natures by the enemy. What I have learned and continue to learn, is that fear is simply an emotion, a feeling that need not be paid attention to, unless it is something real like a fire in the house or someone breaking in, or being stripped of our health or finances. And then, even in these situations, God can steady our hearts and instruct us what to do, leading our hearts to peace. If God tells us not to fear, then it is possible not to give in to fear.

The Bible tells us that when we are afraid we are to do something. We are to put our trust in God, in His care and keeping. It is a training process—training our hearts and minds to trust, rather than to fear. Since fear is an emotion, it need not be listened to, and is to be replaced by God's Word. Sometimes we have to do this many times throughout the day before it becomes a habit. We are such fearful sheep at times, and God knows this. He has compassion on us and is constantly reassuring us that He is with us. Let us choose today, when fear assails us, to think of a scripture verse to counteract it. This will give your mind time to settle down, and you will be better able to make a sound decision about how to handle the fear.

DECEMBER 18

*"For everything that was written in the past was written to
teach us, so that through the endurance taught in the Scriptures
and the encouragement they provide we might have hope."
"May the God of hope fill you with all joy and peace as
you trust in Him, so that you may overflow with hope by
the power of the Holy Spirit" (Romans15:4 &13).*

THE GOD OF HOPE

GOD IS THE God of all hope. Hope is having the expectation that something good is going to happen. We have the expectation that God will perform His Word. We have the expectation that because of our faith in Christ, we will have eternal life, and that when we die our bodies will be one day resurrected. We expect that this will happen because God is our Father, and He will take care of us and provide for our needs. God's Word tells us that we can securely hold on to our hope, because it is an anchor of the soul that is both sure and steadfast. Why can we have hope in this life and not despair? We can have hope because God will not lie to us. The Bible says that it is *"impossible for God to lie."* So we can conclude that every word that is in our Bible is God-breathed and is true. We can place our complete confidence in it. God also tells us that we will never be disappointed for having hope. Therefore, we will keep holding firmly to the hope that is set before us with joy.

DECEMBER 19

*"In You our ancestors put their trust; they trusted and You
delivered them. To You they cried out and were saved; in You
they trusted and were not put to shame"* (Psalm 22:4-5).

MY DELIVERER

IT IS SO good to know that when we are in trouble we can cry
out to the Lord and He will hear and answer us. Our trust
in Him is not in vain. I like today's verse so much because it
reminds me of my own father who loved and trusted God. He trusted, and
God delivered him out of his troubles. So I take my Daddy as an example
of what to do when I am in need. God can be trusted to help us with anything that brings trouble into our lives. He can be trusted that He will come
through and deliver us again and again. Sometimes deliverance doesn't mean
He takes us out of the situation, but that He enables us to maneuver victoriously through it. I choose to put all my trust in my Deliverer, Jesus! I know
and have experienced His faithful deliverance. I will not be disappointed.

DECEMBER 20

*"I keep my eyes always on the LORD. With Him at my
right hand, I will not be shaken" (Psalm 16:8).*

EYES ON JESUS

WHEN WE FACE times in our lives of great uncertainty, it is vitally important not to allow ourselves to be swept away by the terrible waves. God tells us what perspective we are to have and to walk in through times like these. We must make a conscious decision about what we are going to put our focus on. The enemy would love to have us focus on our fearful situation, our feelings, our loss, our dilemma, because if we stay in that place long enough, we will certainly become over-whelmed. God knows this, and that is why He had David write this passage for us in Psalms. It is just for us. We must choose to set the Lord always before us, whether we are in a trying time or a good time. We are to place our focus on Jesus. He is our center—our hub. Everything must revolve around Him and His heart. We pray about everything like He told us to, and He will give us the proper perspective on how to see and handle our circumstance. Eyes on Jesus! Why? Because when we purpose to keep our hearts and thoughts on Him and His Word, we will not be easily shaken, rattled, or afraid.

December 21

"to open their eyes, so they may turn from darkness to light and from the power of Satan to God. Then they will receive forgiveness for their sins and be given a place among God's people, who are set apart by faith in Me" (Acts 26:18).

The Gospel

WHEN YOU SHARE Jesus with someone, do you ever wonder if you told them the whole gospel, hoping you didn't miss something you should have said? I believe sometimes we can become so worried whether or not we explained it the "right way." We may tremble at the thought that their eternal destiny hangs in the balance, and what we say can change their life forever. Did we make the gospel clear enough for them to understand? My friends, the gospel is so simple. Let's not complicate it. A little child can understand it.

I love the way the Apostle Paul shared the gospel with King Agrippa in the Book of Acts. First, he says, we are to preach the good news so that people's spiritual eyes would be opened. When their eyes are opened, they can receive the truth. We tell them to turn from their darkness to God's light. To turn from the power of the devil, to the power of God. Why? So that they may receive forgiveness for their sins through faith in Christ's death and resurrection. They will receive their inheritance as a child of God. So simple. Faith in Jesus. Just believing on Him for forgiveness. It's not so much having the perfect wording to share, or exact prayer with the listener, because God is steadfastly looking at the cry of their heart. If they believe, they will receive eternal life.

The next step is to teach them how to grow in Christ and in their new faith. They are born again by the Holy Spirit and have received a new nature, but they must be taught how to walk out their Christian walk. Once they are saved they are sealed by the Holy Spirit of promise. Now the wonderful journey of faith begins.

Remember, the main thing is to preach Jesus and Him crucified and raised again from the dead, so that all sins can be forgiven.

DECEMBER 22

"But He knows the way that I take; when He has tested me, I will come forth as gold" (Job 223:10).

OUR TESTS

THE TESTS THAT we go through do not just come to us arbitrarily. Each test is carefully and thoughtfully planned and prepared by God Himself. Each of them is designed to accomplish a specific purpose in our lives. I truly believe this. God does nothing without knowing the end result. You see, He knows the way that each of us takes. He knows the choices we make, and the motives that lie behind them. He watches us and knows when we need to go through a test. And so, we are tested and tried in an area that God wants us to mature in. We will be tested until we pass the test. We then will come forth as gold. Our faith will have grown a little more pleasing to the Father. Welcome, therefore, tests for they are producing righteousness in us.

DECEMBER 23

*"With joy you will drink deeply from the fountain
of salvation" (Isaiah 12:3 NLT)!*

DON'T LOSE YOUR JOY

*I*T IS SO easy to lose our joy in this world with so much stress and continual problems. Yet over and over God tells us to rejoice and be glad. How often do we obey His request? I find myself praying, *"Lord, restore to me the joy of my salvation."* I believe what happens is that we forget how wonderful God is, and what He really has done for us. When we think about it, that we have been given a gift—not just any gift, but the gift of eternal life in Jesus Christ; we are connected to the very life of God. It is a free gift to receive and to begin enjoying right now. For Christ, Himself, is that eternal life. We can enjoy the fruits of this life as we walk with Him and abide in His Word.

Knowing that along with this free gift, that we don't have to labor for, comes complete forgiveness of sins, also a place reserved for us in heaven, an inheritance that never fades away, and the fruit of the Spirit. One of these fruits is joy. I believe when we mediate on the truths of our free gift and the love that God has for us, and as we begin to be thankful and grateful, we will find our joy returning. Jesus said that out of our belly shall flow rivers of living water. This living water is the Holy Spirit's presence which brings us joy! So we can take the first step in igniting joy back in us again by remembering the gift, being grateful for it, and reveling in the goodness and mercy of God.

*"He was despised and rejected by mankind, a man of suffering, and
familiar with pain. Like one from whom people hide their faces
He was despised, and we held Him in low esteem" (Isaiah3:3).
"Of the greatness of His government and peace there will be no end. He
will reign on David's throne and over his kingdom, establishing and
upholding it with justice and righteousness from that time on and forever.
The zeal of the LORD Almighty will accomplish this"(Isaiah 9:6-7).*

MESSIAH

*T*HE DEVOUT JEWISH people were waiting for their Messiah
and believed He would come to them. However, they were only
looking for Messiah to come as their deliverer and ruling King.
He would rescue them from their enemies, and then set up His kingdom on
earth. There were many prophecies in the Old Testament that foretold the
coming of this Messiah, and the Jewish people clung to this hope. But they
missed the complete picture of who He was and would be. They were so intent
on looking for Messiah to come as their ruling King, that they were blinded
to the prophecies that foretold that He would first come as a suffering servant,
and then the second time as reigning King. So when Messiah was born in a
lowly stable, they over-looked His appearance and did not believe.

Later, Messiah performed many miracles in their midst, proving He
was sent from God, yet they still would not believe. One day He spoke to a
woman who came out to the well to draw water and told her of living water
and eternal life. She said, *"I know that Messiah is coming"* (who is called
Christ). *"When He comes, He will tell us all things."* Messiah was right there
in front of her and He said, *"I who speak to you am He"* (John, chapter 4).

This man who spoke so graciously was Jesus the Christ. All who come to
Him today can receive salvation and forgiveness of sins because of His sacrificial death on the cross, His burial and resurrection from the dead. Now
we are looking for Him to return a second time as ruling King, to reign in
righteousness and justice. He first stepped into our world as Savior, but will

soon come as King. Will you take Him as your Messiah Redeemer? Then you will take part in His Kingdom which will have no end.

DECEMBER 25

"The wages of sin is death, but the gift of God is eternal life [which is the life of God Himself] through Jesus Christ our Lord" (Romans 6:23).

THAT HOLY NIGHT!

GOD WAS PATIENTLY waiting to give mankind the greatest surprise they would ever receive. He must have anticipated with unspeakable joy, the day He could finally give and unveil the extravagant, majestic, wondrous gift to mankind—Jesus!

And He must have leaped for joy at the thought that all mankind could now be His own once again through the sacrificial gift He was sending—the Lamb, Jesus.

The Day on planet earth arrived! The angels could not help but burst out loud in angelic song and praise. The brightest star ever to be seen arose in the dark night sky. Wise men, Kings saw it, and followed it. It was a sign of God's precious surprise—Baby Jesus.

Shepherds heard and saw the hosts of the Lord singing—how magnificent! They were announcing the coming of the highest, greatest, magnificent, superior gift that God would unwrap before mankind—His Son, Jesus.

The News got out! God had bent down over the entire earth, and upon His most beloved and prized creation—mankind. He was proclaiming that Peace was to be finally made between God and man. Unlimited kindness, inexhaustible mercy and grace—continuous forgiveness—Good Will was to be available to all men. And God gave us a Savior, Jesus.

That Holy Night marked the giving of God's Mystery gift. Mary held Him close and pondered over God's plan with awe and wonder. The unwrapping of the life, death and resurrection of Jesus took about 33 years, and still to this day we are unwrapping more and more—it continues forever, treasures found in this one Supreme Surprise gift of God, King Jesus!

Singing glory to God in the Highest!!!

December 26

"For a great and effective door is opened unto me, and there are many adversaries" (1 Corinthians 16:9 KJ2000 Bible).

Opportunities/Adversaries

Sometimes, when God opens a door for us, and places a platform before us that will greatly further the gospel, there will come into our life those that will oppose and withstand what we are doing. They will come against us in hopes that we will back down, come off our platform, and go out the door. The Bible says in 1 Peter 5:8, that we are to be alert to what's going on around us because our adversary, the devil, walks about looking for someone he can take down and devour. We are to be wise concerning the schemes of Satan because he is searching to trip us up and take us out of the race. He hates us standing up for righteousness and preaching the gospel of Christ. Sometimes he uses men to bring accusations and opposition into our life. These people are poisonous and try to tear us down in some way or discredit our calling. God says to resist such opposition, and to stand firm in our faith, continuing to pursue the course He has placed us on.

DECEMBER 27

"Praise be to the God and Father of our Lord Jesus Christ, the Father of compassion and the God of all comfort, who comforts us in all our troubles, so that we can comfort those in any trouble with the comfort we ourselves receive from God" (2 Corinthians 1:3-4).

COMFORT OTHERS

WE MAY ASK, *"What good can come out of all my suffering?"* There are numerous positive results if we allow God to do His work in us. He is always working with us, transforming our hearts and minds, getting rid of the old bad stuff, and renewing us with the good. When we suffer, whatever situation we find ourselves in pain over, God always gives us a way in which we can be encouraged while going through it. He will bring someone or something into our lives that will cheer us on and bring us some comfort. When we realize what has brought us some comfort in our particular trial, we can be used to comfort another who may be experiencing similar suffering. Being able to lift up another who is struggling is one of the "good" things that can come out from our own suffering.

When I lost my only child, my 22 year old son, I was bent over in the extreme pain that accompanies grief. God, in His mercy and goodness, brought people, books, even pets and other things into my life to help and encourage me on my grief journey. Over the years I have experienced much healing. The very things that have brought me some hope when my life was so dark, I find myself sharing with other moms who have also lost a child. God always uses what we have been through or are going through, to minister to another.

DECEMBER 28

"We do not want you to be uninformed, brothers and sisters, about the troubles we experienced in the province of Asia. We were under great pressure, far beyond our ability to endure, so that we despaired of life itself" (2 Corinthians 1:8).

BEYOND MEASURE

HAVE YOU EVER been *"burdened beyond measure, above strength, so that despair filled your heart?"* There is nothing as scary as feeling like you have no hope in a circumstance of your life. The enemy of our soul whispers to us to give up, give in, throw the towel in, there is no hope for you. However loud the enemy's voice is though, I've got good news! God's voice is louder! Paul tells us in this passage that this is exactly where he and his fellow believers were at. It looked like there was no hope at all in sight. Death was staring at them in the face. But God undergirds Paul's faith and reminds him not to trust in his own devices of deliverance, nor in his own calculations about his struggle. No. He was to firmly place his trust in God, who is mighty and who raises the dead. He is the One who can and will deliver him!

We, Beloved, may be needing to stop trying to figure it all out, and just trust God with the whole matter that is causing us so much distress and grief. He is bigger than we are. He sees all the angles of the problem and He knows all the answers.

December 29

"For no matter how many promises God has made, they are 'Yes' in Christ. And so through Him the 'Amen' is spoken by us to the glory of God" (2 Corinthians 1:20).

In Him, Yes!

God so delights in blessing us, and He is willing and ready to confirm and perform His promises to us. You may ask, what are His promises? Every book in the Bible from Genesis to Revelation is packed full of things that God has said we can have, or that He will do for us. God is saying, yes, you can depend upon Me to come through. You see God is not wishy-washy. He doesn't say He will do something one day, and then neglect to do it the next. God comes through on His promises. Some of His promises have conditions that need to be met before they are fulfilled. One of these is, in order to receive God's free gift of eternal life, we must believe and receive it. Some of God's promises require nothing on our part, such as when He blesses us with extra finances, or a good friend, or a hug from a loved one. These things bless us, and God said that He would bless us. This is one of His promises to us.

Next time you sit down to study God's Word, look for those precious promises and write them down. Then make a note if they have a condition to their fulfillment, or if there is no requirement. Much of the time *faith* is a requirement in receiving from God. God is always ready to bless us, and all we need to do is believe and receive.

December 30

"'Martha, Martha,' the Lord answered, 'you are worried and upset about many things, but few things are needed— or indeed only one. Mary has chosen what is better, and it will not be taken away from her'" (Luke 10:41-42).

One Thing

ONE EVENING WHEN I was spending time with Jesus, He began to speak to my heart about really knowing Him. He showed me that I knew Him, but there was so much more. There were deeper places in Him He wanted to take me. Over the years, I have studied His Word, preached and taught, active in ministry for Him, but God wanted me to know and experience Him on a deeper level. When it comes right down to it, all that really matters is our relationship with God and our intimacy with Him. Let us not just settle on knowing Jesus in our minds, having the knowledge about Him, but let us hunger and thirst to know Him more intimately and experience Him, His heart, His ways. We can only do this by spending time with Him alone. Sometimes, God will allow things to come into our life that will cause our life to come to a screeching halt in order for us to seek after His face more diligently. Mary, in this passage, chose to place her focus on the Savior, and Jesus calls this the *"one thing that is needful."* It is an absolute necessity for us as believers in Christ, to grow in our intimacy with Him, getting to know and love Him more and more.

DECEMBER 31

*"And even if our gospel is veiled, it is veiled to those
who are perishing" (2 Corinthians 4:3).
"No one can come to Me unless the Father who sent Me draws
them, and I will raise them up at the last day" (John 6:44).*

COVERED BY A VEIL

*D*ID YOU REALIZE that we could not come to Christ on our own? When we were in the world without Christ, our hearts were blinded by the devil. We could not grasp nor understand spiritual things. Our hearts were so depraved that we didn't even realize it. Only God can open our eyes to see that we are a sinner in need of a Savior. Unredeemed man will not come to God on his own accord. God says that *"No one seeks God."* We have a veil that covers our spiritual eyes, and we are completely blinded until the Father, as in John 6:44 says, draws us to Jesus. That word *"draw"* in the original Greek means *"to drag."* Sometimes the Father has to drag us to His Son because we won't come to the light on our own. Once we come to the Son we have the choice to receive His redemption for us. And then, we can't even respond to this choice unless God gives us the grace for that also. Ephesians 2:8 tells us that *"by grace we have been saved through faith"* and even that faith is provided for by God. Therefore, when we pray for those who don't know Christ yet, I believe we need to ask God to draw them by His Holy Spirit to Himself, open their eyes to their need of a Savior, and give them the grace to respond positively.

LEAP YEAR

*"Worry weighs a person down; an encouraging word
cheers a person up" (Proverbs 12:25 NLT).*

SPEAK THAT WORD OF HOPE

OH, HOW WE all need an encouraging word these days. Just in our daily living and the stresses we face, can cause our hearts to be anxious. Add to this, personal and family problems, health issues, financial struggles, the cares of the world, and fears of the unknown. All these elements can weigh our hearts down so heavily and cause us to lose hope. If we are under the burden of anxiety, soon anxiety takes on the face of depression. How a good word can lift us up and make us feel hopeful and unafraid. Be aware of those around you who need a good word. Don't be timid in giving them that word of hope, joy and goodness. If you need those same words for yourself, find a friend and share with them how you are feeling. Tell them you need a hopeful word. Ask them to speak life into you. Again, don't be timid on sharing your needs with those who love you. And then, of course, God's Word is filled with words of powerful hope and courage. Speak life into your own life.

*"Let not your heart be troubled, you believe in God, believe
also in Me" (John 14:1).*

Bonus Devotions

"I am the vine; you are the branches. If you remain in Me and I in you, you will bear much fruit; apart from Me you can do nothing" (John 15:5).

Without Him, We Can Do Nothing

*I*T WAS A Sunday, and from the moment I awoke, until the end of the day, I felt agitated, worried, and overwhelmed. It was nearing Thanksgiving and I had so much to do, along with my sister's and my nephew's birthdays coming up. I had an appointment scheduled the day we would drive up to my sister's home. The upcoming Tuesday I had a ladies' Bible study, and that Friday I would be speaking and singing for a group of dear moms who had lost a child. There has been such unrest in our country and the elections and voting brought extreme tension in the air. The Corona Virus was still regarded as a threat, so places were closed down, and we still had to wear masks. So crazy a time. I had just completed and published a new book. So much was stirring around in me and around me.

This particular Sunday, I began to tremble and anxiety filled my heart. I felt some panic arise within me. Then, right at that moment I knew something was wrong. I was feeling that my life was out of balance. God was calling for my attention. I ran to Him and cried out, and told Him I felt agitated and fears were creeping in. As clear as could be, I heard Him say that I was doing way too much, and living my tomorrows for today. Of course, I was, and so I would be overwhelmed; I was not created to live this way. Jesus held me close and whispered that He loved me, and that I didn't have to be concerned about anything at that moment, but just to focus back on Him and being in my present moments. Today's scripture leaped out at me, and I knew that truly without Christ empowering me, and strengthening me for the tasks at hand, I can do nothing. My complete dependence is solely on His grace. So, God taught me once again that day, and I listened and obeyed. Order once again came into my life.

iH

Lightning Source UK Ltd.
Milton Keynes UK
UKHW010630020421
381430UK00001B/155